ENCYCLOPEDIA OF ISLAMIC DOCTRINE

VOLUME 5
SELF-PURIFICATION:
STATE OF EXCELLENCE
(*TAZKIYAT AL-NAFS* / *TASAWWUF, IHSAN*)

SHAYKH MUHAMMAD HISHAM KABBANI

AS-SUNNA FOUNDATION OF AM

As-Sunna Foundation of America
© 1998, 2nd edition, Shaykh Muhammad Hisham Kabbani

Edited by Gabriel F. Haddad, Ph.D. (Columbia), Alexandra Bain, Ph.D. (Victoria), Karim K. Tourk, Jennifer McLennan

Library of Congress Cataloging in Publication Data

Kabbani, Shaykh Muhammad Hisham.
Encyclopedia of Islamic Doctrine Vol. 5. Self-purification : State of Excellence (*tazkiyat al-nafs / tasawwuf, ihsan*)
[Arabic title: *al-Musuat al-islami aqida ahl al-sunnah wa al-jamaat*]
p.   cm.
    Indices.
Islam—doctrines. 2. Heretics, Muslim. 3. Wahhabiyah.
I. Kabbani, Shaykh Muhammad Hisham. II. Title.

ISBN: 1-871031-86-9

Published by
As-Sunna Foundation of America Publications
607A W. Dana St.
Mountain View, CA 94041
e-mail: asfa@sunnah.org
www: http://sunnah.org

Distributed by
KAZI Publications
3023 W. Belmont Avenue
Chicago, IL 60618
Tel: 773-267-7001; FAax: 773-267-7002
e-mail: kazibooks@kazi.org
www: http://www.kazi.org

BP
166
oK33
1998
v. 5

CONTENTS

INTRODUCTION

What does self-purification (*tazkiyat al-nafs / tasawwuf*) mean? What is the proof from the Quran and hadith in regard to self-purification? It is known that Sufi spiritual leaders were responsible for the spread of Islam in the Indian subcontinent, Central and Southeast Asia, Central, North and South Africa, as well as some parts of Russia, Europe, and America today. Where did the Sufis originate? When did they first appear? What was the position of the Companions, Islamic schools of law and scholars of the Community (*umma*) in regard to self-purification? This second volume is devoted to the principles of self-purification (*tazkiyat al-nafs*) and the methods of the people of self-purification who achieved much.

Today Islam is taught only with words by people who do not care to practice it purely nor to purify themselves in practice. This was described in many hadiths that state, "They will order people and not heed their own warning, and they are the worst of people."[1] Similarly, the Prophet (ﷺ) said, "I do not fear for you only the anti-Christ." They asked, "Then who else are you afraid of?" He said, "The misguided scholars."[2] The Prophet (ﷺ) also said, "What I fear most for my nation is a hypocrite who has a scholarly tongue."[3]

Such was not the way of the Companions, including the

---

1 Reported on the authority of Umar, Ali, Ibn Abbas, and others. These were collected by Abu Talib al-Makki in the chapter entitled "The Difference between the scholars of the world and those of the hereafter" in his *Qut al-qulub fi muamalat al-mahbub* (Cairo: Matbaat al-maymuniyya, 1310/1893) 1:140-141.

2 Ahmad narrated it in his *Musnad*.

3 Narrated by Ahmad in his *Musnad* with a good chain.

Companions of the Porch (*Ahl al-Suffa*), concerning whom the following verse was revealed:

> *[O Muhammad,] keep yourself content with those who call on their Lord morning and evening seeking His Face; and let not your eyes pass beyond them, seeking the pomp and glitter of this life; nor obey any whose hearts whom We have permitted to neglect the Remembrance of Us, the one who follows his own desires, whose case has gone beyond all bounds (18:28).*

Nor was this the way of Abu Bakr al-Siddiq, about whom Bakr ibn Abd Allah said, "Abu Bakr does not precede you for praying much or fasting much, but because of a secret that has taken root in his heart."[4] Nor was this the way of the Tabiin such as Hasan al-Basri, Sufyan al-Thawri, and others of the later generations of Sufis who looked back to them for models. Al-Qushayri relates that al-Junayd said, "Self-purification (*tasawwuf*) is not the profusion of prayer and fasting, but wholeness of the breast and selflessness."[5]

Nor was this the way of the recognized imams who emphasized asceticism (*zuhd*) and true fear of Allah (*wara*) in addition to the fulfillment of obligations. Imam Ahmad composed two books with those two qualities as their respective titles. The latter placed the knowledge of saints above the knowledge of scholars, as is shown by the following report by his student Abu Bakr al-Marwazi:

> I heard Fath ibn Abi al-Fath saying to Abu Abd Allah (Imam Ahmad) during his last illness, 'Invoke Allah for us that he will give us a good successor (*khalifa*) to succeed you.' He continued, 'Who shall we ask for knowledge after you?' Ahmad replied, 'Ask Abd al-Wahhab.' Someone who was present there related to me that he said, 'But he does not have much learning–' Abu Abdullah replied, "He is a saintly man (*innahu rajulun salih*), and such as he is granted success in speaking the truth."[6]

---

4 Related by Ahmad with a sound chain in *Kitab fadail al-sahaba*, ed. Wasi Allah ibn Muhammad Abbas (Mecca: Muassasat al-risala, 1983) 1:141 (#118).

5 Al-Qushayri, *Risalat kitab al-sama* in *al-Rasail al-qushayriyya* (Sidon and Beirut: al-Maktaba al-asriyya, 1970) p. 60.

6 Ahmad, *Kitab al-wara* (Beirut: Dar al-kitab al-arabi, 1409/ 1988) p. 10.

In a celebrated edict (*fatwa*), cited further down, the Shafii scholar al-Izz ibn Abd al-Salam gives the same priority to the gnostics, or Knowers of Allah (*arifin*), over the jurists. Imam Malik places the same emphasis on inner perfection in his saying, "Religion does not consist in the knowledge of many narrations, but in a light that Allah places in the breast." Ibn Ata Allah quoted Ibn Arabi as saying, "Certainty (*al-yaqin*) does not derive from the evidences of the mind, but pours out from the depths of the heart."

This is why many of the imams of religion cautioned against the mere thirst for knowledge at the expense of the training of the ego. Imam Ghazali left the halls of learning in the midst of a prestigious career in order to devote himself to self-purification. At its outset, he wrote his magisterial *Ihya ulum al-din*, which begins with a warning to those who consider religion to consist merely of jurisprudence (*fiqh*).

One of the early Sufis and the greatest of the hadith masters (*huffaz*), of his time, Sufyan al-Thawri (d. 161), sounded the same warning. He addressed those who use the narration of hadith for religion, when he said, "If hadith was no good it would have vanished just as goodness has vanished . . . Pursuing the study of hadith is not part of the preparation for death, but a disease that preoccupies people." Dhahabi comments:

> By Allah he has spoken the truth . . . Today, in our time, the quest for knowledge and hadith no longer means for the hadith scholar the obligation of living up to it, which is the goal of hadith. He is right in what he said because pursuing the study of hadith is other than the hadith itself.[7]

It is for "the hadith itself," for the purpose of living up to the *sunna* of the Prophet (ﷺ) and the Holy Quran that the great masters of self-purification forsook the pursuit of science as a worldly allurement, and placed above it the acquisition of perfect character (*ihsan*). This is in accordance with the well-

7 Dhahabi as cited in Sakhawi, *al-Jawahir wa al-durar fi tarjamat shaykh al-islam Ibn Hajar* (al-Asqalani), ed. Hamid Abd al-Majid and Taha al-Zayni (Cairo: Wizarat al-awqaf, al-majlis al-ala li al-shuun al-islamiyya, lajnah ihya al-turath al-islami, 1986) p. 21-22.

known hadith of Aisha concerning the disposition of the Prophet (ﷺ). An example is Abu Nasr Bishr al-Hafi (d. 227), who considered the study of hadith a conjectural science in comparison to the certitude in belief imparted by visiting Fudayl ibn Iyad (d. 187).[8] Both *ihsan* and the process that leads to it are known as *tasawwuf*, as illustrated in the following pages.

---

8 See Ibn Sad, *Tabaqat* (ed. Sachau) 7(2):83; al-Arusi, *Nataij al-afkar al-qudsiyy*a (Bulaq, 1920/1873); and Abd al-Wahhab al-Sharawi, *al-Tabaqat al-kubra* 1:57.

1. SELF-PURIFICATION: DEFINITIONS, TERMINOLOGY AND HISTORICAL OVERVIEW

1.1. SELF-PURIFICATION (*TASAWWUF*) AMONG THE SALAF

It is made clear in the hadith narrated by Umar ibn al-Khattab about Gabriel meeting the Prophet (ﷺ) that one who wishes to fully follow the way of mainstream Islam cannot stop at merely adhering to the rules of faith (*iman*).[1] The journey involves the adoption of principles that lead to excellence (*ihsan*). Hence, the Saved Group follows one of the many schools of personal ethics (*suluk*), in accordance with the guidelines of the Sharia and the strict applications (*azaim*) of the *sunna* (modes of conduct signifying one's complete deter-mina-tion to please his Lord according to the Prophet's model). These schools are collectively known as the science of self-purification (*tasawwuf*).

In the first century after the Hijra, renunciation of the world (*zuhd*) grew as a reaction against the worldliness in the society. This reaction was rooted in Allah's order to His right-eous Messenger to purify people:

> *A Messenger . . . who shall . . . instruct them in Scripture and Wisdom, and sanctify them (2:129).*

> *We have sent among you a Messenger of your own,*

---

[1] In Bukhari and Muslim through various chains. Nawawi included it in his collection of forty hadiths (#2).

> rehearsing Our Signs, and purifying you, and
> instructing you in Scripture and Wisdom (2:151).

> A Messenger from among themselves, rehearsing
> unto them the Signs of Allah, sanctifying them, and
> instructing them in Scripture and Wisdom (3:164).

> Purify and sanctify them; and pray on their
> behalf, verily thy prayers are a source of security for
> them (9:103).

> A Messenger from among themselves, to rehearse
> to them His Signs, to sanctify them, and to instruct
> them in Scripture and Wisdom (62:2).

The adherents to this way held tightly and firmly to the prophetic way of life as it was reflected in the lives of his Companions and their Successors, in the ways they purified their hearts and character of bad manners, and the ways they impressed on themselves and those around them the manners and upright moral stature of the Prophet (ﷺ). Examples of these one-man schools of purification are listed by Abu Nuaym and others as "The Eight Ascetics," and include: Amir ibn Abd Qays, Abu Muslim al-Khawlani, Uways al-Qarani, al-Rabi Ibn Khuthaym, al-Aswad ibn Yazid, Masruq, Sufyan al-Thawri, and Hasan al-Basri, among many others.

The Prophet (ﷺ) himself attested to the power of such saints and their benefit to people, as witnessed by the many hadiths related about Uways al-Qarani.[2] In the following hadith, the Prophet (ﷺ) orders the people, if they meet Uways, to have him ask forgiveness on their behalf, and declares that Uways' intercession will earn entry into paradise for large numbers of people:

> The Prophet (ﷺ) said, "Uways ibn Amir will dawn
> upon you with the assistance (imdad) of the people of
> Yemen from the tribe of Murad and Qaran. He was a
> leper and was healed except in a tiny spot. He has a
> mother whose rights he keeps scrupulously. If he took
> an oath by Allah, Allah would fulfill it. If you are able
> to let him ask forgiveness for you, do it."

---

2 Imam Ahmad reports some of them in his book al-Zuhd.

"More people will enter paradise through the intercession of a certain man from my Community than there are people in the tribes of Rabia and Mudar." Al-Hasan al-Basri said, "That is Uways al-Qarani."[3]

Through slow evolution and as a reaction against the increasing worldliness of the social environment, Muslims flocked to saints and their followers until their methods evolved into a school of practical thought and moral action with their own structure of rules and principles. These became the basis used by Sufi scholars to direct people on the Right Path. The world soon witnessed the development of a variety of schools for purification of the ego (*tazkiyat al-nafs*). Sufi thought, as it spread everywhere, served as a dynamic force behind the growth and fabric of Islamic education. This tremendous advance occurred from the 1st century after the Hijra to the 7th, and paralleled with the following developments:

1 Development of the foundations of law and jurisprudence (*fiqh*), through the recognized imams;
2 Development of the foundations of doctrine and beliefs (*aqida*) through al-Ashari and others;
3 Development of the science of hadith (sayings of the Prophet (ﷺ)), resulting in the six authentic collections and innumerable others;
4 Development of the arts of writing and speaking Arabic (*nahw* and *balagha*).

1.2. THE PATH (*TARIQA*)

Path (*tariqa*) is a term derived from the Quranic verse: *"Had they kept straight on the path (tariqa), We would have made them drink of a most limpid water"* (72:16).

The meaning of "path" in this verse is elucidated by the hadith of the Prophet (ﷺ), related by Bukhari and Muslim, ordering his followers to follow his *sunna* and the *sunna* of his successors. Like *tariqa* in the verse, the meaning of *sunna* in the hadith is "path" and "way." *Tariqa* thus came to be a term

3 Ahmad, *al-Zuhd* (Beirut: Dar al-kutub al-ilmiyya, 1414/ 1993) p. 416, 414.

applied to groups of individuals belonging to the school of thought pursued by a particular scholar or "shaykh," as such a person was often called.

Although the shaykhs applied different methods in training their followers, the core of each one's program was identical. The situation was not unlike what happens in institutions of medicine and law today. The approaches of the various universities may be different, but the body of law and the practice of medicine remain essentially the same. When they graduate from either of these faculties, each student bears the stamp of the particular school he attended.

In a similar way, the student of a particular shaykh will bear the stamp of that shaykh's teaching and character. Accordingly, the names given to the various schools of Sufi thought differ according to the names and perspectives of their founders. This variation manifests itself in a more concrete fashion in the different supererogatory devotions, known as *awrad*, *ahzab* or *adhkar*, used as the practical methodology of spiritual formation. Such differences, however, have nothing to do with the religious principle. In basic principle, the Sufi schools are essentially the same, and the differences in names among schools of law (*madhahib*) refer to methods and not to the essence of religion, which is uniform.

The Sufi regimen under which individuals undertook the path to Allah was a finely-honed itinerary that charted the course of inward and outward progress in religious faith and practice. Following the tradition of the Companions of the Prophet (ﷺ) who used to frequent his company named "the People of the Porch" (*Ahl al-Suffa*). The practitioners of this regimen lived a communal life. Their dwelling-places were the alcove-schools (*zawiya*), border fort-schools (*ribat*), and guest-houses (*khaniqa*) where they gathered together on a regular basis and on specific occasions dedicated to the traditional festivals of the Islamic calendar (*id*).

These structures often evolved into celebrated educational institutions. For example, there were the two fort-schools (*ribat*) founded by the Sufi scholar Abd Allah Ibn al-Mubarak in Merv—which endured for a long time—and Cairo's Khaniqa Baybarsiyya, another Sufi school where the great hadith scholar Ibn Hajar al-Asqalani was headmaster and head lecturer as well as holding the chief judgeship of Syria and Egypt for the last forty years of his life.

Sufis also gathered in informal associations around the shaykh, called *suhba*, and assemblies to invoke the names of Allah and recite the *adhkar* (plural of *dhikr*, "remembrance" of Allah) inherited from the prophetic Tradition. Yet another reason for their gathering was to hear inspired preaching and moral exhortations (*wiaz*). The shaykhs instructed their students to actively respond to Allah and His Messenger; to cleanse their hearts and purify their souls from the lower desires prompted by the ego, and to reform erroneous beliefs. All this was accomplished by adhering to the prophetic *sunna*. The methods of remembering Allah that they instilled in their students were the very same methods passed down from the Prophet (ﷺ). In this way, the shaykhs promoted upright behavior, through both word and deed, and encouraged believers to devote themselves to Allah wholeheartedly. The aim of their endeavor was nothing less than obtaining Allah's satisfaction and inspiring love for His Prophet (ﷺ). In short, what they aimed for was a state where Allah would be pleased with them even as they were pleased with Allah.

The shaykhs were therefore radiant beacons that dispelled darkness from the believer's path, and the solid cornerstones upon which the *umma* could build the foundations of an ideal society. The ideal here was the spirit of sacrifice and selflessness that characterized their every effort. These values, in time, imbued the entire social fabric of Islam. The guesthouses, for example, were, more often than not, found in neighborhoods of the poor and economically disadvantaged. For this reason they became remedies for many social ills.

As a result of such teaching and training it is seen that many students of Sufi shaykhs graduated from their course of studies fully empowered to relieve other people's burdens as well as to strive to illumine the way of Truth. Furthermore, through their training and self-discipline, they developed the manifest and decisive will to do so. Genuine scholars and teachers of *tariqa* leave no stone unturned in conducting their *jihad*, a word which means both the physical struggle against disbelievers and the spiritual struggle against the unseen allurements that trap the soul.

1.3. JIHAD AND SUFI *MUJAHIDIN*

History books are filled with the names of Sufi *mujahidin* (those who struggle) and martyrs (*shuhada*) who have devoted their lives to confronting the enemies of Islam, calling mankind to the Presence of Allah, and calling back those who deviated from the true path and the *sunna* of the Prophet (ﷺ). They accomplished this with wisdom, and they were effective. Their names and stories are too numerous to list in the span of a single book, even in hundreds of volumes. Suffice it to mention a few examples from modern history as cited by the author of *The Reliance of the Traveller*:

> Among the Sufis who aided Islam with sword as well as pen, according to B.G. Martin's *Muslim Brotherhoods in Nineteenth Century Africa*, are such men as the Naqshbandi shaykh Shamil Daghestani, who fought a prolonged war against the Russians in the Caucasus in the nineteenth century; Sayyid Muhammad Abdullah al-Somali, a shaykh of the Salihiyya order who led Muslims against the British and Italians in Somalia from 1899 to 1920; the Qadiri shaykh Uthman ibn Fodi, who led jihad in Northern Nigeria from 1804 to 1808 to establish Islamic rule; the Qadiri shaykh Abd al-Qadir al-Jazairi, who led the Algerians against the French from 1832 to 1847; the Darqawi *faqir* al-Hajj Muhammad al-Ahrash, who fought the French in Egypt in 1799; the Tijani shaykh al-Hajj Umar Tal, who led Islamic jihad in Guinea, Senegal, and Mali from 1852 to 1864; and the Qadiri shaykh Ma al-Aynayn al-Qalqami, who helped marshal Muslim resistance to the French in northern Mauritania and southern Morocco from 1905 to 1909.
>
> Among the Sufis whose missionary work Islamized entire regions are such men as the founder of the Sanusiyya order, Muhammad Ali Sanusi, whose efforts and jihad from 1807 to 1859 consolidated Islam as the religion of peoples from the Libyan Desert of sub-Saharan Africa; the Shadhili shaykh Muhammad Maruf and Qadiri shaykh Uways al-Barawi, whose efforts spread Islam westward and inland from the East African Coast; and the hundreds of anonymous Naqshbandi shaykhs who taught and

> preserved Islam among the peoples of what is now the southern Soviet Union and who still serve the religion there despite official pressure. It is plain from the example of these and similar men that the attachment of the heart to Allah, which is the main emphasis of Sufism, does not hinder spiritual works of any kind, but may rather provide a real basis for them. And Allah alone gives success. [4]

The reader is also referred to Benningsen's *Mystics and Commissars* for the role of Sufis in preserving Islam in the Soviet Union, and *Lion of Daghestan* for their jihad against the Czars before that. Let it also be added that it is the Naqshbandis who preserved Islam in China both from when it spread to the Malay peninsula–and in the darkest days of Mao Tse-Tung's so-called "Cultural Revolution." In all of the above there is ample evidence that *tasawwuf*, far from encouraging escapism and quietism which impede social progress, upheld the highest values of social consciousness as well as religious inquiry and science. In fact, the Sufis provide adequate testimony to the unremitting jihad and struggle against social injustice and social inaction that took place over the centuries.

1.3.1. MODERN MISUNDERSTANDINGS

It is well-known that many people in our time have misunderstood *tasawwuf*. Some people believe it is against Islam and not mentioned in the Sharia, the Quran or the *sunna*. On the other hand, followers of the recognized, major schools of law and of the Imams who came later, such as Nawawi, Ibn Hajar, al-Subki, al-Suyuti, Ibn Hajar al-Haytami, and even Ibn Taymiyya and Ibn Qayyim (despite their having opposed the Mainstream doctrine in so many respects), accepted it and knew that *tasawwuf* has its roots deep in the Quran, the *sunna* and the Sharia. These scholars accepted *tasawwuf* because they knew the reality of the meaning of the term, not because of the standing or age of the term itself.

The term *tasawwuf* was not known in the time of the Prophet (ﷺ). However, even though the name may be younger than that time, the essence of it is part and parcel of the religion and cannot be separated from it.

4 Nuh Keller, *Reliance of the Traveller*, p. 863.

Another reason for misunderstanding the reality of *tasawwuf* is that some people are mixing true *tasawwuf* with pseudo-*tasawwuf*, which denies the necessity of the Sharia and makes up its own rules, claiming for itself an amorphous, ahistorical kind of authority that is not rooted in any precedent. These are not Sufi (*mutasawwif*) but pseudo-Sufi (*mustaswifa*) in the words of the great master Ali al-Huwjiri (d. 469?).[5] Enemies of *tasawwuf*, however, often blur the difference between Sufis and pseudo-Sufis (*mustaswifa*) in their references to *tasawwuf* in order to be rid of both, as they have known Sufis to stand against their false teachings.

An example is the Mutazili sect's aversion to Sufis, which led them to deny the miracles (*karamat*) of saints, as they never saw this sign of truth among themselves. Nowadays, there are people like the Mutazila, who want to create their own definition of Islam, to decide what fits into it and what does not, mixing right with wrong. They do so that they might rid themselves of the essence of Islamic teachings which exposes the incompleteness and error of what they have inherited.

The purpose of *tasawwuf* is first to purify the heart of bad desires and inclinations, and of the dirtiness that accumulates due to sin and wrongdoing. The purpose of *tasawwuf* is then to remove these bad manners and sins, to clean the self, and adorn and decorate the heart with the good behavior and good manners that are demanded by the Holy Quran and the *sunna* of the Prophet (ﷺ). Its ultimate purpose is to help the believer to reach the state of *ihsan*, or excellence of character, of which the Prophet (ﷺ) was the perfect example and the goal towards which each of his Companions strove to achieve.

1.4. THE NECESSITY FOR THE DEVELOPMENT OF ISLAMIC SCIENCES AFTER THE TIME OF THE PROPHET (ﷺ)

To take one example, in the time of the Prophet (ﷺ) there was no need for the science of grammar (*ilm al-nahu*) to be taught, even to a child. A child in the cradle of Islam, raised in the land of Hijaz, could read a poem or Arabic text without any

---

5 Al-Huwjiri, *Kashf al-mahjub*, trans. R.A. Nicholson (Karachi: Dar al-ishaat, 1990) p. 35.

need for diacritical marks (*tashkil*). It came naturally as they were raised knowing it. Later, however, when many non-Arabs entered Islam, and the Quran was being read incorrectly, it became necessary to create new disciplines to assist new Muslims in reading the Quran, so grammar was developed and diacritical marks were established.

The state of perfection (*ihsan*), the state of austerity (*zuhd*), the state of great fear of Allah (*wara*), and the state of Godwariness (*taqwa*) were naturally practiced by the Companions, because they were in company of the Prophet (ﷺ) and those states were a direct result of their association with him. It is for this reason that they are called Companions, because they were the associates of the Prophet (ﷺ) and it was their association with him that allowed them to be purified.

After the Companions, it became necessary to establish a school with a foundation, like the science of grammar (*ilm al-nahu*), as the many people who entered Islam at that time did not have the opportunity to meet the Prophet (ﷺ) or the Companions, and did not know the true path of Islam. It was necessary to establish schools that would develop the spiritual disciplines aiming at the states named above. These matters were combined under the main discipline of the science of self-purification (*ilm al-tasawwuf*).

It is essential to understand that *tasawwuf* is not something new to Islam nor something innovated. Rather, it is something taken from the Prophet (ﷺ) and from the Companions and its roots are deep in Islam. It is not the case as some enemies of Islam, orientalists and their students, have said. They have innovated many new names for *tasawwuf* in order to attack the science and state of *ihsan*, though it is mentioned by the Prophet (ﷺ) in his hadith. They attempted to apply the term "superstition" (*shawaza*) to the science of *tasawwuf*.

It is well-known that any term may be used to name a science and one is free to define or use any term one wishes; thus the science of perfection of character (*ilm al-ihsan*) is not changed by giving it a different name. It is dearly hoped that no one will be prevented or forbidden from learning this important science due to prejudice against the term *tasawwuf*. If the term is problematic to someone, let him give it a different name, but let him learn the science, by whatever name he wishes to call it.

The term *tasawwuf*, which is used to refer to the ways of cleansing the heart, denotes the same concept as *tazkiyat al-nafs* in the Quran. Both have the same subject-matter as the sciences of asceticism (*zuhd*) and perfection of character (*ihsan*). The terms *zuhd, tazkiya* and *ihsan* were all used in the time of the Prophet (ﷺ). Later, these terms were defined with extensive detail, and refined according to the guidelines of the Quran and the hadith, as were the other Islamic sciences already mentioned.

1.5. THE LINGUISTIC ROOTS
OF THE WORD *TASAWWUF*

There are four roots given to the word *tasawwuf*. The first is from the Arabic word *safa* or *safw*, which means purity. The Prophet (ﷺ) compared the world to a little rainwater on a mountain plateau of which the *safw* had already been drunk and from which only the dregs (*kadar*) remained.[6] He called Sham [Damascus] Allah's purest of lands (*safwat Allah min biladih*).[7] Ibn al-Athir defines the word in his dictionary *al-Nihaya* as "the best of any matter, its quintessence, and purest part."[8]

Another root is derived from the People of the Porch (*Ahl al-Suffa*), who were those who lived in the mosque of the Prophet (ﷺ) during his life and who were mentioned in the Quran in the following verse:

> *[O Muhammad,] keep yourself content with those who call on their Lord morning and evening seeking His Face; and let not your eyes pass beyond them, seeking the pomp and glitter of this life; nor obey any whose hearts whom We have permitted to neglect the*

6 In Ibn Asakir from Ibn Masud. Al-Qushayri and al-Huwjiri mention it in their chapters on *tasawwuf*, respectively in *Kashf al-mahjub* (Nicholson trans. p.) and *al-Risala*: Rabia Harris trans., *Sufi Book of Spiritual Ascent* (Chicago: ABC International Group, Inc., 1997), p. 270.

7 Tabarani related it and Haythami authenticated the chain through Irbad ibn Sariya in *Majma al-zawaid*, chapter on the merits of Syria.

8 Ibn al-Athir, *al-Nihaya*, s.v. *s-f-w*.

> *Remembrance of Us, the one who follows his own*
> *desires, whose case has gone beyond all bounds*
> (18:28).

This verse emphasizes how much the believers have to keep themselves in the state of *dhikr*, or recollection of Allah on the tongue, in the mind and through the heart. This root is sometimes compared to *ahl al-saff*, or "the People of the Rank," in the sense of "first rank," as the first rank is blessed and the Sufis are the elite of the Community.

The third of these roots is *al-suf* or wool, as it was the manner of the pious people of Kufa to wear it. The fourth linguistic root is from soft sponge (*suffat al-kaffa*) in reference to the Sufi whose heart is very soft due to its purity.

1.5.1. THE PRIMACY OF THE HEART
OVER ALL OTHER ORGANS

The heart is the seat of sincerity in a person without which none of his actions are accepted. The Prophet (ﷺ) said, according to Bukhari, "Surely there is in the body a small piece of flesh; if it is good the whole body is good and if it is corrupted the whole body is corrupted and that is the heart." He said in two other hadiths narrated by Muslim, "Surely Allah does not look at your bodies nor at your faces but He looks at your hearts," and "No one will enter Paradise who has even an atom of pride in his heart." Many other hadiths explicitly state the primacy of the heart:

• Abu Hurayra narrates: I said, "O Allah's Apostle! Who will be the foremost people in gaining your intercession on the Day of Resurrection?" Allah's Apostle said, "O Abu Hurayra! I knew that no one would ask me about this before you because of your longing for the knowledge of hadith. The foremost of people in gaining my intercession on the Day of Resurrection is he who said, 'There is no deity but Allah,' purely and sincerely from his heart (*qalb*) or his soul (*nafs*)."[9] Ibn Hajar said in his commentary on Bukhari:

> The Prophet (ﷺ) mentioned the heart for emphasis, as Allah said of the sinner, "*Verily his heart is sin-*

---

9 Bukhari related it (English 1:79).

ful" (2:283) . . . "Foremost" alludes to their different
order of entry into Paradise as distinct from their different ranks of sincerity, the latter being emphasized
by his saying "from his heart" although it is clear that
the seat of sincerity is the heart. However, the attribution of the action to that organ effects more emphasis.[10]

• One of the Companions named Wabisa relates that all the
people used to ask the Prophet (ﷺ) about the good things, but
he resolved to ask him about the evil things. When he came to
him the Prophet (ﷺ) poked him in the chest with his fingers
and said three times, "O Wabisa, fear of Allah is here." Then he
said, "Ask for your heart's decision, no matter the decision this
one and that one gives you."[11]

• From Ibn Umar: The Prophet (ﷺ) said, "Everything has a
polish, and the polish of hearts is the remembrance of Allah.
Nothing saves one from Allah's punishment more than the
remembrance of Allah." They said, "Not even jihad for Allah's
sake?" He said, "Not even if you strike with your sword until it
breaks."[12]

• Ibn Umar relates: I was sitting with the Prophet (ﷺ) when
Harmala ibn Zayd al-Ansari of the Banu Haritha tribe came to
him. He sat in front of Allah's Messenger, peace be upon him,
and said, "O Messenger of Allah, belief is here"—and he pointed to his tongue—"and hypocrisy is here"—and he pointed to
his heart—"and I don't perform the remembrance of Allah
except little." Allah's Messenger remained silent. Harmala
repeated his words, whereupon the Prophet (ﷺ) seized
Harmala's tongue by its extremity and said, "O Allah, give him
a truthful tongue and a thankful heart, and grant him to love
me and to love those who love me, and turn his affairs towards
good." Harmala said, "O Messenger of Allah, I have two broth-
ers who are hypocrites; I was with them just now. Shall I not
point them out to you (so you will pray for them)?" The Prophet
(ﷺ) said, "(Yes,) whoever comes to us in the way you have come,
we shall ask forgiveness for them as we asked forgiveness for

10 Ibn Hajar, *Fath al-bari* (1989 ed.) 1:258 and 11:541.
11 Related in Ahmad, Tabarani, Abu Yala, and Abu Nuaym.
12 Bayhaqi relates it in *Shuab al-iman* 1:396 #522; al-Mundhiri in *al-Targhib*
2:396; and Ibn Abi al-Dunya.

you; and whoever keeps to this path, Allah becomes his protector."[13]

• From Ibn Umar also, the Prophet (ﷺ) said, "Don't speak much rather than make *dhikr* of Allah; speaking much without *dhikr* of Allah hardens the heart, and no one is farther from Allah than the hard-hearted."[14]

Thus it is clear that the Prophet (ﷺ) tied everything to the good condition of the heart. When one leaves bad manners and takes on good manners, then he will have a perfect and healthy heart. That is what Allah mentioned in the Quran, *"The Day wherein neither wealth nor sons will avail but only he will prosper who brings to Allah a sound heart"* (26:88-89). Allah mentions the hearts of His true knowers (*ulama*) when He said, *"Know here are signs self-evident in the hearts of those who have been endowed with knowledge, and none but the unjust reject our signs"* (29:49).

What are the diseases of the heart? Imam Suyuti said in his book on the Shadhili *tariqa*, "The science of hearts, the knowledge of its diseases such as jealousy, arrogance and pride, and leaving them, are an obligation on every Muslim."[15] The exegetes have said that jealousy (*hasad*), ostentation (*al-riya*), hypocrisy (*al-nifaq*) and hatred (*al-hiqd*) are the most common bad manners, to which Allah referred when He said, *"Say, the things that my Lord has indeed forbidden are: shameful deeds (fawahish) whether open or secret"* (7:33). Allah's mentioning "whether open or secret" is the evidence for the need to not merely make the exterior actions correct, but to cleanse that which is hidden in a person's heart and is known only to his Lord.

Tasawwuf is the science and knowledge whereby one learns to purify the self of the ego's bad desires, such as jealousy, cheating, ostentation, love of praise, pride, arrogance, anger, greed, stinginess, respect for the rich and disregard of the poor.

---

13 *Al-hafiz* Abu Nuaym narrated it in *Hilyat al-awliya*. Ibn Hajar said in *al-Isaba* (2:2 #1659): "Its chain of transmission is acceptable and Ibn Mindah also extracted it. We have narrated the same through Abu al-Darda in the *Fawaid* of Hisham ibn Ammar." Al-Tabarani also narrated through Abu al-Darda. Haythami said of that chain: "It contains one unknown narrator, but the rest are trustworthy."

14 Tirmidhi related it and said: a rare hadith (*gharib*); also Bayhaqi in the *Shuab* 4:245 #4951.

15 Suyuti, *Tayid al-haqiqa al-aliyya wa-tashyid al-tariqa al-shadhiliyya*, ed. Abd Allah ibn Muhammad ibn al-Siddiq al-Ghumari al-Hasani (Cairo: al-Matbaa al-islamiyya, 1934), p. 56.

Similarly, one must purify the external self. The science of *tasawwuf* teaches one to look at oneself, to purify oneself according to the Holy Quran and the *sunna* of the Prophet (ﷺ), and to dress oneself with the perfect attributes (*al-sifat al-kamila*). These include: repentance (*tawba*), Godwariness (*taqwa*), keeping to the straight way (*istiqama*), truthfulness (*sidq*), sincerity (*ikhlas*), abstention (*zuhd*), great piety (*wara*), reliance on Allah (*tawakkul*), contentment with the Decree (*rida*), surrender to Allah (*taslim*), good manners (*adab*), love (*mahabba*), remembrance (*dhikr*), watchfulness (*muraqaba*), and other qualities too numerous to mention here.

Just as the science of hadith has dozens of classifications of hadith, the science of *tasawwuf* has numerous classifications of both the good characteristics (*akhlaq hasana*), which are obligatory for the believer to develop, and the bad ones (*akhlaq dhamima*), which it is necessary to eliminate to attain the state of *ihsan*. Through the science of *tasawwuf*, the heart, precious essence, and lifeblood of Islam are made manifest to us. For Islam is not only an external practice, but also has an internal life. On this Allah says, *"Leave the outwardness of sin and its inwardness"* (6:120), and *"Among the believers are men who have been true to their Covenant with Allah"* (33:23). This means that not all believers are included in the selected group of those who "kept their covenant with Allah." It means a person can be a believer, but not among those who have kept their covenant until he has reached a state of cleanliness; the state of *ihsan*, perfection of behavior, which the Prophet (ﷺ) mentioned in the Hadith. This, as should by now be clear, is what became well-known later as the science of *tasawwuf*.

2. PROOF FROM THE QURAN

2.1. ALLAH DESCRIBES SELF-PURIFICATION (*TAZKIYAT AL-NAFS*) AS A DUTY OF THE PROPHET (ﷺ)

As mentioned previously, the evidence for *tasawwuf* from the Quran is the same as the evidence for *tazkiyat al-nafs* or self-purification, which we have established above as the definition of *tasawwuf*. Allah says:

> He is the One Who raised among the people of Makka a Messenger from among themselves who recites to them His communications and purifies them, and teaches them the Book and the Wisdom, although they were before certainly in clear error (62:2).

The term used here is *wa yuzakkihim* (purifies them). The various root meanings of the word *tazkiya* in Arabic are:

zaka :   "he cleansed" or "he was clean"
yuzakki : "to clean" and "to purify"
tazkiya : "purification"
zakat :   "Islamic poor-tax," "charity," "purity"
azka :   "the purest"
zaki :   "pure, innocent."

Allah says in another verse, "*By the soul and the proportion and order given to it, and its inspiration as to its wrong and its right; truly he succeeds who purifies it, and he fails that corrupts it"* (91:7-10). This verse states the necessity of purifying and cleaning the ego (*nafs*) in order to succeed in this life and the next. This is precisely the goal of *tasawwuf.* Following are verses related to other means and ends to such self-purification.

2.2. ALLAH ORDERS BELIEVERS TO FIND A MEANS OF APPROACH TO HIM, TO ACCOMPANY THE *SADIQIN*, AND HE PROMISES TO GUIDE THE *MUHSININ*

Allah orders, *"O believers, be wary of Allah and find a means to approach Him and strive in His Way that perhaps you may be of the successful"* (5:35). This verse means that a person must strive in Allah's way, not in the ego's way, nor towards the ego and its desires, if he wishes to be successful. It indicates the necessity of following the footsteps of the Prophet (ﷺ) as the means to approaching Allah Almighty, and of taking him and those who know him as guides.

Allah also says, *"O ye who believe, fear Allah and keep company with those who are truthful"* (9:119). This verse substantiates the need to accompany and associate with the best of Allah's servants. The *sadiqin* are the ones who reached one of the highest stations of faith according to the verse, already mentioned, *"Among the believers are men who have been true to their Covenant with Allah and of them some have died and some still wait but they have never changed their determination (in the least)"* (33:23). This means that in every era there are people who hold fast to the Covenant of Allah. These are the Friends of Allah mentioned in other verses, including, *"Nay they are the Friends of Allah, no fear shall come upon them neither shall they grieve"* (10:62). One of the Friends of Allah is al-Khidr, whom the Prophet Moses (ﷺ) was ordered to accompany and learn from.

Allah says, *"Those who are striving in Our Way, We will guide them to Our paths, for verily Allah is with those who do good"* (29:69). Most, if not all, of the great scholars of Islam practiced *tazkiyat al-nafs* and tried to reach the state of *ihsan* exemplified by the saints referred to above. They are the pious exemplars who spread Islam in Central Asia, India, Pakistan, Turkey, Bosnia, Indonesia, Malaysia, China, Indo-China, Spain, Eastern Europe, and most of Africa. All of these scholars practiced *tasawwuf* and used its methods to spread Islam in these countries. Through their states of *zuhd, wara, taqwa* and *tazkiya*, Sufis became like magnets drawing masses of people to Islam.

2.3. ALLAH DESCRIBES SOMEONE WHO LEARNS DIRECTLY FROM HIS PRESENCE (AL-KHIDR)

Allah eloquently describes the meeting of Prophet Moses (﷽) with Khidr (﷽):

> *So they found one of Our servants on whom We had bestowed mercy from Ourselves and whom We had taught knowledge from Our Own Presence. Moses said to him, "May I follow you on the condition that you teach me something of the Higher Truth that you have been taught?" The other said, "Surely you will not be able to have patience with me"* (18:66-67).

From these two verses, it is clear that even though Moses (﷽) was a prophet, and the only prophet to speak with Allah directly (*kalimullah*), Khidr possessed knowledge that Moses (﷽) did not have. Prophet Moses (﷽) sought to obtain this knowledge from him, because he knew Khidr was receiving knowledge directly from the Presence of Allah (*ilm ladunni*) as one of Allah's Friends.

Allah also says, *"Follow the way of those who turn to Me"* (31:15). Yusuf Ali correctly comments on this verse saying, "That is the way of those who love Allah." The state of love is related to the heart, not to the mind. Three of the many proofs that believers should follow a guide, or "teacher of upbringing" (*shaykh al-tarbiya)* in technical terms, are found in order to keep company with the Truthful, from the verses of Prophet Moses' encounter with Khidr, and in the order to follow the path of Allah's true lovers.

2.4. THE SUPERIORITY OF LOVE IN WORSHIP

Ibn Qayyim al-Jawziyya compiled some of the sayings of the great Sufis regarding love and its priority in sound worship:[1]

- Junayd said:

> I heard al-Harith al-Muhasibi say, love is when you incline completely towards something and then the preference of that thing over yourself and your soul and your possessions, then the compliance with that inwardly and outwardly, then your knowing of your shortcoming in your love to Him.

- Abdullah ibn al-Mubarak said:

> Whoever is given a portion of love and he has not been given an equivalent amount of awe, has been cheated.

- Yahya bin al-Muadh al-Razi said:

> An atom's weight of love is more beloved to me than to worship seventy years without love.

- Abu Bakrah al-Qattani said:

> There was a discussion about love in Makka during the pilgrimage season and the shaykhs were speaking about it. Junayd was the youngest of them in age. They said to him, "Say what you have O Iraqi." He lowered his head in deference and his eyes filled with tears, then he said, "A slave taking leave of himself, connected with the remembrance of his Lord, standing with the fulfillment of his duties, looking at Him with his heart, whose heart is burned by the light of His Essence, his drink is clear from the cup of His love, and if he talks it is by Allah, and if he utters it is from Allah, and if he moves it is by the order of Allah, and if he is silent he is with Allah, and he is by Allah, he is for Allah, he is with Allah (*fa huwa billahi wa lillahi wa maallahi*)." The shaykhs cried out and said, "There is nothing above that, may Allah strengthen you, crown of the Knowers!"

1 Ibn Qayyim, *Rawdat al-muhibbin wa nuzhat al-mushtaqin* (Beirut: Dar al-kutub al-ilmiyya, 1983) p. 406-409.

Junayd's words are related in one of the foundational texts that provides evidence for the miracles (*karamat*) of the saints, the hadith *qudsi* (sacred saying) related in Bukhari, on the authority of Abu Hurayra, the Messenger of Allah said Allah said:

> Whosoever shows enmity to one of My friends (*wali*), I shall be at war with him. My servant draws not near to me with anything more loved by Me than the religious duties I have enjoined upon him, and My servant continues to draw near to Me with supererogatory works so that I shall love him. When I love him I am his hearing with which he hears, his seeing with which he sees, his hand with which he strikes, and his foot with which he walks. Were he to ask something of Me, I would surely give it to him, and were he to ask refuge in Me, I would surely grant him it . . .

• Love was mentioned to Dhul-Nun and he said:

> Enough, do not discuss this question as the ego (*nafs*) will hear it and take its claim in it. For the disobedient one, fear and sorrow are better! Love is for the one who already has fear and is free of all impurity.

• Dhul-Nun also said:

> For everything there is punishment, and the punishment of the knower of Allah is the cutting from him of his remembrance of Allah (*dhikrullah*).

•Junayd referred to this distinction of levels in his answer when he was told, "Over there are a people who say, they are definitely reaching the station of goodness by the leaving of deeds." He said:

> Are they talking about the cancellation of (obligatory and other) deeds? Nay, whoever commits adultery and steals is in a better condition than the one who says such a thing. For certainly Allah's knowers

(*al arifina billah*) took the deeds from Allah and returned to Him with these deeds to Him, and if I had lived a thousand years I would never decrease from the good deeds the least bit.

• Junayd also said:

The knower of Allah is not considered a knower until he becomes like the earth; it is the same to him whether the good person or the bad person steps on him; or like the rain, he gives without discrimination to those whom he likes and those he dislikes.

• Sumnun said:

The lovers of Allah have gained the honor of both the world and the hereafter. The Prophet (ﷺ) said, "The human being is with the one he loves." They are with Allah in this world and the next.

• Yahya ibn Muadh also said:

He is not a truthful one who pretends he loves Him and trespasses His boundaries.

• He also said;

The knower of Allah leaves this worldly life and he does not have enough of two things: crying over his own self, and his longing for his Lord.

• Another seeker of self-purification said;

The knower of Allah does not become a knower until if he has been given the treasures of Sulayman it will not busy him with other than Allah for the blink of an eye.

2.5. MORE VERSES AND COMMENTARIES ON SELF-PURIFICATION (*TASAWWUF*)

Some of the verses referring to purification and self-purification in the Quran have already been mentioned. Allah says:

> *(A Messenger) who shall rehearse Your signs to*
> *them, instruct them in the Book and wisdom and puri-*
> *fy them (2:129).*

> *A similar (favor have you already received), in*
> *that we have sent among you a Messenger of your own,*
> *rehearsing to you Our signs, and purifying and sanc-*
> *tifying you . . . (2:151).*

> *Those will prosper who purify themselves and glo-*
> *rify the Name of their Lord and pray (87:14).*

> *And whoever purifies himself does so to his own*
> *soul's benefit; and to Allah is the journeying (35:18).*

In all of these verses, Allah Almighty refers to the characteristics of the Sufis (*mutasawwif,*) or those who are busy purifying themselves. They are always remembering their Lord, by
recalling His Names and Attributes, and they are attentive to
their prayers. This is the essence of *tasawwuf*, and also the
essence of Islam. The reader is reminded again that this is only
a technical term, and can be replaced by any synonym. If someone claims to follow or practice Islam, this struggle to purify
the self is incumbent upon him, as it is so clearly ordered in
these verses. Indeed it is meaningless to claim that there could
be any surrender to Allah without the pursuit of self-purification. That is why some scholars, among them Imam Ghazali
and Imam Suyuti, have considered *tasawwuf* a religious obligation (*wajib*).[2] Whether one is successful or not in this pursuit
is in Allah's hands, but its necessity is incumbent on every
Muslim man or woman.

2.6. VERSES ABOUT THE STATE OF PERFECTED CHARACTER (*IHSAN*)

After the verses that address self-purification, let us now

---

2 Ghazali's opinion is cited in *The Reliance of the Traveller*, p. 12. For Suyuti, see
below, Chapter 4: Sayings and Writings of the Imams and Scholars.

turn to quote some verses that address the state of *ihsan* or excellence. Allah said:

> For the Mercy of Allah is near to those who are good *(muhsinin)* (7:56).

> For Allah is with those who restrain themselves and who are good (16:128).

> Is there any reward for Excellence *(ihsan)* other than Excellence? (55:60).

> And He rewards those who do good with what is best (53:31).

> Allah commands justice, the doing of good *(ihsan)*, giving to kith and kin, and He forbids all indecent deeds and evil and rebellion: He instructs you that you may receive admonition (16:90).

> Nay, whoever who submits his whole self to Allah and is a muhsin (in the state of ihsan), his reward is with his Lord, on those shall be no fear nor shall they grieve (2:112).

> Whoever submits his whole self to Allah and is in a state of ihsan has grasped indeed the firmest hand-hold, and to Allah will all things return (31:21).

> Who can be better in religion than one who submits his whole self to Allah and does good in the way that Allah likes . . . (4:125).

Verses about the state of *ihsan* are numerous, but what has been quoted is sufficient. The meaning of *ihsan*, as the Prophet (ﷺ) defined it, is praying with humility and submission *(khudu* and *khushu)* as if the believer is seeing Allah and is aware that He is seeing him. In his "Book of Definitions" *(Kitab al-tarifat)* al-Jurjani (d. 816) said:

> Al-*ihsan*: verbal noun denoting what one ought to do in the way of good. In Sharia it means to worship

Allah as if you see Him, and if you do not see Him, He sees you. It is the attainment of true worship-in-servanthood predicated on the sight of the divine lordship with the light of spiritual sight (*al-tahaqquq bi al-ubudiyya ala mushahadat hadrat al-rububiyya bi nur al-basira*). That is: the sight of Allah as He is described by His attributes and through His very attribute, so that one will see Him with certitude, not literally (*fa huwa yarahu yaqinan wa la yarahu haqiqatan*). That is why the Prophet (ﷺ) said, "As if you were seeing Him." For one sees Him from behind the veil of His attributes.[3]

The word *ihsan* and its derivatives have the following meanings in the dictionary:

hasuna: "become, seem, make excellent, beautiful"
ihsanan: "(to do) excellently"
ahsana: "he did a great good"
ihsan: "kindness"
husna: "reward"
hasan: "excellent, beautiful"
hisanun: "beautiful ones"

"To become beautiful" in the first of these meanings means to decorate oneself with good attributes, to beautify inwardly and outwardly. When used as an adjective, it means kindness as a trait or an internal attitude as well as composure.

It should be clear by now that the state of *ihsan* mentioned in the Holy Quran is a very high state, which Gabriel showed to be an intrinsic part of the religion, and which he placed at the same level as the states of *islam* (submission) and *iman* (faith). The religion consists of three states: *islam, iman* and *ihsan*, each of which has its own definition. That is why it is mentioned in the Holy Quran in so many places, and why the Prophet (ﷺ), when asked about it by Gabriel, gave it the same importance as he gave to *islam* and *iman*.

This is the meaning of the whole science of *tasawwuf*. Those who oppose it may change the term if it suits their needs, since terms do not change the basic nature or the fundamental real-

---

3 Al-Sharif Ali ibn Muhammad al-Jurjani, *Kitab al-tarifat* (Beirut: Dar al-kutub al-ilmiyya, 1408/1988) p. 12.

ity of a thing. As the adage goes, "a rose by any other name would smell as sweet."

3. PROOF FROM THE HADITH

M uslim narrated:

Umar—may Allah be well pleased with him—also said: While we were sitting with Allah's Messenger— Allah's blessings and peace be upon him—one day, all of a sudden a man came up to us. He wore exceedingly white clothes. His hair was jet-black. There was no sign of travel on his person. None of us knew him. He went to sit near the Prophet (鑾) leaning his knees against the knees of the Prophet (鑾) and placing his hands on his thighs.

He said, "O Muhammad! tell me about *islam* (submission)." Allah's Messenger (鑾) said *"Islam* (submission) is to bear witness that there is no god but Allah, and that Muhammad is the Messenger of Allah; to perform the prayer; to pay the poor-tax; to fast during Ramadan; and to make the pilgrimage to the House if you are able to go there." The man said, "You have spoken the truth." We wondered at him; how could he be asking and confirming the Prophet (鑾) at the same time? Then he said, "Tell me about *iman* (belief)." The Prophet (鑾) said, *"Iman* (belief) is to believe in Allah, His Angels, His Books, His messengers, and the Last Day; and to believe in what has been decreed, both its good and its evil." The man said, "You have spoken the truth. Now tell me about *ihsan* (excellence)." The Prophet (鑾) replied, *"Ihsan* (excellence) is to worship Allah as if you see Him, for if you do not see Him, He certainly sees you."

The man said, "Now tell me about the Hour." The Prophet (鑾) replied, "The one who is being asked knows no more about it than the questioner." He said, "Then tell me about its signs." He replied, "The slave-girl will give birth to her mistress, and you will see the barefoot, naked, destitute herdsmen outdo each other in building tall structures." Then he left and time passed. Later he said to me, "O Umar, do you know who that was asking questions?" I said, "Allah and His Messenger know best." He said, "He was none other than Gabriel. He came to you to teach you your religion."

3.1. UMM AL-AHADITH:
THE HADITH OF GABRIEL

As said earlier, the term *tasawwuf* is a technical term that originated from the various meanings. It has deep roots in the *sunna* of the Prophet (ﷺ), since its origin is *ihsan*, the state of excellence that is mentioned in the hadith of Gabriel, which is known to all scholars as the "source of the *sunna* and of all hadith" (*umm al-sunna wa umm al-ahadith*).

In this hadith, Gabriel has divided religion into categories or main branches from which all religion, all hadith, and all *sunna* flow. He emphasized each branch by asking each question separate from the other. The first branch was related to his question "What is *islam* (submission)?" The second was related to the question "What is *iman* (faith)?" The third is related to the question "What is *ihsan* (excellence)?" It cannot be said that religion is only *islam*, or only *iman* or only *ihsan*. Each of these branches is essential to the religion, and none can be left out. The Prophet (ﷺ), in his answers to these questions, confirmed this and said to his Companions after Gabriel left, "Gabriel came to teach you your religion."

Islam, iman, and *ihsan* may be called three pillars of religion. The first pillar represents the practical side of the religion, including worship, deeds and other obligations. That pillar is the external side of the self, and is related to the body and the community. Scholars call the first pillar Sharia. Scholars learned to specialize in this, and it was given the name of the "science of jurisprudence" (*ilm al-fiqh*). The second pillar represents belief in the mind and heart. This is belief in Allah, His Messengers, His Books, the Angels, the Last Day, and Destiny. This became known to the scholars as *ilm al-tawhid*. The third pillar represents *tasawwuf*.

3.2. THE THIRD COMPONENT OF RELIGION: PERFECTION OF CHARACTER (*IHSAN*)

Ihsan, the third aspect of the religion is known as the spiritual aspect of the heart. It is intended to make one aware when combining the first and second components, and to remind that one is always in the Presence of Allah, and that one should consider this in all thoughts and actions. If one cannot see Him —because no one can see Allah in this life—then one must keep the continuous awareness of Allah's Presence in the heart. One must know that He is aware of every moment and detail in one's worship and one's belief. By doing these things, one will attain a state of excellence, a state of high quality, and will taste the spiritual pleasure and light of knowledge that Allah will direct to your heart. That is what scholars have termed the science of truth or *ilm al-haqiqa*, known in the time of the Companions, as *al-siddiqiyya*, or the Path of the truthful saints. Only later did it become known by the name of *tasawwuf*.

The preceding may be summarized by saying that *islam* prescribes the behavior of a Muslim, *iman* relates to the beliefs and defines them, and *ihsan* refers to the state of the heart that determines whether one's *islam* and *iman* will bear fruit in this life and the next. This is supported by the hadith in Bukhari mentioned above:

> Verily there is in the body a small piece of flesh; if it is good the whole body is good and if it is corrupted the whole body is corrupted and that is the heart.

Ihsan is divided into many parts, including all the good traits of a believer such as Godwariness (*taqwa*), fear of Allah (*wara*), abstention (*zuhd*), reverence (*khushu*), humility (*khudu*), patience (*sabr*), truthfulness (*sidq*), reliance (*tawakkul*), good character (*adab*), repentance (*tawba*), turning to Allah (*inaba*), forbearance (*hilm*), compassion (*rahma*), generosity (*karam*), humbleness (*tawadu*), modesty (*haya*), courage (*shajaa*), etc.

All of these are the qualities of the Prophet (ﷺ), and "His

character was the Quran," according to Aisha's saying.[1] The Prophet (鑾), in his turn, impressed these qualities on all his Companions so that they became shining examples of how human beings should exist in perfect harmony with the Creator and with each other.

In his explanation of the hadith of Gabriel, Imam Nawawi refers to *ihsan* in terms of *maqam al-mushahada* (the station of witnessing) and *maqam al-siddiqin* (the station of the most truthful saints), which are two of the branches of *tasawwuf*. Following is the complete text of Nawawi's commentary on the hadith of Gabriel.

3.3. IMAM NAWAWI'S COMMENTARY ON GABRIEL'S HADITH

3.3.1. "TELL ME ABOUT *IMAN* (BELIEF)."

Iman, lexically, means conviction of a general nature. Legally it is an expression for a specific conviction in the belief in Allah, His Angels, His Books, His Messengers, the Last Day, and whatever is decreed, both its good and its evil. Islam is a word signifying the performance of the legal obligations. These are the external actions that one applies oneself to do.

Allah the Exalted has differentiated belief (*iman*) from submission (*islam*) and this is also in the hadith. He said, "The Arabs say, 'We believe.' Say, 'You do not believe, but say We submit'" (49:14). This is because the hypocrites prayed, fasted, and paid alms while denying everything in their hearts. When they claimed belief, Allah declared their claim a lie because of the denial in their hearts, but He confirmed their claim of submission because of their performance of the duties entailed by it.

Allah says, "*If the hypocrites come to you and say, 'We bear witness that you truly are Allah's Messenger,' Allah knows better than they that you are indeed His Messenger, and Allah witnesses that the hypocrites are liars*" (63:1). They are liars in their claim of bearing witness to the Message while their hearts are denying it. The words of their mouths does not match the con-

---

tents of their hearts, whereas the condition of bearing witness to the Message is that the tongue confirm the heart. When they lied in their claim, Allah exposed their lie.

Since belief is also a condition for the validity of submission, Allah the Exalted distinguishes the submitter (*muslim*) from the believer (*mumin*) by saying *"We brought out the believers who dwelled in it and found none left in it but one house of submitters"* (51:35-36). This distinction links belief and submission in the way of a condition and its fulfillment.

Lastly, Allah named prayer by the name of "belief" (*iman*) when He said *"It was not Allah's purpose that your belief should be in vain"* (2:143) and *"You knew not what the Book was nor what was belief (faith, iman)"* (42:52). He means prayer.

3.3.2. "AND TO BELIEVE IN WHAT-HAS-BEEN-DECREED (*QADAR*), BOTH ITS GOOD AND ITS EVIL."

The word is pronounced both *qadar* and *qadr*. The way of the People of Truth (i.e. *Ahl al-Sunna wa al-Jamaa*) is to firmly believe in Allah's decree. The meaning of this is that Allah—Glorified and Exalted is He—has decreed matters from pre-eternity and that He—Glorified and Exalted is He—knows that they shall take place at times known to Him— Glorified and Exalted is He—and at places known to Him; and they do occur exactly according to what He has decreed—Glorified and Exalted is He.

Know that there are four kinds of decrees:

1 The decree in the divine foreknowledge. It is said concerning it: Care (*inaya*) before friendship (*wilaya*), pleasure before birth, and continual harvest proceeds from the first fruits. Allah the Exalted said, *"He is made to turn away from it who has been made to turn away"* (51:9). In other words, one is turned away from hearing the Quran and from believing in this life who was driven from them in pre-eternity. Allah's Messenger said—Allah's blessings and peace be upon him: "Allah does not destroy except one who is already destroyed."[2]

2 Muslim, *Iman* #208: "None perishes with Allah except he who is bound for destruction." Ibn Hajar said (*Fath al-bari, Riqaq* Ch. 31 #6491): "I.e. he who is adamant in clinging to evil in his resolve, his speech, and his deed, and avoids good by design, speech, and deed."

2 The decree in the Preserved Tablet. Such decree may be changed. Allah said: *"Allah erases what He will, and He consolidates what He will, and with Him is the Mother of the Book"* (13:39). We know that Ibn Umar used to say in his invocations, "O Allah, if You have foreordained hardship for me, erase it and write felicity for me."

3 The decree in the womb concerning which the angel is ordered to foreordain one's sustenance and term of life, and whether he shall be unfortunate or prosperous.

4 The decree which consists in joining specific forewritten matters to the appointed times in which they are to befall, for Allah the Exalted has created both good and evil and has ordained that they should befall His servant at times appointed by Him.

The evidence that Allah Almighty created both good and evil is His saying: "The guilty are in error and madness. On the day they are dragged to the fire on their faces, they will be told, *"Taste the touch of hell."* Lo! We created every thing with proportion and measure (qadar)" (54:47-49). That verse was revealed concerning the proponents of absolute freewill or Qadariyya who were thus told: "That belief of yours is in hellfire."

As further evidence of what has been decreed the Exalted said, *"Say: I seek refuge in the Lord of the Cleaving from the evil of what He has created"* (113:1). The reading of that oath at the time something good befalls Allah's servant will repel (foreordained) evil before it reaches him. There is also in the hadith: "Good deeds and upholding family ties repel a bad death and eventually turn it into a good one;"[3] "Invocation and affliction are suspended between heaven and earth, vying, and invocation repels affliction before the latter is able to come down."[4]

The proponents of absolute freewill [the Mutazila] claimed that Allah the Exalted has not foreordained matters, that His knowledge does not precede them, that they begin to exist only when they occur and that He—Exalted is He—knows them only at that time. They lied concerning Allah. Exalted is He above their

---

3 Tirmidhi, *Zakat* #28.

4 Cf. Ibn Majah, *Muqaddima* #10, *Fitan* #66; Tirmidhi, *Witr* #21, *Qadar* #6; Ahmad 5:277, 280, 282; Ibn Hibban.

lying utterances, and higher than that. They went into oblivion.

Now the latter-day Qadariyya say that the good is from Allah while the bad is from other than Him. Allah is also Exalted high above such a statement. In a rigorously authenticated hadith the Prophet (ﷺ) said, "The believers in absolute freewill are the Zoroastrians of this Community."[5] He named them Zoroastrians because their school of thought resembles that of Zoroastrian dualism. The dualists claim that good is effected by light and evil by darkness, and thus earned their name. Similarly the proponents of freewill ascribe the good to Allah and the bad to other than Him, whereas He—Exalted is He—is the creator of both good and evil.

The Imam of the Two Sanctuaries said in his "Book of Guidance to the Definitive Proofs Concerning the Foundations of Belief" that some of the Qadariyya said, "It is not we but you (Ahl al-Sunna) who are the Qadariyya because of your belief in the so-called decree."[6] Juwayni answered these ignoramuses that they had ascribed the power of decree to themselves, and whoever claimed, for example, the power of evil and ascribed it to himself, he has earned its attribute, rather than one who ascribes it to other than himself and denies any authorship of it.

3.3.3. "TELL ME ABOUT IHSAN (EXCELLENCE)."

This is the station of true vision (maqam al-mushahada). Whoever is able to directly see the King shies away from turning to other than Him in prayer and busying his heart with other than Him.

The station of ihsan is the station of the most truthful saints (maqam al-siddiqin) to which we have referred in our commentary on the hadith of intention:[7]

---

5 Abu Dawud, Tabarani, Ahmad, Bukhari in his Tarikh, and others.

6 Abu al-Maali Rukn al-Din Abd abd al-Malik ibn Abd Allah ibn Yusuf al-Juwayni al-Naysaburi Al-Shafii al-Ashari (419-478), Kitab al-irshad ila qawati al-adilla fi usul al-itiqad. He was Ghazali's shaykh and author of the fifteen-volume Nihayat al-matlab fi dirayat al-madhhab (The utmost of what is sought on understanding the evidence of the Shafii school) as well as other works in tenets of faith, theology, fundamentals of Islamic methodology, and Shafii fiqh (jurisprudence). See al-Subki's Tabaqat al-shafiiyya al-kubra 5:165.

7 Al-Muhasibi said, "Truthfulness (sidq), as an attribute of a servant of Allah, means evenness in the private and the public person, in visible and hidden behavior. Truthfulness is realized after the realization of all the stations (maqamat) and states

3.3.4. "HE CERTAINLY SEES YOU."

He sees your heedlessness if you are heedless in prayer and chatting to your self.

3.3.5. "TELL ME ABOUT THE HOUR."

This answer indicates that the Prophet (ﷺ) did not know the Hour. Knowledge of the Hour is among the matters whose knowledge Allah has reserved for Himself. He said: "*Allah has with Him the knowledge of the Hour*" (31:34) and "*It is heavy in the heavens and the earth. It comes not to you save unawares*" (7:187) and "*What can convey its knowledge unto thee (How canst thou know)? It may be that the Hour is nigh*" (34:63, 42:17).

As for he who claims that the age of the world is 70,000 years and that 63,000 years remain, it is a false statement reported by al-Tawkhi in the "*Causes of Revelation*" from certain astrologers and mathematicians. Moreover, whoever claims that the term of the world is 7,000 years, this is a bold affirmation concerning the Unknown, and it is not permitted to believe it.

3.3.6. "TELL ME ABOUT ITS SIGNS."

Another report has "to her master." Most commentators say that this is a sign of the multiplicity of slave-girls and their offspring. A child by the slave-girl's master is like her master, because the owner's possessions go to his children. Some say that the meaning refers to slave-girls giving birth to kings. The mother would then fall under her child's sovereignty. Another meaning is that a person may have a son from his slave-girl before selling her away; then the son grows up and buys his own mother. That is one of the conditions of the Hour.

(*ahwal*). Even sincerity (*ikhlas*) is in need of truthfulness, whereas truthfulness needs nothing, because although real sincerity is to seek Allah through obedience, one might seek Allah by praying and yet be heedless and absent in his heart while praying. Truthfulness, then, is to seek Allah Almighty by worshipping with complete presence of heart before Him. For every truthful one (*sadiq*) is sincere (*mukhlis*), while not every sincere one is truthful. That is the meaning of connection (*ittisal*) and disconnection (*infisal*): the truthful one has disconnected himself from all that is other-than-Allah (*ma siwa Allah*) and he has fastened himself to presence-before-Allah (*al-hudur billah*). That is also the meaning of renunciation (*takhalli*) of all that is other-than-Allah and self-adornment (*tahalli*) with presence-before-Allah, the Glorified, the Exalted."

3.3.7. "YOU WILL SEE THE BAREFOOT, NAKED, DESTITUTE HERDSMEN OUTDO EACH OTHER IN BUILDING TALL STRUCTURES."

Its meaning is that the Bedouins who live in the desert and their like from among the needy and the poor will become experts in erecting tall structures. The world will become bountiful for them and they will end up vying in luxury with their buildings.

3.3.8. "AND HE (THE PROPHET) WAITED (*LABITHA*) A LONG TIME."

The reports also say: "I waited [*labithtu*] a long time." Both are sound. In Abu Dawud and Tirmidhi's narrations, Umar says, "After three days," and in Baghawi's *Sharh al-tanbih*, "After three days or more," which apparently means after three nights had passed. All this apparently contradicts Abu Hurayra's statement in his narration (in Bukhari), "The man turned around and left, after which Allah's Messenger said—Allah's blessings and peace be upon him—'Bring that man back to me' and they looked to bring him back, but they found no-one. Then he said—'Allah's blessings and peace be upon him, that was Gabriel.'"

It is possible to reconcile the two versions of the event by considering that Umar may not have been present at the time of the Prophet's disclosure—Allah's blessings and peace be upon him – but that he had already risen and left the gathering by that time. So the Prophet (ﷺ) spoke on the spot to those who were present, and they in turn told Umar after three days, since he had not been present at the time the rest of the Companions had been informed.

3.3.9. "THAT WAS GABRIEL. HE CAME TO YOU TO TEACH YOU THE PRESCRIPTIONS OF YOUR RELIGION."

There is an indication in that statement that *islam, iman,* and *ihsan* are all named "religion" (*din*).

The hadith also provides a proof that belief in Allah's decree is an obligation that one should avoid probing matters, and that contentment with what comes to pass is an obligation.

A man came up to Ahmad ibn Hanbal—may Allah be well pleased with him–and said, "Admonish me." He answered him:

If Allah the Exalted has taken upon Himself the provision of all sustenance, why do you fret? If indeed compensation for all things belongs to Allah, why be stingy? If indeed there is a Paradise, why rest now? If indeed there is a fire, why disobey?

If the questioning of Munkar and Nakir is true, what good is human company?[8] If the world is bound for extinction, what peace of mind is there in it? If indeed there is a Reckoning, what good are possessions? And if all things are decreed to pass and measured out, what good is fear?

The author of *Maqamat al-ulama* (The Stations of the Learned) mentions that the world is divided into twenty-five parts:

- Five related to what is decreed to pass and measured out: sustenance, children, parents, power, and age;
- Five related to personal effort (*ijtihad*): paradise, hell, decency, spiritual chivalry, and writing;
- Five related to habit: eating, sleeping, walking, coupling, and voiding excrement.
- Five related to natural constitution: abstention, purity, altruism, beauty, and dignity.
- Five related to inheritance: wealth, relations, forbearance, truthfulness, and loyalty.[9]

None of the above contradicts the saying of the Prophet (ﷺ) whereby "Everything is bound to pass and measured out."[10] Rather, it means that some of these matters are determined by (secondary) causes,

---

8 Cf. The Sufi shaykh Ibn Ata Allah: "When Allah alienates you from the company of His creatures, know that He wishes to open for you the door of His own intimacy." (*Kitab al-hikam* #93.)

9 This is Imam Ghazali.

10 Hadiths: *kullu shayin bi qadar*: "Everything is measured out..." Muslim, *Qadar* Ch. 4 # 18, also Ahmad; *kullu shayin bi qadain wa qadar*: "Everything is bound to pass and measured out..." Tabarani in "*al-Awsat*": Haythami said in *Majma al-zawaid* that it contains unknown sub-narrators.

while others are not, and everything is bound to pass and measured out.

3.4. THE SCHOOL OF PERFECTION OF CHARACTER (*IHSAN*) AND SELF-PURIFICATION (*TAZKIYA*)

The school of which the Companions partook did not die with the passing of the Prophet (鬱). On the contrary, his methods and knowledge were turned over to his Companions, and each of them, in turn, became a school from which the *umma* learned the Prophet's methods and knowledge. Over time, these schools developed and formalized their methods, and created the distinct science of *tasawwuf*. The schools of *tasawwuf* developed alongside the schools of Sharia, and likewise came to pass their knowledge and science to succeeding generations of Muslims. Similarly, as the Sharia developed within the framework of Islam, the Quran and the *sunna* even though it encompassed many areas not mentioned verbatim in these sources, so too did *tasawwuf* develop a complicated and extended framework within the Book and the *sunna*; never did it step out of the bounds of these parameters.

3.5. THE RELATIONSHIP BETWEEN THE LAW (*SHARIA*) AND THE TRUTH (*HAQIQA*)

The name "science of reality," or *ilm al-haqiqa*, is sometimes given to *tasawwuf*. Imam Ahmad said, upon hearing al-Harith al-Muhasibi speak, "I never heard on the science of realities (*ilm al-haqaiq*) such words as those uttered by that man."[11] The meaning of this expression is that the reality of the servant's worship concerns the spiritual condition of his heart, while the performance of his worship satisfies his external obligations. The second is the object of Sharia, and its exponents are many, while the first is the object of the truth (*haqiqa*), and its exponents are few.

An example of the fulfillment of both the Sharia and *haqiqa* is prayer. It is obligatory to offer prescribed prayer (*salat*) with all the required movements and details according to the

---

11 Related with a sound chain by al-Khatib al-Baghdadi in his *Tarikh Baghdad* 8:214, and by al-Dhahabi in *Mizan al-itidal* 1:430.

Sharia. This is known as "the body of the prescribed prayer (*jasad al-salat*)." On the other hand, one of the essentials of prayer is to keep the heart in Allah's Divine Presence and know that He is looking at you throughout the prescribed prayer (*salat*). Such is the Reality and Essence of prescribed prayer. During the practice of *salat*, people may carry out the outward obligations of the prescribed prayer, but their hearts may not be involved. To pray from the heart is to strive for the state of *ihsan*; to keep the heart pure and clean of bad manners, and to remain immune to the distractions of this world. The Prophet (鏒) prayed this way, because he said he came to take people away from the attractions and distractions of this world, and he cursed them in many of his hadiths.

By analogy, the external form of *salat* is its body, and humility (*khudu*) and self-effacement (*khushu*), its soul. What is the benefit of a body without a soul? If prescribed prayer (*salat*) is movement without presence, then it is to move like a robot. As the soul needs the body to sustain it, so too does the body need the soul to give it life. The relationship between the divine law and the *truth* is like the relationship of body and soul. The perfect believer who has reached a state of *ihsan* is the one who can join the two.

The Prophet (鏒) also expressed this distinction, in his hadith:
Knowledge is of two kinds: knowledge established in the heart and knowledge on the tongue.[12]

Al-Izz ibn Abd al-Salam al-Maqdisi (not Shaykh al-Islam al-Sulaymi) explained this to refer respectively to *haqiqa* and Sharia:

> Knowledge is of two kinds: knowledge of externals (*ilm al-zahir*) which applies to the divine law, and knowledge of internals (*ilm al-batin*) which applies to the truth. The Prophet (鏒) said, "Knowledge is of two kinds . . ."[13]

Imam Al-Shafii alluded to the same distinction in his say-

---

12 Narrated by Ibn Abd al-Barr, *Jami bayan al-ilm wa fadlih* 1:190; al-Mundhiri, al-Targhib 1:103; al-Khatib al-Baghdadi, *Tarikh Baghdad* 4:346; and others.

13 Al-Izz ibn Abd al-Salam, *Bayn al-sharia wa al-haqiqa aw hall al-rumuz wa mafatih al-kunuz* (Cairo: matbaat nur al-amal, n.d.) p. 11.

ing, "Knowledge is of two kinds: knowledge of beliefs and knowledge of bodies."[14]

Therefore the essential understanding of *tasawwuf* is to combine the divine law and the truth, soul and body, externals and internals. Due to the immense difficulty of fulfilling *tasawwuf*, its methods are sometimes called war against the ego or *jihad al-nafs*.

3.6. THE GREATER JIHAD: JIHAD AGAINST THE EGO (*JIHAD AL-NAFS*)

Allah declares in the Quran that He accepts acts of worship only from those who purify themselves (*qad aflaha man zakkaha* 91:9), achieve soundness of the heart (*illa man ata Allaha bi qalbin salim* 26:89), and show a humble spirit (*innaha lakabiratun illa ala al-khashiin* 2:45). Together, these are generally called "purification of intention." That is why the great scholars like Bukhari, Shafii, Nawawi and others, began their books of jurisprudence with the hadith of intention, "Actions are judged according to intention."

An act outward act of worship that is performed without pure intention, is not considered worship—including fighting and dying in defense of Muslims. The Prophet (صلى الله عليه وسلم) said of one such warrior, "He is a companion of the fire." They are called in Sharia, *shahid al-fasad* (corrupt martyr). Purification of intention is vital in all five pillars of Islam. It is for this reason that the words *jihad al-akbar* (the greater jihad) are sometimes used to refer to the jihad of self-purification.

Ibn Qayyim al-Jawziyya writes in *al-Fawaid*:

> Allah said, *"Those who have striven for Our sake, We guide them to Our ways"* (29:96). He has thereby made guidance dependent on jihad. Therefore, the most perfect of people are those of them who struggle the most for His sake, and the most obligatory of jihads (*afrad al-jihad*) are the jihad against the ego, the jihad against desires, the jihad against satan, and the jihad against the lower world (*jihad al-nafs wa jihad al-hawa wa jihad al-shaytan wa jihad al-dunya*). Whoever struggles against these four, Allah

---

14 Suyuti related it in the introduction to his book *al-Tibb al-nabawi*, as mentioned by al-Ajluni in *Kashf al-khafa* 2:89 (#1765).

will guide them to the ways of His good pleasure which lead to His paradise, and whoever leaves jihad, then he leaves guidance in proportion to his leaving jihad.

Al-Junayd said, "Those who have striven against their desires and repented for our sake, we shall guide them to the ways of sincerity, and one cannot struggle against his enemy outwardly (i.e. with the sword) except he who struggles against these enemies inwardly. Then whoever is given victory over them will be victorious over his enemy. Whoever is defeated by them, his enemy defeats him."[15]

Competition and rivalry are allowed, to encourage excellence in worship. Allah established levels among the believers, as is written in His book, and as is clear from countless hadiths. The reward of jihad is immense, as attested to by the Prophet (ﷺ) in the hadith where he says if he could, he would ask Allah to bring him back to life so that he could go back and die as a martyr, many times over. Yet, with respect to *tasawwuf*, those who remember Allah, including perfect scholars who are true knowers of Allah, are superior to the *mujahidin*. For example, although Zayd ibn Haritha and Khalid ibn Walid were great generals, their demise was less serious for Islam, than that of Abu Musa al-Ashari or Ibn Abbas. For this reason the Prophet (ﷺ) explicitly declared the superiority of those who remember Allah, in the following two authentic hadiths in which the Prophet (ﷺ) said:

"Shall I tell you something that is the best of all deeds, constitutes the best act of piety in the eyes of your Lord, elevates your rank in the hereafter, and carries more virtue than the spending of gold and silver in the service of Allah, or taking part in jihad and slaying or being slain in the path of Allah?" They said, "Yes!" He said, "Remembrance of Allah."[16]

Even if one strikes disbelievers and idolaters with his sword until it breaks, and he is completely dyed

---

15 Ibn Qayyim al-Jawziyya, *al-Fawaid*, ed. Muhammad Ali Qutb (Alexandria: Dar al-dawa, 1412/1992) p. 50.

16 Related on the authority of Abu al-Darda by Ahmad, Tirmidhi, Ibn Majah, Ibn Abi al-Dunya, al-Hakim who declared it sound, and Dhahabi confirmed him, Bayhaqi, Suyuti in *al-Jami al-saghir*, and Ahmad also related it from Muadh ibn Jabal.

with their blood, the Rememberers of Allah are above him one degree.[17]

3.6.1. HADITH ON THE JIHAD AGAINST THE EGO

The hadith master Mulla Ali al-Qari relates in his book *al-Mawduat al-kubra*, also known as *al-Asrar al-marfua*:

> Suyuti said: al-Khatib al-Baghdadi relates in his "History" on the authority of Jabir, The Prophet (ﷺ) came back from one of his campaigns saying, "You have come forth in the best way of coming forth; you' have come from the lesser jihad to the greater jihad." They asked, "And what is the greater jihad?" He replied, "The striving (*mujahadat*) of Allah's servants against their idle desires."
>
> Ibn Hajar al-Asqalani said in *Tasdid al-qaws*, 'This saying is widespread and it is a saying by Ibrahim ibn Ablah according to Nisai in al-Kuna. Ghazali mentions it in the *Ihya* and al-Iraqi said that Bayhaqi related it on the authority of Jabir and said: "There is weakness in its chain of transmission."[18]

The *hafiz* Ibn Abu Jamra al-Azdi al-Andalusi (d. 695) says in his commentary on Bukhari, entitled *Bahjat al-nufus*:

> Umar narrated that a man came to the Prophet (ﷺ) asking for permission to go to jihad. The Prophet (ﷺ) asked, "Are your parents alive?" He said that they were. The Prophet (ﷺ) replied, "Then struggle to keep their rights" (*fihima fa jahid*) . . . There is in this hadith evidence that the *sunna* for entering the path and undertaking self-discipline is to act under the expert guidance, so that he may be shown the way that is best for him to follow, and the soundest for the particular wayfarer. For when that Companion wished to go out to jihad, he did not content himself with his own opinion in the matter but sought advice from one more knowledgeable than him and more expert. If this is the case in the lesser jihad, then what about the greater jihad?[19]

---

17 Related on the authority of Abu Said al-Khudri by Ahmad (3:75), Tirmidhi (#3376), Baghawi in *Sharh al-sunna* (5:195), Ibn Kathir in his *Tafsir* (6:416), and others.

18 Ali al-Qari, *al-Asrar al-marfua* (Beirut 1985 ed.) p. 127.

19 Ibn Abu Jamra, *Bahjat al-nufus sharh mukhtasar sahih al-bukhari* 3:146.

Ibn Hibban relates in his *Sahih* from Fadala ibn Ubayd:

The Prophet (ﷺ) said in the Farewell Pilgrimage:
" . . . the *mujahid* is he who struggles against himself
(*jahada nafsah*) for the sake of obeying Allah."[20]

Al-Haythami related the following version and declared it
sound:

The strong one is not the one who overcomes people, the strong one is he who overcomes his ego (*gha-
laba nafsah*).[21]

---

20 Tirmidhi, Ahmad, Tabarani, Ibn Majah, al-Hakim, and Qudai also relate it.
The contemporary hadith scholar Shuayb al-Arnaut confirmed that its chain of transmission is sound in his edition of Ibn Hibban, Sahih 11:203 (#4862).

21 Al-Haythami, in the chapter on *Jihad al-nafs* in his *Majma al-zawaid*.

4. SAYINGS AND WRITINGS OF THE IMAMS AND SCHOLARS ABOUT SELF-PURIFICATION (*TASAWWUF*)

4.1. HASAN AL-BASRI (D. 110 AH)

Hasan al-Basri was one of the early Sufis in both the general and the literal sense, as he wore a cloak of wool (*suf*) all his life. The son of a freedwoman (of Umm Salama, the Prophet's wife) and a freedman (of Zayd ibn Thabit the Prophet's stepson), this great Imam of Basra was a leader of saints and scholars in his day. He was widely known for his strict and encompassing embodiment of the *sunna* of the Prophet (ﷺ). He was also famous for his vast knowledge, his austerity and asceticism, his fearless remonstrances of the authorities, and his appeal both in discourse and appearance.

Ibn al-Jawzi wrote a 100-page book on his life and manners entitled *Adab al-Shaykh al-Hasan ibn Abi al-Hasan al-Basri*. He mentions a report that, when he died, al-Hasan left behind a white, wool cloak (*jubba*) that he had worn exclusively for twenty years, winter and summer, and that was still in a state of immaculate beauty, cleanliness, and quality.[1]

In a book he devoted to the sayings and the deeds of Sufis, Ibn Qayyim relates:

> A group of women went out on the day of *id* and went about looking at people. They were asked, "Who is the most handsome person you have seen today?" They replied, "It is a shaykh wearing a black turban." They meant Hasan al-Basri.[2]

---

1 Ibn al-Jawzi, *Sifat al-safwa* 2(4):10 (#570).

2 Ibn al-Qayyim, *Rawdat al-muhibbin wa nuzhat al-mushtaqin* (The garden of the lovers and the excursion of the longing ones) p. 225.

The hadith master Abu Nuaym al-Isfanahi (d. 430) mentions that it is al-Hasan's student, Abd al-Wahid ibn Zayd (d. 177), who was the first person to build a Sufi *khaniqa*, or guesthouse and school in Abadan on the present-day border of Iran with Iraq.[3]

It was on the basis of Hasan al-Basri and his students' fame as Sufis that Ibn Taymiyya stated, *"Tasawwuf's* place of origin is Basra."[4] This is a misleading assertion. Rather, Basra is chief among the places renown for the formal development of the schools of purification that became known as *tasawwuf*, and whose principles were none other than the Quran and the *sunna*, as has already been demonstrated at length.

Ghazali relates al-Hasan's words on *Jihad al-nafs* that Hasan al-Basri said:[5]

> Two thoughts roam over the soul, one from Allah, one from the enemy. Allah shows mercy on a servant who settles at the thought that comes from Him. He embraces the thought that comes from Allah, while he fights against the one from his enemy. To illustrate the heart's mutual attraction between these two powers the Prophet (ﷺ) said, "The heart of a believer lies between two fingers of the Merciful"[6] . . . The fingers stand for upheaval and hesitation in the heart . . . If man follows the dictates of anger and appetite, the dominion of satan appears in him through idle passions [*hawa*] and his heart becomes the nesting-place and container of satan, who feeds on the ego's desires (*hawa*). If he does battle with his passions and does not let them dominate his *nafs*, imitating in this the character of the angels, at that time his heart becomes the resting-place of angels and they alight upon it.

A measure of the extent of Hasan al-Basri's extreme Godwariness and scrupulousness (*wara*) is offered by his following statement, also quoted by Ghazali:

---

3 Abu Nuaym al-Isfahani, *Hilyat al-awliya* 6:155.

4 Ibn Taymiyya, *"al-Sufiyya wa al-fuqara,"* al-*Tasawwuf* in *Majmua al-fatawa al-kubra* 11:16.

5 Hasan al-Basri, in the section of his *Ihya* entitled *Kitab riyadat al-nafs wa tahdhib al-akhlaq wa mualajat amrad al-qalb* (Book of the training of the ego, the disciplining of manners and the healing of the hearts diseases).

6 Narrated by Muslim, Ahmad, Tirmidhi, and Ibn Majah.

Forgetfulness and hope are two mighty blessings
upon the progeny of Adam; but for them the Muslims
would not walk in the streets.[7]

4.2. IMAM ABU HANIFA (D. 150 AH)

Ibn Abidin relates that Imam Abu Hanifa said, "If it were
not for two years, I would have perished." He comments:

> For two years he accompanied Sayyidina Jafar al-
> Sadiq and he acquired the spiritual knowledge that
> made him a gnostic in the Way . . . Abu Ali Daqqaq
> (Imam Qushayri's shaykh) received the path from
> Abu al-Qasim al-Nasirabadi, who received it from al-
> Shibli, who received it from Sari al-Saqati who
> received it from Maruf al-Karkhi, who received it
> from Dawud at-Tai, who received the knowledge, both
> the external and the internal, from the Imam Abi
> Hanifa.[8]

4.3. SUFYAN AL-THAWRI (D. 161 AH)

Ibn Qayyim al-Jawziyya and Ibn al-Jawzi relate that
Sufyan al-Thawri said:

> If it were not for Abu Hashim al-Sufi (d. 150) I
> would have never perceived the presence of the sub-
> tlest forms of hypocrisy in the self . . . Among the best
> of people is the Sufi learned in jurisprudence.[9]

Ibn al-Jawzi also narrates the following:

> Abu Hashim al-Zahid said, "Allah has stamped
> alienation upon the world in order that the friendly
> company of the seekers (muridin) consist solely in
> being with Him and not with the world, and in order
> that those who obey Him come to Him by means of
> avoiding the world. The People of Knowledge of Allah
> (ahl al-marifa billah) are strangers in the world and
> long for the hereafter."[10]

---

7 In Ghazali, trans. T.J. Winter, *The Remembrance of Death* p. 18.

8 Ibn Abidin, *Hashiyat radd al-muhtar ala al-durr al-mukhtar* 1:43.

9 Ibn Qayyim, *Madarij al-salikin*; Ibn al-Jawzi, *Sifat al-safwa* (Beirut: Dar al-kutub al-ilmiyya, 1403/1989) 1 (2):203 (#254); Abu Nuaym, *Hilyat al-awliya*, s.v. "Abu Hashim al-Sufi."

10 Ibn al-Jawzi, *op. cit.*

4.4. IMAM MALIK (D. 179 AH)

The scholar of Madina, he was known for his intense piety and love of the Prophet (ﷺ). He held the Prophet (ﷺ) in such awe and respect that he would not mount his horse within the confines of Madina out of reverence for the ground that enclosed the Prophet's body, nor would he relate a hadith without first performing ablution. Ibn al-Jawzi relates:

> Abu Musab said: "I went in to see Malik ibn Anas. He said to me, 'Look under my place of prayer or prayer-mat and see what is there.' I looked and I found a certain writing. He said, "Read it.' (I saw that) it contained (the account of) a dream which one of his brothers had seen and which concerned him. He said (reciting what was written), 'I saw the Prophet (ﷺ) in my sleep. He was in his mosque and the people were gathered around him, and he said, "I have hidden for you under my pulpit (*minbar*) something good–or: knowledge, and I have ordered Malik to distribute it to the people."' Then Malik wept, so I got up and left him."[11]

Just as Abu Hanifa and Sufyan al-Thawri implicitly asserted the necessity to follow the Sufi path to acquire perfection, Imam Malik explicitly enjoined *tasawwuf* as a duty of scholars in his statement:

> He who practices *tasawwuf* without learning the divine law corrupts his faith, while he who learns the divine law without practicing *tasawwuf* corrupts himself. Only he who combines the two proves true (*man tasawwafa wa lam yatafaqqah fa qad tazandaqa wa man tafaqqaha wa lam yatasawwaf fa qad tafassaqa wa man jamaa baynahuma fa qad tahaqqaqa*).

This is related by the *muhaddith* Ahmad Zarruq (d. 899), the hafiz Ali al-Qari al-Harawi (d. 1014), the *muhaddith* Ali

---

11 Ibn al-Jawzi, *Sifat al-safwa* 1(2):120. in the chapter entitled "Layer 6 of the People of Madina."

ibn Ahmad al-Adawi (d. 1190) and Ibn Ajiba (d. 1224), and others.[12] Ibn Ajiba explains:

> Shaykh Ahmad Zarruq said, "*Tasawwuf* has over two thousand definitions, all of which go back to the sincerity of one's self-application to Allah . . . Each one's definition corresponds to his state and the extent of his experience, knowledge, and taste, upon which he will ground his saying, "*Tasawwuf* is such-and-such."
>
> It follows that every one of the saints quoted [in Abu Nuaym's *Hilyat al-awliya*] who has a part of sincere self-application (*sidq tawajjuh*) has a part in *tasawwuf*, and each one's *tasawwuf* consists in his sincere self-application. As a rule, sincere self-application is a requirement of religion since it forms both the manner and the content of the acts that Allah accepts. Manner and content are not sound unless sincerity of self-application is sound. "*He approves not ingratitude in His servants, but if you are thankful, he will approve it in you*" (39:7).
>
> Therefore Islam necessitates deeds, and there is no self-purification (*tasawwuf*) without knowledge of the law (*fiqh*), as Allah's external rulings are not known except by knowledge of the law; and there is no knowledge of the law without self-purification, as there is no deed without sincerity in self-application, and there is neither without belief. Hence the divine law requires all of them by definition, just as the body and the soul necessitate each other, as one cannot exist or be complete in the world except in conjunction with the other. That is the meaning of Imam Malik's saying, "He who practices *tasawwuf* without learning the divine law . . ."[13]

4.5. IMAM SHAFII (D. 204 AH)

Al-hafiz al-Suyuti relates in *Tayid al-haqiqa al-aliyya* that Imam Al-Shafii said:

12 Ali al-Qari, *Sharh ayn al-ilm wa-zayn al-hilm* (Cairo: Maktabat al-thaqafa al-diniyya, 1989) 1:33; Ahmad Zarruq, *Qawaid al-tasawwuf* (Cairo, 1310); Ali al-Adawi, *Hashiyat al-Adawi ala sharh Abi al-Hasan li-risalat Ibn Abi Zayd al-musammat kifayat al-talib al-rabbani li-risalat Ibn Abi Zayd al-Qayrawani fi madhhab* Malik (Beirut?: Dar ihya al-kutub al-arabiyah, <n.d.>) 2:195; Ibn Ajiba, *Iqaz al-himam fi sharh al-hikam* (Cairo: Halabi, 1392/1972) p. 5-6.
13 Ibn Ajiba, *Iqaz al-himam* 5-6.

I accompanied the Sufis and received from them
but three words: their statement that time is a sword;
if you do not cut it, it cuts you; their statement that if
you do not keep your ego busy with truth it will keep
you busy with falsehood; their statement that depri-
vation is immunity.[14]

The *muhaddith* al-Ajluni also relates that Imam Shafii
said:

Three things in this world have been made lovely
to me: avoiding affectation, treating people kindly,
and following the way of *tasawwuf*.[15]

4.6. IMAM AHMAD IBN HANBAL (D. 241 AH)

Muhammad ibn Ahmad al-Saffarini al-Hanbali (d. 1188)
relates from Ibrahim ibn Abd Allah al-Qalanasi that Imam
Ahmad said about the Sufis, "I don't know people better than
them." Someone said to him, "They listen to music and they
reach states of ecstasy." He said, "Do you prevent them from
enjoying an hour with Allah?"[16]

Imam Ahmad's admiration of Sufis is borne out by the
reports of his awe before al-Harith al-Muhasibi. Yet he also
expressed caution about the difficulty of the Sufi path for those
unprepared to follow it. It may not be for everyone to follow the
way of those about whom Allah instructed His Prophet (ﷺ),
"And keep yourself content with those who call their Lord early
morning and evening, seeking His Countenance . . ." (18:28).

4.7. AL-HARITH AL-MUHASIBI (D. 243 AH)

Al-Harith al-Muhasibi was one of the earliest authors of
Sufi treatises and the teacher of al-Junayd. Abd al-Qahir al-
Baghdadi, Taj al-Din al-Subki, and Jamal al-Din al-Isnawi all
reiterate that "Upon the books of al-Harith ibn Asad al-
Muhasibi on *kalam, fiqh*, and hadith rest those among us who
are *mutakallim* (theologian), *faqih* (jurist), and Sufi."[17] His

14 Suyuti, *Tayid al-haqiqa al-aliyya* p. 15.
15 Al-Ajluni, *Kashf al-khafa wa muzil al-albas* 1:341 (#1089).
16 Al-Saffarini, *Ghidha al-albab li-sharh manzumat al-adab* (Cairo: Matbaat al-
Najah, 1324/1906) 1:120.
17 Abd al-Qahir al-Baghdadi, *Kitab usul al-din* p. 308-309; Taj al-Din Subki,
Tabaqat al-Shafiiyya 2:275; Jamal al-Din al-Isnawi, *Tabaqat al-shafiiyya* 1:(#9)26-27.

extant works include:
- *Kitab al-riaya li huquq Allah* (Book of observance of the rights of Allah)[18]
- *Kitab al-tawahhum* (Book of imagination), a description of the Day of Judgment
- *Kitab al-khalwa* (Book of seclusion)
- *Risalat al-mustarshidin* (Treatise for those who ask for guidance)
- *Kitab al-riaya li-huquq Allah* (Book of the observance of the rights of Allah)
- *Kitab fahm al-quran* (Book of the understanding of Quran)
- *Kitab mahiyyat al-aql wa manahu wa ikhtilaf al-nas fihi* (Book of the nature and meaning of the mind and the differences among people concerning it)
- *al-Masail fi amal al-qulub wa al-jawarih wa al-aql* (The questions concerning the works of the hearts, the limbs, and the mind)
- *Kitab al-azama* (The book of magnificence)
- *al-Wasaya wa al-nasaih al-diniyya wa al-nafahat al-qudsiyya li nafi jami al-bariyya* (The spiritual legacies and counsels and the sanctified gifts for the benefit of all creatures).

The following is a passage from *al-Wasaya* in which al-Muhasibi describes his search for the truth among the various groups of Muslims, his embarking on the Sufi path, and the characteristics of Sufis as opposed to non-Sufis:

> It has been clearly stated that this Community will be divided into seventy-odd groups, one of them the Saved One, and Allah knows about the rest. I spent a part of my life studying the differences of this Community, looking for the clear method and the straight path, searching for knowledge and acting upon it, guided on the path of the hereafter by means of the directions of the scholars. I understood a great deal of Allah's speech (the Quran) through the interpretation of the jurists. I contemplated the conditions

---

18 Shaykh al-Islam al-Izz ibn Abd al-Salam wrote an abridgment of it. Al-Subki mentions it in *Tabaqat al-shafiiyya*. A copy of it is at the Chester Beatty Library, ms. 3184 (2).

of this *umma*, looked at its ways of thinking and discourses and understood from this what has been predestined for me.

I saw their divisions as a deep ocean where many people have drowned, and very few were saved. I saw that every group claims that salvation is to those who follow them and destruction is to anyone who opposes them. Then I saw that people are of different types:

• Among them is the one who possesses the knowledge of the hereafter–he is hard to find and very scarce.

• Another type is the ignorant; staying away from him is a blessing.

• Another type is the one who pretends to be a scholar, while he is infatuated with this world, and preferring it in reality to all else.

• Another type is one with knowledge, identified with the religion, but using his knowledge as a way to rise and gain prestige, trading his religion for the refuse of this world.

• Another type is one who is carrying knowledge not knowing the real meaning of what he is carrying.

• Another type is one who appears as an ascetic, searching for virtue, yet he is helpless, and his knowledge cannot penetrate the hearts of the listeners, and his views are not reliable.

• Another type is one attributed intelligence and learning, while he is missing abstinence-through-fear-of-Allah (*wara*) and Godwariness (*taqwa*).

• Another type are the followers of their passions and lower desires, those who humiliate themselves for the sake of this world, seeking its highest position.

• Another type are the human devils preventing people from seeking the hereafter, who fight like dogs over this world (*dunya*), cherish it, and want nothing but to get more and more out of it, who therefore are in this world alive, but in reality they are dead; what is right is wrong according to them and and they consider the living and the dead equal.

I searched for myself in those types and I became perplexed. So I headed for the guidance of the guided ones, asking for support and guidance, and took knowledge for a guide. I pondered and examined things carefully, until it was clear to me—based on the Book of Allah, the *sunna* of His Prophet (ﷺ), and the Consensus of the Community—that following one's desires makes one blind to guidance and such a one loses his way to the truth, and protracts his stay in blindness.

So I began removing idle desires (*hawa*) from my heart, and concentrated on the divisions of the *umma*, in search of the Saved Group, attentive to those who had followed destructive desires and the perished groups, careful not to step anywhere before being sure, seeking the way of salvation for my soul.

Then I found—as the *umma* agrees is stated in the Book of Allah—that the way of salvation is in holding to Godwariness (*taqwa*), in performing obligations, in fearing Allah regarding what He has permitted and what He has forbidden (*wara*) and the limits which He has set, in sincerity to Allah through obedience and following the example of His Messenger. I sought the knowledge of obligations (*faraid*) and the prophetic habits (*sunan*) from the scholars of narrations, and I found within them both agreement and division, but I found that all of them agree that the knowledge of obligations and the *sunna* are to be found among those who know Allah and know His orders, the Knowers of Allah who act according to His good pleasure, greatly fearing to trespass what He has forbidden, modeling themselves after the example of His Messenger, and preferring the Hereafter over the world: these are the ones who are holding fast to the commands of Allah and the ways of the Messengers.

So I looked among this Community for these types of servants whose standing is agreed upon and who are known for their accomplishments, and sought to take from their knowledge, and found out that they are exceedingly rare and fewer than few, and that their kind of knowledge is fading, as Allah's Messenger said, "When Islam started it was a stranger, and it shall become a stranger again, just as it started, so glad tidings to the strangers"[19]—and they are alone with their religion. I felt that my calamity worsened for the loss of the righteous saints

19 Muslim, *Iman*; Ahmad 4:73.

(al-awliya al-atqiya), and I was afraid that death might come to me suddenly, while I am still disturbed over the division of this umma. So I started to search for a scholar: and I had no choice but to find one, and I did my best, until the One who is Affectionate towards His Creation arranged for me to meet a group of them.

I found in them the signs of taqwa and the qualities of wara and the preference of the next world over this one. I found that their instructions and their counsel is in accordance with the actions of the leaders of guidance, and I found them gathered together to give good counsel to the Community, not encouraging anyone to disobey Him nor losing hope in His Mercy. They are always open and patiently accept hardships and difficulties, content with destiny and thankful in prosperity. They make creation love their Lord in perfect repentance by reminding them of His favors and bounties, and they encourage them to refer all their affairs to Allah, knowledgeable of the Greatness of Allah, knowledgeable of His Book and the sunna, learned in His religion, knowledgeable of what He likes and dislikes, cautious and avoiding novelties and whims, refraining from extremes and exaggerations, despising disputations and arguments, cautiously refraining from backbiting and oppression, opposing their desires, taking account of themselves, controlling their senses, cautious in their food, their clothing and all their situations, avoiding anything that is doubtful, avoiding lustful desires, content with the minimum of food, cutting down on what is indifferent, doing-without in what is permissible, wary of Judgment, afraid of Resurrection, busy with their own lot, hard upon themselves not on others. Every one of them has his own business that keeps him preoccupied, everyone of them is knowledgeable in the affairs of the hereafter and the description of the Day of Judgment, the abundant reward and the painful punishment. That is what caused them continuous sorrow and ceaseless worries and kept them from the happiness of this world and its pleasures.

This group has embodied the manners of this religion, and drawn the definitive lines for Godwariness in a way that made my chest contract with awe, and made it clear to me that the conduct of religion and the sincerity of *wara* is an ocean which someone like myself cannot fathom. I came to realize the extent of their virtues, to see clearly their concern, and I became more and more certain that they are the ones who are striving on the Path of the hereafter, the true followers of the example of the Messengers, the source of light to those who ask for enlightenment from them, and guidance to those who seek guidance.

So I became interested in their way, benefitting from them, accepting their code of conduct, enjoying their obedience. I don't see anything equal to them, and I prefer no one over them, so Allah blessed me with a kind of knowledge whose truthfulness became clear to me and whose completeness I have seen. I hope that salvation will come to those who accept it or adopt it, and I am positive that support will come to anyone who will practice.

I have found crookedness in those who oppose this way, and rust has accumulated on the heart of anyone who ignores or denies it. I found that the supreme proof is with the one who understands it and I found out that adopting it and acting according to it is an obligation upon me, so I have believed in it in my inner self and kept it inside my conscience and made it the foundation of my religion, and built my deeds on it, and experienced different states within it.

I have asked Allah to give me the ability to thank Him for the Bounty He has bestowed on me and to give me the strength to perform the tasks related to what He has taught me, knowing my shortcomings and knowing that I can never thank Him enough.[20]

4.7.1. IMAM AHMAD'S AWE BEFORE AL-MUHASIBI

Here is the account of the first time Imam Ahmad heard al-Muhasibi speak directly:

> Ahmad ibn Hanbal disliked al-Harith's specula-tions in theology and the books he wrote on it. He used to warn people against al-Harith. Muhammad ibn Ahmad ibn Yaqub was told by Muhammad ibn Nuaym al-Dabbi, I heard Imam Abu Bakr Ahmad ibn

---

20 Al-Muhasibi, *Kitab al-wasaya*, ed. Abd al-Qadir Ahmad Ata (Cairo, 1384/1964) 27-32.

Ishaq—al-Sibji—saying, I heard Ismail ibn Ishaq al-Sarraj say: Ahmad ibn Hanbal told me one day, "I hear that this Harith is often at your house. What if you invited him while placing me somewhere I could hear him without being seen?" I answered him, "Certainly, O Abu Abd Allah!" and I was happy with this first step on his part. I went and asked al-Harith to come to us that very night, and to do so as his companions would be present also. "O Ismail, they are many, so you will serve them nothing other than oil and dates, and only as much as you are able." I followed his instructions and went to Abu Abd Allah to inform him. He came after sunset, went up to a small room and began to recite his usual devotions (*wird*). Al-Harith and his companions arrived, ate, and stood for the night prescribed prayer, and they did not pray after it. Then they sat silently in front of al-Harith and remained speechless until the middle of the night. One of them then asked al-Harith a question and al-Harith began to speak. His companions listened to him as if afraid to scare a bird away. Some wept. Others let out small cries as he spoke. Then I went to the room to enquire about Abu Abd Allah and found that he had passed out after weeping much. I went back down. They continued thus until the morning at which time they got up and went their way. I went back up to see Abu Abd Allah. He was a changed man. "What do you think of these people now, O Abu Abd Allah?" I asked. He said, "As far as I know, I have never seen their like, nor heard on the science of realities (*ilm al-haqaiq*) such words as those uttered by that man. However, despite what I just said, in truth I don't see fit for you to keep their company. Then he got up and left.[21]

Al-Subki explained Imam Ahmad's ambiguous reaction thus:

Consider this account carefully and know that Ahmad ibn Hanbal did not consider it wise for this man (al-Sarraj) to join their company because he was not one to raise himself to their state. In truth they were in a difficult path which all cannot equally

21 Al-Khatib al-Baghdadi, *Tarikh Baghdad* 8:214.

undertake and which makes one fear for one who undertakes it. Otherwise, would Ahmad have wept and praised al-Harith the way he praised him?[22]

Someone might raise the following objections:

Q. Al-Harith and his companions prayed the night prescribed prayer (salat al-isha) while Ahmad was present. How could Ahmad have not joined the prescribed salat, especially knowing that Ahmad's position was that joining the group prayer is obligatory?

A. Ahmad was with the group, but "upstairs" from the group, more likely in a separate room from where he could hear, but not necessarily see, al-Muhasibi, as the report mentions. Furthermore:

• It is not ascertained in the report that he did not pray behind him.
• It is possible that he did not have his ablution.
• It is possible that they delayed the night prescribed prayer past the beginning of its time and that by the time they prayed he had already finished.

The first possibility is the least that can be said. Any of these possibilities are more likely than to say, he deliberately did not pray behind him because, among other reasons, it is known that Ibn Umar prayed behind al-Hajjaj ibn Yusuf al-Thaqafi, who was a tyrant and shed the blood of the innocent. It is also known that Ibn Umar prayed behind the People of Innovation such as the Khawarij. He used to say, "Prescribed prayer (salat) is an excellent deed (hasana), and I don't care who takes part in it with me," and "whoever says, 'Hasten to the prescribed prayer,' (hayya ala al-salat), I respond to him [with yes]."[23]

To say that Imam Ahmad did not pray behind al-Muhasibi deliberately is tantamount to ascribing Imam Ahmad one of these views:

• Either he considered Al-Muhasibi worse than al-Hajjaj

22 Subki, Tabaqat al-shafiiyya 2:279.
23 This is related in Sunan al-Bayhaqi (3:121), al-Mughni (2:186-187) and elsewhere.

and the Khawarij, which is absurd and impious; or
- He left the practice of the Companion Abd Allah ibn Umar, although the Hanbali school of law is in great part a revival of the latter's, and this is unlikely.

Q. Why did Ahmad mention science of realities (ilm al-haqaiq), which is a Sufi term?

A. Imam Ahmad apparently acknowledged Sufi terminology. There is no more to say about this. Suggesting that it is unlikely is perfectly acceptable, but suggesting that it is impossible is not. Again, the end of the argument is that the report is sound according to the criteria of hadith masters, so let us leave speculation in favor of solid evidence.

Q. Why did al-Dhahabi not accept the authenticity of the account?

A. Al-Dhahabi made some equivocal comments in his *Mizan al-itidal* about the above account, but he does not question the authenticity of its chain of transmission. He authenticates it, yet expresses disbelief in it.[24] However, his subjective rejection, even though informed by his knowledge of his subject (his biography of Imam Ahmad is about 300 pages long) does not stand in the face of the evidence.

It is clear that Dhahabi admired al-Muhasibi by calling him "of great rank" in *Siyar alam al-nubala*:

> The Ascetic, the Knower . . . I say, al-Muhasibi is of great rank, and he briefly touched upon speculative theology, so he was reproached for it.[25]

All Sufi masters are scholars of *sunna*, otherwise they would not qualify as Sufi masters. On the other hand, many great Islamic scholars who did not claim to be Sufi masters greatly admired these people and saw clearly that they were of Allah's elect or *awliya*. History, including the present day, is replete with Islamic scholars, from the *muftis* of nations to the shaykh al-Azhar university, and from ministers of Islamic edu-

---

24 "The chain of transmission of this story is sound, but the report itself is rejected, for my heart does not accept it. I think it unlikely that one such as Ahmad would do this." Dhahabi, *Mizan al-itidal* 1:430 (#1606).

25 Al-Dhahabi, *Siyar alam al-nubala*, ed. Muhammad ibn Hasan Musa (Jeddah: Dar al-andalus, 1995) #508.

cation to presidents of leagues of Islamic scholars. All of these have seen and understood that the Sufi masters carried the *sunna* better than those who just memorized the divine law. Many of the Sufi masters themselves reached top positions among the Islamic scholars of their day.

Today, some believe they see a conflict between what they imagine to be masters of *tasawwuf* on the one hand, and non-Sufi scholars on the other. This is an artificial dichotomy that does not actually exist in the Community of the Prophet (ﷺ). However, some uninformed or ill-intentioned brethren will pick and choose a few quotes that illustrate differences among the scholars, in order to fuel disunity and create the illusion of what they name a "history of conflict."

In reality, representative scholars from the recognized schools of law have vindicated those who follow *tasawwuf* from the slander directed against them from certain quarters of the Islamic world. Why then are some still found today combing the books of Islamic literature to try to reintroduce insignificant and long-settled issues and cast doubts regarding the ways of Islam? They mention, for example, Ibn al-Jawzi's censure of excesses in *Talbis iblis* as if it was a wholesale condemnation of *tasawwuf*. They forget that he wrote entire books on the early Sufis, including Rabia al-Adawiyya and Ibrahim al-Adham. Or, they mention Imam Ahmad's disagreement with in Muhasibi's method, forgetting that he greatly admired al-Muhasibi's Sufi discourses. They cite al-Dhahabi's report of Abu Zura's censure of al-Muhasibi and Dhahabi's lament on the descending level of hadith scholarship in Sufi books, forgetting that Dhahabi admired al-Muhasibi and expressed the greatest respect for Sufis.

It is strange that Dhahabi should be quoted to illustrate anti-Sufi views when he explicitly said about one of the Sufis who came under the most attack, Ibn al-Farid, "Don't hasten to judge him." This is Dhahabi's notice on Ibn al-Farid in *Mizan al-itidal*:

> He related hadith from al-Qasim ibn Asakir; he cries out frank union with Allah in his poetry, and

this is a great calamity. Therefore, examine his compositions carefully and do not hasten (to judge), rather, keep the best opinion of Sufis (*hassin al-zanna bi al-Sufiyya*).[26]

Here are more examples of Dhahabi's praise of Sufis:

[#506] al-Abdi, known as Qasim al-Jui (d. 248): the Imam, the exemplar, the saint, the *muhaddith* . . . the Shaykh of the Sufis and the friend of Ahmad ibn al-Hawari. He is known as al-Jui.
[#506] . . . I say, the ascetics (*zuhhad*) of that time were al-Jui in Damascus, al-Sari al-Saqati in Baghdad, Ahmad ibn Harb in Naysabur, Dhu al-Nun in Egypt, and Muhammad ibn Aslam in Tus. Where are the likes of such masters? Only the dust will fill my eyes, or what is under the dust!
[#969] Shihab al-Din al-Suhrawardi: the shaykh, the imam, the scholar, the *zahid*, the knower, the *muhaddith*, Shaykh Al-Islam, the Peerless One of the Sufis.
[#512] I say, if you see the Sufi dedicated to hadith, then trust him, and when you see him staying away from hadith then do not be pleased with him. [27]

This is in an indirect praise of all Sufis, since all of them are dedicated to hadith and constantly referring back to it. These lines show that Dhahabi was in no way against *tasawwuf*. Rather, he objected to characteristics of some Sufis that he saw did not accord with his understanding of the *sunna*. He overlooked the difference between adherents and those who claim to be adherents to *tasawwuf*, although he mentions it elsewhere.

4.7.2. DHAHABI'S SUFI HADITH TEACHERS
The Sufis among Dhahabi's hadith teachers are too many to count. Here are some of their names as listed by Dhahabi himself:
• Ahmad ibn Ishaq Abu al-Maali al-Abarquhi (d. 701), who said in his last illness while he was in Makka, "I will die in this

26 Al-Dhahabi, *Mizan al-itidal* 3:214.
27 Dhahabi, *Siyar alam al-nubala*.

illness because the Prophet (ﷺ) promised me that I would die in Makka."[28]

• Ahmad ibn Abd Allah al-Qadi Shuqayr (d. 715) the Hariri Sufi[29]

• Ahmad ibn Abd al-Rahman al-Shahrazuri al-Sufi al-Qadiri (d. 701)[30]

• Ahmad ibn Abd al-Munim Rukn al-Din Abu al-Abbas al-Qazwini al-Tawusi al-Sufi (d. 704)[31]

• Ahmad ibn Ali al-Qadi al-Jayli al-Dimashqi al-Sufi (d. 724)[32]

• Ahmad ibn Muhammad Najm al-Din Abu al-Abbas ibn Sasra (d. 723) the Shafii chief judge (*qadi al-qudat*) and chief religious teacher (*shaykh al-shuyukh*) in Damascus. He disapproved of Ibn Taymiyya and presided at his trial in Damascus in 705.[33]

• "My friend" Sharaf al-Din Ahmad ibn Nasr Allah al-Faqih al-Sufi (d. 730), from *khaniqa al-tawawis*.[34]

• al-Shaykh Abu Ishaq Ibrahim ibn Barakat al-Baalbaki, known as Ibn al-Qurashiyya (d. 740): "One of the remarkable Qadiri *fuqara*, a man of religion, perspicuity, perfection, amiability, and rare benefits."[35]

• al-Shaykh Abu Ishaq Ibrahim ibn Dawud al-Hakkari al-Kurdi al-Muqri al-Sufi al-Zahid (d. 712), the father of Shams al-Din and Imad al-Din[36]

• The leader and shaykh Sadr al-Din Abu al-Majami Ibrahim ibn Muhammad al-Juwayni al-Khurasani al-Sufi al-Muhaddith (d. 720). Dhahabi relates that the Mongol ruler Ghazan Khan became Muslim at his hands. He adds, "He was held in extremely high reverence by the Sufis due to the station of his father, Sad al-Din ibn Hammuwayh (or Hamawayh)."[37]

---

28 Al-Dhahabi, *Mujam shuyukh al-Dhahabi, al-mujam al-kabir*, ed. Muhammad Habib al-Hayla (Taif: Maktabat al-Siddiq, 1408/1988) 1:37.
29 *Ibid.* 1:48.
30 *Ibid.* 1:58.
31 *Ibid.* 1:72.
32 *Ibid.* 1:77.
33 *Ibid.* 1:91. Cf. Ibn Kathir, *al-Bidaya* 14:37, 106-107; Subki, *Tabaqat* 9:20-22.
34 Al-Dhahabi, *Mujam shuyukh al-Dhahabi*, 1:104.
35 *Ibid.* 1:131.
36 *Ibid.* 1:136.
37 *Ibid.* 1:157-158.

Sad al-Din (d. 678) was *shaykh al-shuyukh* in Damascus.[38]

• "My shaykh" Ibrahim ibn Munir al-Baalbaki al-Abid al-Zahid al-Sayyah (d. 725).[39]

• Ishaq ibn Ibrahim ibn Muzaffar al-Misri al-Waziri al-Muqri al-Muaddib al-Sufi (d. 719), the teacher of the orphans[40]

• Aqush Abu Muhammad Husam al-Din al-Qutbi al-Yunini (d. 720), "He was one of the Sufis of al-Asadiyya, he was pious and recited the Quran often."[41]

• "My companion" Izz al-Din al-Hasan ibn Ahmad al-Irbili the physician (d. 726), "He was one of the Sufis of Duwayrat Hamd."[42]

• Husayn ibn Mubarak al-Mawsili al-Sufi (d. 742). "He was a man of good and a pious man. He wrote many books of learning and books about the *sunna*, and he kept company with the *fuqara*."[43]

• Abu Sad al-Khidr ibn Abd Allah al-Juwayni al-Dimashqi al-Sufi (d. 674). "He was the shaykh of the *khaniqa sumaysatiyya* . . . He wrote a two-volume history filled with benefits and wonders."[44]

• Umm Muhammad Zaynab bint Ali al-Wasiti (d. 695). "A woman versed in servanthood, fasting, staunch, humble, worshipful. Her brother Imam Taqi al-Din ibn al-Wasiti used to visit her seeking to obtain her blessing (*yaqsud ziyarataha wa al-tabarruk biha*)."[45]

• Zayn al-Arab bint Abd al-Rahman al-Dimashqiyya al-Sulamiyya (d. 704). She was the shaykha of the *ribat* in al-Kharimiyyin.[46]

• Abu Ali Suwanj ibn Muhammad al-Turkumani al-Dimashqi al-Faqir (d. 694)[47]

• Abu al-Barakat Shaban ibn Abi Bakr al-Irbili al-Sufi al-

---

38 *Ibid*. 1:322.
39 *Ibid*. 1:160.
40 *Ibid*. 1:163.
41 *Ibid*. 1:184.
42 *Ibid*. 1:209.
43 *Ibid*. 1:216.
44 *Ibid*. 1:222.
45 *Ibid*. 1:253.
46 *Ibid*. 1:258.
47 *Ibid*. 1:277.

Qadiri al-Zahiri al-Zahid (d. 711). "He was a man of good, perspicuous, modest, refined, who did not read nor write."[48]

• Abu Ghanim Zafir ibn Jafar al-Sulami al-Dimashqi (d. 615). "He was one of the *fuqara* of the *maqsura* (saint's shrine) of the Halabiyyin."[49]

• Sharaf al-Din Abu Muhammad Abd Allah ibn Abd al-Halim Ibn Taymiyya al-Harrani al-Hanbali (d. 727). "Frugal in his eating and clothing, of many qualities, he used to reproach certain things to his brother (Taqi al-Din Ibn Taymiyya) and consider them blameworthy on his part."[50]

• Ibn Abu Nasr Abd Allah ibn Muhammad ibn Nasr ibn Abd al-Razzaq ibn al-Shaykh Abd al-Qadir al-Jili (i.e. al-Jilani) al-Hanbali al-Faqih al-Sufi (d. 708)[51]

• Abu al-Majd Abd al-Rahman ibn al-Muhaddith Abi Abd Allah al-Isfarayini al-Dimashqi Al-Shafii (d. 701). "He was the shaykh of the *khaniqa shihabiyya*."[52]

• Zayn al-Din Abd al-Rahman ibn Muhammad al-Zahid, Khatib Yalda (712). "He was perspicuous, saintly, worshipful, and kept himself secluded from the people."[53]

• Abu al-Qasim Abd al-Samad ibn Qadi al-Qudat Abd al-Karim al-Harastani al-Dimashqi Al-Shafii (d. 694). "He learned jurisprudence and attended the schools, then he became an ascetic . . . People held him in veneration and miracles are related about him. I have heard that my shaykh Zayn al-Din al-Fariqi mentioned that Ibn al-Harastani had told him of the fall of the Tartars before it took place in 680."[54]

• Izz al-Din Abd al-Aziz ibn Umar al-Hamawi al-Ghassani al-Sufi (d. 720).[55]

• Abu Muhammad Abd al-Ghaffar ibn Muhammad al-Maqdisi al-Sufi (d. circa 700).[56]

• Abu Nasr Abd al-Latif ibn Nasr al-Shaykhi al-Sufi al-Halabi (d. 697). "He was *shaykh al-shuyukh* in Aleppo."[57]

---

48 *Ibid.* 1:298.
49 *Ibid.* 1:314.
50 *Ibid.* 1:323-324.
51 *Ibid.* 1:339.
52 *Ibid.* 1:379.
53 *Ibid.* 1:381.
54 *Ibid.* 1:393-394.
55 *Ibid.* 1:399.
56 *Ibid.* 1:405.
57 *Ibid.* 1:415.

• Najm al-Din Abd al-Malik ibn Abd al-Qahir Ibn Abd al-Ghani Ibn Taymiyya al-Harrani al-Shahid al-Sufi (d. 720).[58]

• Abu Amr Uthman ibn Abi Bakr al-Faqir al-Salih (b. 674). "A reciter of the Quran, he is erudite and a man of good, decency, and seclusion from people. I have kept his company since childhood."[59]

• "The Unique Leader, the Knower and Hadith Scholar" Abu Abd Allah Najm al-Din Ali ibn Muhammad al-Azdi al-Hilali al-Dimashqi Al-Shafii (d. 729). "He used to recount beneficial matters, and he held the saints in excellent esteem– may Allah make him and me of their number."[60]

• Abu Hafs Umar ibn Abi al-Qasim al-Yunini al-Salawi al-Sufi (d. 707). "He kept company with the *fuqara*."[61]

• Umm Muhammad Aisha Bint Rizq Allah al-Biladiyya al-Maqdisiyya (d. 711). "She was one of the women devotees who wept much, showed humility, and kept to the recitation of devotions (*awrad*)."[62]

• al-Fulk al-Sufi, Ali ibn al-Fulk al-Alawi al-Hasani al-Wasiti al-Muammar (b. 600).[63]

• "The *faqih* and knower" Abu al-Qasim al-Fadl ibn Isa al-Ajluni al-Hanbali al-Masmari (d. 735). "He was of high stature and wore a large turban and handsome clothes. He was a good interpreter of dreams. People venerated him as a saint."[64]

• Abu Abd Allah Muhammad ibn Ahmad al-Maqdisi al-Salihi (d. 705). "He was known as Shamlaj al-Faqir."[65]

• Muhammad ibn Ahmad al-Mawsili al-Salihi al-Faqir (d. 723). "He was perspicuous, of simple life, a man of decency and good."[66]

• Diya al-Din Abu Abd Allah Muhammad ibn Ahmad al-Faqir (d. 713).[67]

• Al-Imam al-Khayyir Shams al-Din Abu Abd Allah Muhammad ibn Ahmad al-Khallati Al-Shafii al-Sufi (d. 706).[68]

---

58 *Ibid.* 1:421.
59 *Ibid.* 1:441.
60 *Ibid.* 2:49.
61 *Ibid.* 2:83.
62 *Ibid.* 2:90.
63 *Ibid.* 2:100.
64 *Ibid.* 2:101.
65 *Ibid.* 2:139-140.
66 *Ibid.* 2:143.
67 *Ibid.* 2:146.
68 *Ibid.* 2:148.

- Abu Abd Allah Muhammad ibn Jawhar al-Muqri al-Mujawwid al-Talafazi al-Sufi al-Mulaqqan (d. 696).[69]
- "The Imam, the Judge, the Exegete, the Savant, the Ascetic" Jamal al-Din Muhammad ibn Sulayman al-Naqib al-Balkhi al-Dimashqi al-Hanafi (d. 698). "He compiled a very long commentary of Quran in ninety-nine volumes in which he enclosed the Quranic readings, the contexts of revelation, the linguistic explanations, the sayings of the exegetes, those of the Sufis, and their *haqaiq* (spiritual realities)."[70]
- Abu Abd Allah Muhammad ibn Sulayman al-Faqih Al-Shafii (d. 699). "He was the caretaker of the grave of al-Sayyida Nafisa (the greatest female saint of Egypt)."[71]
- Abu Abd Allah Muhammad ibn Abd Allah ibn al-Saqil al-Harrani (d. 713). "He was one of the *fuqara* of the *ribat* of Ibn al-Askaf."[72]
- "The brilliant savant and *usul* specialist" Safi al-Din Muhammad ibn Abd al-Rahim al-Hindi Al-Shafii (d.715). "He was versed in prayer, worship, *tasawwuf*, and excellent belief." He spoke against Ibn Taymiyya at the latter's trial in Damascus.[73]
- "*Qadi al-qudat*, the Paragon of Islam, the standard-bearer of the *sunna*, my shaykh" Jamal al-Din Abu al-Maali Muhammad ibn Ali al-Ansari al-Zamalkani al-Dimashqi Al-Shafii (d. 727). 2:244. He replaced Safi al-Din al-Hindi in the trial against Ibn Taymiyya, against whom he subsequently wrote a refutation of Ibn Taymiyya's position on divorce, and a refutation of his views on the Visitation to the Prophet (ﷺ) (*al-ziyara*).[74]
- Abu Abd Allah Muhammad ibn Muhammad al-Muhaddith al-Zahid al-Kikhi al-Sufi (d. 684).[75]
- "The righteous man of good, the Imam, the Knower, the Muhaddith" Abu Abd Allah Badr al-Din Muhammad ibn

69 *Ibid.* 2:181.
70 *Ibid.* 2:193.
71 *Ibid.* 2:195.
72 *Ibid.* 2:205.
73 *Ibid.* 2:216.
74 Ibn Kathir, *al-Bidaya* 14:75; Subki, *Tabaqat* 9:162.
75 Al-Dhahabi, *Mujam shuyukh al-Dhahabi*, 2:244.

Masud Ibn al-Tuwwazi al-Halabi Al-Shafii (d. 705). "He was the Shaykh of Hims and the Deputy Judge there, and the shaykh of the *khaniqa*."[78]

• "The Imam, the Reciter, the Perfecter, the Residue of the Salaf" Muwaffaq al-Din Abu Abd Allah Muhammad ibn Abi al-Ala al-Rabbani al-Nasibi Al-Shafii al-Sufi" (d. 695). "The shaykh of the Sufis and *fuqara* in Baalbak.[79]

• "The Speaker, the Ascetic, the Blessing to Mankind" Abu Abd Allah Muhammad ibn Abi al-Fadl al-Jabari al-Sufi (d. 713). "The Imam of Masjid al-Halabiyyin in Cairo."[80]

• Al-Shaykh al-Imam al-Mufti al-Zahid al-Arif Zahir al-Din Abu al-Mahamid Mahmud ibn Ubayd Allah al-Zanjani Al-Shafii al-Sufi (d. 673). "He kept company with Shaykh Shihab al-Din al-Suhrawardi and heard from him *Awarif al-maarif*, and from Abd al-Salam al-Dahiri he heard Abu Nasr al-Sarraj's *al-Luma*."[81]

• "The Imam, the reliable Muhaddith, the Knower, the Linguist, the Ascetic" Safi al-Din Abu al-Thana Mahmud ibn Abi Bakr al-Tannukhi al-Armuwi al-Shami Al-Shafii al-Sufi (d. 723).[82]

• Al-Alim al-Zahid Taqi al-Din Abu Bakr ibn Sharaf al-Salihi Nazil Hims (d. 728). "He was a *mutasawwif*, possessed eloquence, nobility, an intimate knowledge of matters at hand, and a large share of excellent qualities."[83]

• Abu Bakr ibn Sanjar al-Alai al-Shayzari al-Sufi (no dates).[84]

Many of the masters of hadith whom Dhahabi listed in his *Tadhkirat al-huffaz* are Sufis, including:[85]

• Abu Abd Allah Muhammad Ibn al-Banna al-Sufi
• Abu al-Hasan b. Jahdam al-Sufi

---

76 Ibn Kathir, *al-Bidaya* 14:131-132; Ibn Hajar, *al-Durar al-kamina* 4:193; al-Subki, *Tabaqat* 9:191.
77 Al-Dhahabi, *Mujam shuyukh al-Dhahabi*, 2:267.
78 *Ibid*. 2:282-283.
79 *Ibid*. 2:323-324.
80 *Ibid*. 2:325.
81 *Ibid*. 2:331.
82 *Ibid*. 2:335-336.
83 *Ibid*. 2:403.
84 *Ibid*. 2:405.
85 Al-Dhahabi, *Tadhkirat al-huffaz* (Beirut: Dar al-Kutub al-Ilmiyah).

- Abu al-Husayn al-Baghdadi Ahmad b. al-Hasan b. Abd al-Jabbar al-Sufi al-Hakim
- Abu Muhammad Abd al-Aziz b. Ahmad Ibn Muhammad b. Ali al-Tamimi al-Dimashqi al-Sufi al-Wahshi
- Abu Muhammad al-Andalusi al-Maghribi al-Qafasi al-Sufi
- Abu Sad Ahmad b. Muhammad b. Ahmad b. Abdullah b. Hafs al-Ansari al-Harawi al-Malini al-Sufi
- Abu Said Ahmad b. Muhammad b. Ziyad b. Bishr b. Dirham al-Basri al-Sufi
- Abu Yaqub Yusuf b. Ahmad b. Ibrahim al-Sufi
- Ahmad b. Abd Allah b. Ahmad b. Ishaq b. Musa b. Mahran al-Mihrani al-Isfahani
- Al-Sufi al-Ahwal Sibt al-Zahid Muhammad b. Yusuf al-Banna al-Talamanki
- Al-Hafiz Abu Hafs al-Sukkari Ahmad b. al-Hasan al-Sufi
- Ishaq b. Balkuyah al-Sufi
- Ismail b. Sad al-Sufi
- Muhammad b. al-Husayn b. Muhammad b. Musa al-Nishaburi al-Sufi al-Azdi
- Zaynuddin Abu al-Fath Muhammad b. Ahmad b. Abi Bakr al-Abyurdi al-Sufi Al-Shafii al-Isirdi

In conclusion, it may be said that the supposed conflict between the scholars of hadith and the Sufis is a fabrication intended to create division within the Community. Detractors collect a few sayings that raise uncertainty or doubt about *tasawwuf*, and neglect to mention that such criticism falls under the rubric of exception. The rule is that *tasawwuf* is an indication of spiritual rank that brings nothing but honor to its adherent, as attested to by Imam Ahmad, Dhahabi, Sakhawi, Suyuti, al-Izz ibn Abd al-Salam, al-Qari, al-Nawawi, and others Imams of hadith. This is true even of Ibn Taymiyya, who considered himself able to define *tasawwuf* in depth, and prided himself on having received the Qadiri *tariqa*, even as he harbored anti-Sufi inclinations that came to the surface in his attacks against Ibn Arabi and others. Let the reader be warned that to look at the disagreements of great scholars with the intent to criticize is to invite *fitna*. Al-Subki warned:

Beware of listening to what happened between Abu Hanifa and Sufyan al-Thawri, or Malik and Ibn Abi Dhib, or Ahmad ibn Salih and al-Nisai, or Ahmad ibn Hanbal and al-Harith al-Muhasibi [and others in later times]. If you become busy with this I fear death for you. These are notable leaders in religion and their utterances have various explanations which some, perhaps, have misunderstood. As for us, we have no other course but to approve of them and keep quiet concerning what took place between them, just as what is done concerning what took place between the Companions, may Allah be well pleased with them . . . O you who are seeking guidance! Keep to the path of good manners with the past masters. Avoid looking into their disagreements with each other except what provides a clear demonstration. Even then, if you are able to apply to it a good interpretation (of what they meant), then do so, otherwise: leave aside what took place between them, and busy yourself with what concerns you, and leave what does not concern you![86]

4.8. QASIM IBN UTHMAN AL-JUI (D. 248 AH)

He is one of the great saints of Damascus who studied hadith from Sufyan ibn Uyayna. Ibn al-Jawzi relates in *Sifat al-safwa* that al-Jui explained that he got the name al-Jui ("of the hunger") because Allah had strengthened him against physical hunger by means of spiritual hunger. He said:

Even if I was left one month without food I would not care. O Allah, you have done this with me. Therefore complete it for me![87]

Al-Dhahabi writes about him in *Siyar alam al-nubala*:

[#506] al-Abdi, known as Qasim al-Jui: The Imam, the exemplar, the saint, the *muhaddith* . . . the Shaykh of the Sufis and the friend of Ahmad ibn al-Hawari (*al-imam al-qudwa al-wali al-muhaddith Abu Abd Al-Malik Al-Qasim ibn Uthman al-Abdi al-*

---

86 Subki, *Qaida* p. 53.
87 Ibn al-Jawzi, *Sifat al-safwa* 2(2):200 (#763).

Dimashqi, Shaykh as-Sufiyya wa rafiq Ahmad ibn al-Hawari, urifa bi al-Jui).

Ibn al-Jawzi also relates that Ibn Abu Hatim al-Razi said:

> I entered Damascus to see the transcribers of hadith. I passed by Qasim al-Jui's circle and saw a large crowd sitting around him as he spoke. I approached and heard him say:
> Do without others in your life in five matters:
> • If you are present among people, don't be known;
> • If you are absent, don't be missed;
> • If you know something, consider your advice unsought;
> • If you say something, reject your words;
> • If you do something, you receive no credit for it.
>
> I advise you five other things as well:
> • If you are wronged, do not reciprocate it;
> • If you are praised, don't be glad;
> • If you are blamed, don't be distraught;
> • If you are called a liar, don't be angry;
> • If you are betrayed, don't betray in return.

Ibn Abu Hatim said, "I made these words all the benefit I got from visiting Damascus."[88]

4.9. IMAM AL-JUNAYD AL-BAGHDADI (D. 297 AH)

The Imam of the world in his time, al-Junayd al-Baghdadi, said, defining a Sufi:[89]

> The Sufi is the one who wears wool on top of purity, follows the path of the Prophet (ﷺ), endures bodily strains, and leaves behind all that pertains to the world (al-Sufi man labisa al-sufa ala al-safa wa ittabaa tariq al-mustafa wa athaqa al-jasada tam al-jafa wa kanat al-dunya minhu ala qafa).[90]

---

88 Ibid.

89 Al-Junayd, Kitab dawa al-arwah, ed. and trans. A.J. Arberry in Journal of the Royal Asiatic Society (1937).

90 A saying by Abu Ali al-Rudhabari (d. 322) narrated by Suyuti in his book on

4.10. HAKIM AL-TIRMIDHI (D. 320 AH)

Abu Abd Allah Muhammad ibn Ali al-Hakim al-Tirmidhi al-Hanafi, a *faqih* and *muhaddith* of Khorasan and one of the great early authors of *tasawwuf* who is quoted extensively by Ibn Arabi. He wrote many books, of which the following have been published:

- *al-Masail al-maknuna*: The concealed matters
- *Adab al-nafs*: The discipline of the ego
- *Adab al-muridin*: Ethics of the seekers of Allah, or Ethics of Sufi students
- *al-Amthal min al-kitab wa al-sunna*: Examples from the Quran and the *sunna*
- *Asrar mujahadat al-nafs*: The secrets of the struggle against the ego
- *Ilm al-awliya*: The knowledge of the saints
- *Khatm al-wilaya*: The Seal of sainthood
- *Shifa al-ilal*: The healing of defects
- *Kitab manazil al-ibad min al-ibadah, aw, Manazil al-qasidin ila Allah*: The book of the positions of worshippers in relation to worship, or: The positions of the travellers to Allah
- *Kitab marifat al-asrar*: Book of the knowledge of secrets
- *Kitab al-ada wa-al-nafs; wa al-aql wa al-hawa*: The book of the enemies, the ego, the mind, and vain desires;
- *al-Manhiyyat*: The prohibitions
- *Nawadir al-usul fi marifat ahadith al-rasul*: The rare sources of the religion concerning the knowledge of the Prophet's sayings
- *Tabai al-nufus: wa-huwa al-kitab al-musamma bi al-akyas wa al-mughtarrin*: The different characters of souls, or: The Book of the clever ones and the deluded ones
- *al-Kalam ala mana la ilaha illa Allah*: Discourse on the meaning of "There is no god but Allah."

The following excerpt is a transcription of the first two chapters of his *Adab al-muridin* or "Ethics of Sufi students":

tasawwuf entitled *Tayid al-haqiqa al-aliyya* (Cairo: al-Matbaa al-islamiyya, 1352/1934) p. 15.

I. Concerning the *murid* (seeker) and What Helps or Hurts Him in His Journey to Allah Most High, and What His First Step Ought to Be

There are two types of disciples: Those that seek Allah's grace by worshipping Him, fulfilling His commands and avoiding His prohibitions, then turning to perform as many voluntary good works as they can, seeking through them salvation from the fire and attainment of the rewards He has prepared for His workers.

Others approach Allah in worship, fulfill His commands and avoid His prohibitions, then turn to examine their inner self and find in their hearts many diseases, such as love of the world, lust for power, honor, and greatness, greed, the furnace of appetites (*shahawat*), the chatter of vain desires (*hawa*), ambition, envy, love of praise and compliments–all of them worldly bonds blinding the heart.

Such a heart can never find the way to Allah bearing those stains, because in loving the world he parts with His Lord. He is in love with something Allah has removed far from Himself and despised. To ask for greatness is to compare oneself with Allah Most High; in the furnace of desires one faces the greatest seductions; and in the chatter of vain passions lies tyranny itself and aversion to the rights of Allah the Lord of Might and Majesty. That heart is veiled from wisdom and from the understanding of how Allah disposes His affairs.

Such a person is a prisoner of his ego (*asir annafs*). He performs obligations while attached to the world, he avoids prohibitions while attached to the world, and he generally worships Allah at his own convenience. This is a servant who must try to build every matter, every action, and every moment upon sincerity, by working on his ego

Whoso desires the reward of Allah the Lord of Might and Majesty, let him keep to this battle, and let him be sincere in every matter in order to purify his worship.

For whoever seeks Allah Most High, must take pains and ask for sincerity in the secret of his heart until the door is opened for him. When the door opens

and the gift is given, at that time the cost of his journey will be repaid in full. He will be strengthened and
continue on his way, and the further he goes the more
his gift is increased for him and he continues even further. This does not stop until he reaches Allah
through his heart (hatta yasil ilallah qalban). At that
time Allah appoints him according to his degree and
he becomes a friend of Allah (wali Allah). He has
made his heart stand still in the presence of Allah
wherefore he received his appointment. From that
point he proceeds to works with a heart strong with
Allah's strength and rich with Allah's wealth, with a
faultless ego free from sins and devils. He has parted
ways with vain passions and the pursuit of honor and
he has purified himself.

We have dealt with these topics in two books, "The
Training of the Ego" (Riyadat al-nafs) and "The
Practice of the Saints" (Sirat al-awliya), in which are
found, with Allah's permission, cures for all who
aspire to knowledge in this matter.

II. Concerning the Welfare of the Heart and Its Remedies, and the Corruption of the Heart and Its Ills

The welfare of the heart lies in sadness and anxi-
ety, and its remedy in the continuous remembrance
(dhikr) of Allah Most High. The corruption of the
heart comes from joy in the world and contentment in
the states (ahwal) of the ego, and its sickness is the
avoidance of the remembrance of Allah and the turning to whatever distracts one from that remembrance.

Worldly joy is to the ego what water is to the fish.
The life of the fish is in water and if he stays on dry
land he will not live. Similarly if the ego is denied the
joys of the world, it will wither and become feeble, its
power will decrease, its activity will diminish and
cease– for sadness kills its life–until the heart rids
itself of whatever took place in it before and the stains
that ensued.

When the heart reaches Allah the Exalted, He
gives it life. When He gives life to the heart, the ego
experiences the life of the heart with the light of Allah
Most High. Before, the heart was deadened with the

delights and joys of the ego: when its owner tamed the ego and forbade it these joys, his Lord thanked him, because he has done battle for Allah with all his strength, and so Allah has guided his way as He has promised in His Revelation when He said: *"Those who have striven for Our sake, We guide them to Our ways"* (29:69).

When the door is opened for him he continues with his heart on the way to Allah the Almighty. Then come the gifts which repay him the cost of his journey until he reaches Allah, Who revives him with His light in His nearness, and he becomes one of Those Brought Near (*muqarrabin*). At that point he obtains joy in Allah after having once delighted in the world and the ego and its different states. He has gained eminence before the Allah of Might and Majesty.

As for him who discontinues the remembrance of Allah, his heart hardens, because remembrance contains mercy from Allah Most High, which He has promised His servants in His Revelation when He said: *"Remember Me and I will remember you"* (2:152). When mercy comes, the heart moistens and softens, and the heat of the ego is extinguished as it becomes attracted to the mercy which appeared in the heart. The heart loses its hardness and its coarseness and its rudeness.

Now the heart and the ego are partners in this body. The heart's strength lies in gnosis or internal knowledge (*marifa*), reason (*aql*), external knowledge (*ilm*), understanding (*fahm*), intellect (*dhihn*), intelligence (*fitra*), memory (*hafz*), and the life in Allah. Joy in those things motivates the heart, strengthens it, and gives it life.

The strength of the ego comes from material delights and pleasures, sexual gratification, honor and power and high rank, and the satisfaction of every ravenous appetite. Joy in those things motivates the ego and strengthens it. All of these are the soldiers of vain passions, because vain passions rule the ego. The ruler of the heart is internal knowledge, and the other things we have mentioned are its soldiers.

When the ego is flourishing and its joys are thriving, the ego overpowers the heart. At such a time the life of the heart ceases together with those things through which the heart lives. Its joys become worldly. But when the ego is denied these pleasures and sexual contentments, it withers and relaxes its grip, it weakens and dwindles away, while sorrows and anxieties accumulate and bear down on it. Through the anxieties caused by denial and abstention the ego loses its strength, and the heart gains power through the things we have mentioned.

The heart's joy in Allah becomes manifest, and that is why Allah said: *"Say: In the kindness of Allah and in His mercy—in that let them rejoice: It is better than what they gather"* (10:58). It was reported from the Prophet (ﷺ) that he said:

The ego of a human being is a blazing fire even on top of an old neck, except for them whose hearts Allah tests for Godwariness (*taqwa*), and they are few.[91]

It was reported from Anas b. Malik, may Allah be pleased with him, that the Prophet (ﷺ) said:

Even when human beings become old and hoary, two things remain young in them: greed for money, and lust for life.[92]

The Prophet (ﷺ) therefore urges us to remember death, as he said: Remember the destroyer of delights. Remembered often, its power lessens; seldom remembered, its power grows.[93]

It was narrated with its chain of authorities by Abu Hurayra. The meaning is that when you remember death you realize that your lot is to possess nothing, and that you are heading for extinction in the end. If you remember the latter, death becomes an easy thing to you, and if you remember the former, you realize that the little which one has in the world is plenty. For one knows not at what time, in an instant, death suddenly confronts one. Thus death is the "destroyer of delights." Remembering its destruction will do away with false joys and replace them with despondency and sadness.

It is now clear to you that there are two kinds of joy: the joy of the heart in Allah, in His kindness, in His mercy, and the joy of the ego in pleasure and delight. Whoever sincerely desires to reach Allah Most High must look carefully at everything the ego enjoys, whether in matters of religion or in matters of

---

91 Hadith *mursal mawquf* narrated by al-Hakim from *Makhul*, Ibn al-Mubarak from Abu al-Darda, and Daylami from Abu Hurayra. Suyuti cites it in *al-Durr al-manthur* 6:86.

92 Bukhari, Muslim, Ibn Majah, Tirmidhi, Ahmad.

93 Ibn Majah, Tirmidhi, al-Hakim.

the world. Then he must forbid his ego such joy, until it weakens and dies of grief in his breast.

For when someone forbids his ego the enjoyment of worldly pleasures and, on the other hand, indulges it with the enjoyment of religion, as in good works and devotions, the ego will still be pleased, and therefore remain alive and well. The reason is, that person's vain passions continue to be part of every one of his good works. For all his efforts, he remains a confused and sinful person. If he stops his efforts his stains will surely remain with him, and he will never reach Allah Most High through mistakes and vain passions. That is why Allah said: *"Strive for Allah to your utmost power"* (22:78). One's "utmost power" means the eradication of every joy of the ego whether in religion or in the world. Since one finds pleasure in every good work, and since passion remains a party to each of them, it is clear that such acts are not purely for the sake of Allah. It then becomes a duty to turn to some other action that will preclude the pleasure of the ego.

If one does that to his utmost strength and capability, Allah Most High will thank him in this world, and he whom Allah thanks, Allah opens his heart for His light. When that light ascends in the breast, the ego finds in such gifts all that it could not find before, when it was distracted by the pleasures and delights of the world.

Then the need arises to guard the ego lest it start deriving from these gifts a pleasure which will entrap and kill its owner. For when the ego finds pleasure in the gifts of Allah, it prospers and revels after having withered and languished, and therein lies the greatest danger. That is where the majority of the heart's wayfarers to Allah have fallen prey to the ego's treachery. This chapter contains in brief the answers to a thousand questions which are all corollaries and subsections of this one.[94]

4.11. IMAM ABU MANSUR ABD AL-QAHIR AL-BAGHDADI (D. 429 AH)

Imam al-Baghdadi is one of those who possessed an all-encompassing understanding of the multifarious views and

---

94 Al-Hakim al-Tirmidhi, *Adab al -muridin*, ed. Abd al-Fattah Abd Allah Baraka (Cairo: Matbaat as-saadat, 1976) p. 33-41.

beliefs of both Muslims and non-Muslims. He writes in his *Farq bayn al-firaq*:

> Know that Sunnis are divided into eight groups of people . . . the sixth group being the Sufi Ascetics (*al-zuhhad al-Sufiyya*), who have seen things for what they are and therefore have abstained, who have known by experience and therefore have taken heed truly, who have accepted Allah's allotment and contented themselves with what is within reach.
>
> They have understood that hearing, sight, and thought are all accountable for their good and their evil and subject to reckoning to an atom's weight. In consequence they have harnessed themselves with the best harness in preparation for the Day of the Return. Their speech has run the two paths of precepts and subtle allusions in the manner of the People of Hadith but without the pursuit of idle discourse. They neither seek self-display in doing good, nor do they leave doing good out of shyness. Their religion is the declaration of singleness and the disavowal of similitude. Their school is the commital of matters to Allah, reliance upon Him, submission to His order, satisfaction with what they have received from Him, and shunning all objection to Him. "Such is the bounty from Allah, He bestoweth it upon whom He will, and Allah is of infinite bounty" (57:21, 67:4).[95]

Imam Abd al-Qahir al-Baghdadi writes in *Usul al-din*:

> The book *Tarikh al-sufiyya* (History of the Sufis, more commonly known as *Tabaqat al-sufiyya*) by Abu Abd al-Rahman Sulami comprises the biographies of nearly a thousand shaykhs of the Sufis, none of whom belonged to heretical sects and all of whom were of the Sunni community, with the exception of only three of them: Abu Hilman of Damascus, who pretended to be of the Sufis but actually believed in incarnationism (*hulul*); Husayn ibn Mansur al-Hallaj, whose case remains problematic, though Ibn Ata Allah, Ibn Khafif, and Abu al-Qasim al-Nasir Abadi approved of him [as did the Hanbalis Ibn Aqil, Ibn Qudama, and

---

95 Abd al-Qahir al-Baghdadi, *al-Farq bayn al-firaq* (Beirut: Dar al-kutub al ilmiyya, n.d.) 242-243.

al-Tufi]; and al-Qannad, whom the Sufis accused of
being a Mutazili and rejected, for the good does not
accept the wicked.[96]

4.12. IMAM ABU AL-QASIM AL-QUSHAYRI (D. 465 AH)

He was a *muhaddith* who transmitted hadith to thousands
of pupils in Naysabur, where he fought the Mutazila until he
fled to Makka to protect his life. Al-Qushayri was the student
of the great Sufi shaykh Abu Ali al-Daqqaq. He was also a
mufassir who wrote a complete commentary of the Quran.[97]
His most famous work, however, is his *Risala ila al-sufiyya*, or
Epistle to the Sufis. This is one of the early complete manuals
of the science of *tasawwuf*, together with Abu Nasr al-Sarraj's
(d. 378) *Kitab al-luma* (Book of lights), Abu Talib al-Makki's (d.
386) *Qut al-qulub fi muamalat al-mahbub wa wasf tariq al-
murid ila maqam al-tawhid* (The Nourishment of hearts in
dealing with the Beloved and the description of the seeker's
way to the station of declaring Oneness), Abu Bakr al-
Kalabadhi's (d. 391) *al-Taarruf li madhhab ahl al-tasawwuf*
(Defining the school of the People of Self-purification), and Abd
al-Rahman al-Sulami's (d. 411) *Tabaqat al-sufiyya*
(Biographies of the Sufis).

Qushayri gathered definitions for *tasawwuf* from a number
of Sufi shaykhs and included them in his *Risala*. The following
is a translation of his chapter on Sufism (*tasawwuf*):

> Many people have asked, "What is the meaning of
> Sufism?" and "Who is a Sufi?," each one expressing
> what most struck him. A close examination of all this
> material would take us far from our aim of brevity.
> Here we will mention only some of the statements on
> this topic, with the aim of fostering understanding, if
> Allah Most High so wills.
>
> I heard Muhammad ibn Ahmad ibn Yahya al-Sufi
> say . . . that Abu Muhammad al-Jurayri was asked
> about Sufism and said, "Sufism means to take on

---

96 Abd al-Qahir al-Baghdadi, *Usul al-din* p. 315-16.

97 Entitled *Lataif al-isharat bi tafsir al-Quran* (The subtleties and allusions in
the commentary of the Quran).

every sublime moral characteristic from the life of the Prophet (🙼) and to leave behind every lowly one."

I heard Abd al-Rahman ibn Yusuf al-Isfahani say . . . that when questioned about Sufism, Junayd said, "To be a Sufi means that the truth causes you to die to yourself and to live through Him." I heard Abu Abd Rahman al-Sulami say . . . that when asked about the Sufi, al-Husayn ibn Mansur al-Hallaj said, "The Sufi is a person whose essence is one. No one admits him, and he admits no one." And I heard him say . . . that Abu Hamzah al-Baghdadi said, "The sign of the genuine Sufi is that he is poor, after having been rich, abased after having been honored, hidden, after having been famous. The sign of the false Sufi is that he has worldly wealth, after having been poor is honored after having been abased, and becomes famous after having been obscure."

Amr ibn Uthman al-Makki was asked about Sufism. He said, "It is that the servant be engaged at every moment in what is best for him at that moment." Muhammad ibn Ali al-Qassab said, "Sufism is noble traits manifested at a noble time in a noble individual among noble people." Sumnun, asked about Sufism, said, "Sufism means that you own nothing and nothing owns you." Ruwaym answered, "It means giving the self over to Allah Most High for whatever He wants of it." Junayd answered, "It means that you are together with Allah Most High, without other attachments."

I heard Abd Allah ibn Yusuf al-Isfahani say . . . that Ruwaym ibn Ahmad al-Baghdadi said, "Sufism is founded on three traits: clinging to spiritual poverty and the need of Allah; confirming oneself in generosity and concern for others; abandoning resistance to Allah's will and [abandoning] personal preference."

Maruf al-Karkhi said, "Sufism is to seize the realities and despair of what is in the hands of creatures." Hamdun al-Qassar said, "Keep company with the Sufis. With them the ugly person has all sorts of excuses!" Asked about the people of Sufism, Al-Kharraz said, "People who are made to give until they are exhilarated, who are blocked and frustrated until they lose themselves, who then are summoned away from intimate secrets—why, weep for us!"

Junayd said, "Sufism is force without compromise. The Sufis are people of one household. No outsider enters among them. Sufism is a remembrance of Allah and a uniting of parts, an ecstasy and a listening to guidance, an individual work and an emulation of the Prophet (ﷺ). The Sufi is like the earth. Every ugly thing is cast upon it, yet nothing grows out of it but what is pleasant. The Sufi is like the earth upon which walk the righteous and the libertine alike or like the cloud that shades everything or like the rain that gives everything drink. When you see a Sufi whose outward aspect is wealthy, know that his inner aspect is in ruins."

Sahl ibn Abd Allah al-Tustari said, "The Sufi is one whose blood may be shed with impunity and whose property is open to all." Nuri said, "The characteristic of the Sufi is to keep silent when he has nothing and to prefer others over himself when he has something." Kattani said, "Sufism is morality. Whoever is superior to you in morality is superior to you in Sufism."

Abu Ali al-Rudhbari said, "Sufism is to stay at the door of the Beloved even if you are driven away." He also said, "It is the purity of nearness to Allah after the impurity of distance from Him." It is said, "The most repulsive of all repulsive things is a stingy Sufi." And, "Sufism is an empty palm and a good heart." Shibli said, "Sufism is to sit with Allah without concerns." Abu Mansur said, "The Sufi is a pointer *from* Allah Most High while the rest of Creation are pointers *to* Allah Most High."

Shibli said. "The Sufi is cut off from the creation and put in contact with the Truth. He has said [to Moses], '*I have attached you to Myself*' [20:41]. Allah severs the Sufi from everything else, then says to him, '*You shall never see Me*' [7:143]! The Sufis are children in the lap of the truth. Sufism is scorching lightning. Sufism is to be protected against seeing the universe."

Ruwaym said, "Sufis do not disappear due to the virtue of their correcting each other. When they become reconciled to the way they are, there is no good in them." al-Jurayri said, "Sufism is self-observation and holding fast to right behavior." Al-Muzayyin said, "Sufism is yielding to the Truth." Abu Turab al-Nakhshabi said, "The Sufi is polluted by nothing and purifies everything." The Sufi, it is said, is he whom no search wearies nor any cause upsets.

I heard Abu Hatim al-Sijistani say . . . that Dhu al- Nun al-Misri was asked about the Sufis. He said, "They are a people who prefer Allah over everything and whom Allah prefers over everything." Al-Wasiti said, "The Sufis have hints. Then these become actions. Then nothing remains but sorrows!"

Nuri, questioned about the Sufi, said, "He is the one who listens to the spiritual concert and prefers lawful means." I heard Abu Hatim al-Sijistani say that Abu Nasr al-Sarraj said, "Al-Husri was asked, 'In your view, who is a Sufi?' He replied, 'He whom the earth does not bear nor the heavens shade.'"

This points to the state of *mahw*, erasure from the world. It is said that the Sufi is one who, if he meets with two states or two characteristics that are both good, will choose the better of the two.

Shibli was asked, "Why are the Sufis called by that name?" He answered, "Because of the last remaining remnant of their egos. If not for that, no name would attach to them!"

I heard Abu Hatim al-Sijistani say . . . that Ibn al-Jalla was asked, "What is the meaning of calling someone a Sufi?" He said, "We will not recognize this person by the condition of his formal learning. We will recognize that someone who is poor, stripped of means, who is with Allah Most High and without worldly place, but whom the Truth, glory to Him, does not prevent from the knowledge of every place, is to be called a Sufi.'

A dervish said, "Sufism is falling from dignity and blackness of face in this world and the next!" Abu Yaqub al-Mazabili said, "Sufism is a state in which the hallmarks of humanity melt away." Abul Hasan al-Sirwani said, "The Sufi is someone who is concerned with inner spiritual conditions as well as outer devotional exercises."

I heard Abu Ali al-Daqqaq say, "The best thing that has been said on this topic is the statement of the one who said, 'This is a path that is only suitable for people whose souls Allah has used to sweep away their dunghills.'"

In reference to this, he said one day, "If the poor dervish had nothing but a soul and he laid it before the dogs of this gate, no dog would look at it." Abu

Sahl al-Suluki said, "Sufism is the resistance to resistance." Al-Husri said, "The Sufi is not to be found after his nonexistence and does not cease to exist after he has come to be."

There is some ambiguity in this. The meaning of his statement, "He is not to be found after his nonexistence," is that when the calamities of his nature have passed away, those calamities do not return. His statement, "He does not cease to exist after he has come to be," means that when he is occupied with the Truth he does not collapse, like the rest of creation, for the events of life do not affect him.

The Sufi, it is said, is the one who has lost himself in what he has glimpsed of the truth. And it is said, "The Sufi's will is overpowered by direct divine action, but he is veiled by the conduct proper to servanthood." And, "The Sufi is not altered, but if he is altered, he is not polluted."

I heard Abu Abd al-Rahman al-Sulami say . . . that al-Kharraz said, "I was in the mosque of Kairouan one Friday, the day of congregational prescribed prayer, when I saw a man passing among the ranks, saying, "Be charitable to me! I used to be a Sufi, but I was weak. I gave him some money, but he said, 'Go away; for shame! That is not the thing for this problem!' And he would not accept it."[98]

4.13. SHAYKH ABD ALLAH AL-HARAWI AL-ANSARI (D. 481 AH)

A Sufi shaykh, hadith master (*hafiz*), and Quranic commentator (*mufassir*) of the Hanbali school, he was one of the most fanatical enemies of innovation, and a student of Khwaja Abu al-Hasan al-Kharqani (d. 425), the grandshaykh of the early Naqshbandi Sufi path.[99] His life and work are recorded by Dhahabi in his *Tarikh al-islam* and *Siyar alam al-nubala*, Ibn Rajab in his *Dhayl tabaqat al-hanabila*,[100] and Jami in his book in Persian *Manaqib-i Shaykh al-Islam Ansari*.[101]

98 Al-Qushayri, *al-Risala,* as translated by Rabia Harris, *Sufi Book of Spiritual Ascent* (Chicago: KAZI Publications, Inc.1997), p. 280-284.

99 The Naqshbandi chain of masters at the time of al-Kharqani is as follows: Abu Yazid al-Bistami > Abu al-Hasan al-Kharqani > Abu Ali al-Farmadi (Ghazali's teacher) > Abu Yusuf al-Hamadani > Abu al-Abbas al-Khidr > Abd al-Khaliq al-Ghujdawani.

100 Ibn Rajab, *Dhayl ala tabaqat al-hanabila* (Damascus, 1951) 1:64-85.

101 Edited by A.J. Arberry, "Jami's Biography of Ansari" in The Islamic Quarterly (July-December 1963) p. 57-82.

Al-Ansari was a prolific author of Sufi treatises, including:
- *Manazil al-sairin*, on which Ibn Qayyim wrote a commentary entitled *Madarij al-salikin*;
- *Tabaqat al-Sufiyya* (Biographies of the Sufi masters),

which is the expanded version of the earlier work by Abu Abd al-Rahman al-Sulami (d. 411) bearing the same title.

- *Kitab ilal al-maqamat* (Book of the pitfalls of spiritual stations), describing the characteristics of spiritual states for the student and the teacher in the Sufi path;
- *Kitab sad maydan* (in Persian, Book of the hundred fields), a commentary on the meanings of love in the verse: "*If you love Allah, follow me, and Allah will love you!*" (3:31). This book collects al-Harawi's lectures in the years 447-448 at the Great Mosque of Herat (in present-day Afghanistan) and presents his most eloquent exposition of the necessity of following the Sufi path.
- *Kashf al-asrar wa uddat al-abrar* (in Persian, the Unveiling of the secrets and the harness of the righteous), in ten volumes by al-Maybudi, it contains al-Harawi's Quranic commentary.

4.14. HUJJAT AL-ISLAM IMAM GHAZALI (D. 505 AH)

"The Proof of Islam," Abu Hamid al-Tusi al-Ghazali, was the reviver of the Fifth Islamic century, a scholar of *usul al-fiqh*, and an author of the most well-known work on *tasawwuf*, *Ihya ulum al-din* (The revival of the religious sciences). He says in his autobiography, *al-Munqidh min al-dalal* (Deliverance from error):

> The Sufi path consists in cleansing the heart from whatever is other than Allah . . . I concluded that the Sufis are the seekers in Allah's Way, and their conduct is the best conduct, and their way is the best way, and their manners are the most sanctified. They have cleaned their hearts from other than Allah and they have made them as pathways for rivers to run, carrying knowledge of Allah.[102]

102 Al-Ghazali, *al-Munqidh min al-dalal*, p. 131.

As Ibn Ajiba mentions in his *Iqaz al-himam*, al-Ghazali declared *tasawwuf* to be a *fard ayn*, or personal obligation, for every legally responsible Muslim man and woman, "as none but prophets are devoid of internal defects and diseases."[103]

The following is translated from parts of *Ihya ulum al-din*, including:

1 Definitions at the beginning of the book *Kitab sharh ajaib al-qalb* (Book of the explanation of the mysteries of the heart)

2 Section entitled, "The Soldiers of the Heart" in the same book

3 Section entitled, "Satan's domination over the heart through whispering (*al-waswas*)" in the same book

4 Section entitled, "Proofs . . ." from the book *Kitab riyadat al-nafs wa tahdhib al-akhlaq wa mualajat amrad al-qalb* (Book of the training of the ego and the disciplining of manners and the healing of the heart's diseases).[104]

1 Meaning of *nafs*: It has two meanings. First, it means the powers of anger and sexual appetite in a human being . . . and this is the usage mostly found among the people of *tasawwuf*, who take *nafs* as the comprehensive word for all the evil attributes of a person. That is why they say: one has to do battle with the ego and break it, as is referred to in the hadith, *ada aduwwuka nafsuka al-lati bayna janibayk*—"Your worst enemy is your ego which lies between your flanks."[105] It can be found in Bayhaqi's *Kitab al-zuhd* (Book of narrations on asceticism).

The second meaning of *nafs* is the soul, the human being in reality, his self and his person. However, it is described differently according to its different states. If it assumes calmness under command and has removed from itself the disturbance caused by the onslaught of passion, it is called "the satisfied soul" (*al-nafs al-mutmainna*) . . . In its first meaning the *nafs* does not envisage its return to Allah because it has kept itself far from Him; such a *nafs* is

---

103 Ibn Ajiba, *Iqaz al-himam* p. 8.
104 Al-Ghazali's words are cited beginning here.
105 Al-Iraqi says it is in Bayhaqi on the authority of Ibn Abbas and its chain of transmission contains Muhammad ibn Abd al-Rahman ibn Ghazwan, one of the forgers.

from the party of satan. However, when it does not
achieve calmness, yet sets itself against the love of
passions and objects to it, it is called "the self-accus-
ing soul" (*al-nafs al-lawwama*), because it rebukes its
owner for his neglect in the worship of his master . . .
If it gives up all protest and surrenders itself in total
obedience to the call of passions and shaytan, it is
named "the soul that enjoins evil" (*al-nafs al-ammara
bi al-su*) . . . which could be taken to refer to the ego
in its first meaning. . . .

2 Allah has armed soldiers that He has placed in
the hearts and the souls and others of His worlds, and
none knows their true nature and actual number
except He . . . [He proceeds to explain that the limbs
of the body, the five senses, will, instinct, and the
emotive and intellective powers are among those soldiers.] Know that the two soldiers of anger and sexual passion can be guided by the heart completely . . .
or on the other hand disobey and rebel against it completely, until they enslave it. Therein lies the death of
the heart and the termination of its journey towards
eternal happiness. The heart has other soldiers:
knowledge (*ilm*), wisdom (*hikma*) and reflection
(*tafakkur*) whose help it seeks by right, for they are
the Party of Allah against the other two who belong to
the party of shaytan . . .

Allah says, *"Have you seen the one who chooseth
for his god his own lust?"* (25:43), and *"He followed his
own lust. Therefore his likeness is as the likeness of a
dog; if thou attackest him he panteth with his tongue
out, and if thou leavest him he panteth with his tongue
out"* (7:176) and about the person who controlled the
passion of his ego Allah says, *"But as for him who
feared to stand before his Lord and restrained his soul
from lust, Lo! The garden will be his home"* (79:40-41).

Know that the body is like a town and the intellect of the mature human being is like a king ruling
that town. All the forces of the external and internal
senses he can muster are like his soldiers and his
aides. The ego that enjoins evil (*nafs ammara*), that
is, lust and anger, is like an enemy that challenges
him in his kingdom and strives to slaughter his people. The body thus becomes like a garrison-town or
sea-outpost, and the soul like its custodian posted in
it. If he fights against his enemies and defeats them

and compels them to do what he likes, he will be praised when he returns to Allah's presence, as Allah said, "*Allah hath conferred on those who strive with their wealth and lives a rank above the sedentary*" (4:95). . . .

3 The thoughts that stir one's desire are of two kinds: praiseworthy, and that is called "inspiration" (*ilham*), and blameworthy, and that is called "whispering" (*waswasa*) . . . The heart is owned mutually by a satanic force and an angel . . . The angel stands for a creature which Allah has created for the overflowing of benefit, the bestowal of knowledge, the unveiling of truth, the promise of reward, and the ordering of the good . . . The satanic force stands for a creature whose business is to be against all this . . . *Waswasa* against *ilham*, satanic against angelic, and success (*tawfiq*) against disappointment (*khidhlan*).

The Prophet (ﷺ) said, "There are two impulses in the soul, one from an angel which calls towards good and confirms truth; whoever finds this let him know it is from Allah and praise Him. Another impulse comes from the enemy which leads to doubt and denies truth and forbids good; whoever finds this, let him seek refuge in Allah from the accursed devil." Then he recited the verse, "*The devil shows you fear of poverty and enjoins evil upon you*" (2:268).[106]

The Prophet (ﷺ) said, "There is none among you in whom there is not a devil." They said, "Even in you, O Messenger of Allah?" He said, "Even in me, but Allah helped me to overcome him and he has submitted to me, so he doesn't order anything except good"[107] . . . The mutual repelling of the soldiers of the angels and the devils is constant in the battle over the heart, until the heart is conquered by one of the two sides which sets up its nation and settles there . . . And most hearts have been seized by the soldiers of Satan, who fill them with the whispers that call one to love this passing world and disregard the next. . . .

4 The Prophet (ﷺ) said, "The true fighter against unbelief is he who fights against his ego in obeying Allah"(*al-mujahidu man jahada nafsahu fi taat Allah*)[108] . . . Sufyan al-Thawri said, "I never dealt

106 Tirmidhi: *hasan*; Nisai; Iraqi did not weaken it.
107 Muslim.
108 A sound (*sahih*) hadith related by Tirmidhi, Ahmad, Tabarani, Ibn Majah, Ibn Hibban, al-Hakim, and Qudai.

with anything stronger against me than my own ego; it was one time with me, and one time against me" . . . Yahya ibn Muadh al-Razi said, "Fight against your ego with the four swords of training: eat little, sleep little, speak little, and be patient when people harm you . . . Then the ego will walk the paths of obedience, like a fleeing horseman in the field of battle."

4.14.1. THOSE WHO ATTACK IMAM GHAZALI

Today's "Salafis" have revived the practice of attacking Imam Ghazali and belittling those who read his works and rely on him to argue their opinions. This is especially the case with Imam Ghazali's *Ihya ulum al-din*. This book is a major work and a landmark in the study of *tasawwuf* whose immense success and readership is particularly disturbing for the enemies of *tasawwuf*. Some go so far as to claim that Ghazali was mad when he wrote this book; others misconstrue his deathbed reading of Imam Bukhari as a renunciation of *tasawwuf*. Yet others introduce the book's condemnation by a handful of scholars who are known for their anti-Sufi bias. Nevertheless, the book has superceded the clamor of its critics, and its translations continue to increase in number and quality. The following is intended to provide readers with reliable references concerning al-Ghazali's life and works.

Salah al-Din al-Safadi (d. 764), Abu Hayyan al-Andalusi's student, relates in his great biographical dictionary entitled *al-Wafi*, which contains over 14,000 biographies:

> Muhammad b. Muhammad b. Muhammad b. Ahmad, the Proof of Islam, the Ornament of the Faith, Abu Hamid al-Tusi (al-Ghazali), the Shafii jurist, was in his later years without rival.
>
> In 488 he gave up the entirety of his worldly estate (and his professorship at the Nizamiyya, where he had taught since 484) and followed the way of renunciation and solitude. He made the pilgrimage, and, upon his return, directed his steps to Syria, where he abided a while in the city of Damascus, giving instruction in the mosque retreat (*zawiyat al-jami*) which now bears his name in the Western quar-

ter. He then voyaged to Jerusalem, exerting himself greatly in worship and in visiting the holy sites and places. Next he travelled to Egypt, remaining for a while at Alexandria . . .

He returned to his native city of Tus (shortly before 492). Here he compiled a number of valuable books [among them the *Ihya*] before returning to Nishabur, where he was obliged to give lessons at the Nizamiyya (499). He subsequently forsook this and made his way back to his home city, where he assumed the directorship of a retreat (*khaniqah*) for the Sufis and that of a neighboring college for those occupied with learning. He divided his time among good works such as reciting through the Quran and holding lessons for the People of Hearts (the Sufis). . .

It is among the noblest and greatest of books, to the extent that it was said concerning it: If all books of Islam were lost except the *Ihya*, it would suffice for what was lost... They disapproved of him for including in it hadiths which were not established to be authentic, but such inclusion is permitted in works of encouraging good and discouraging evil (*al-targhib wa al-tarhib*). The book remains extremely valuable. Imam Fakhr al-Din al-Razi used to say, "It was as if Allah gathered all sciences under a dome, and showed them to al-Ghazali," or something to this effect. He passed away . . . in 505 at Tabaran . . . the citadel of Tus, where he was interred.[109]

The above clearly negates the fabrication that Ghazali disavowed *tasawwuf* before the end of his life. There are also those who would differentiate between the Ghazali of *usul al-fiqh* and the Ghazali of *tasawwuf*. When they are told that Imam Ghazali's books on the methodology and foundations of Islamic law are considered required reading in the field,[110] they say that he wrote them before the seclusion during which he adopted *tasawwuf*. In reality, the greatest and most comprehensive of the four books he wrote on *Usul al-fiqh* (Principles of Jurisprudence) was composed in the last period of his life, as stated by Dr. Taha al-Alwani:

Imam al-Ghazali's Encyclopedia of Sharia Source

109 Salah al-Din Khalil ibn Aybak al-Safadi, *al-Wafi bi al-wafayat* (Wiesbaden, 1962-1984) 1:274-277 (#176).
110 Such as his *Mustafa, mankhul* and *Shifa al-ghalil*.

Methodology, his fourth book on the subject, and his last word, was *al-Mustasfa*, which has been printed several times in Egypt and elsewhere. Indeed, this is the work he wrote after coming out of his period of meditation and seclusion.[111]

The notice on Ghazali in the *Reliance* states:

> In Damascus he lived in seclusion for some ten years, engaged in spiritual struggle and the remembrance of Allah, at the end of which he emerged to produce his masterpiece *Ihya ulum al-din* [Revival of the Religious Sciences], a classic among the books of the Muslims about internalizing Godfearingness (*taqwa*) in one's dealings with Allah, illuminating the soul through obedience to Him, and the levels of believers' attainment therein. The work shows how deeply Ghazali personally realized what he wrote about, and his masterly treatment of hundreds of questions dealing with the inner life that no-one had previously discussed or solved is a performance of sustained excellence that shows its author's well-disciplined intellect and profound appreciation of human psychology. He also wrote nearly two hundred other works, on the theory of government, sacred law, refutations of philosophers, tenets of faith, Sufism, Quranic exegesis, scholastic theology, and bases of Islamic jurisprudence.[112]

Among Ghazali's scholarly critics, the most vocal was Ibn al-Jawzi, who happened also to hold Sufis in disdain. He dismisses the *Ihya* in four of his works: *Ilam al-ahya bi aghlat al-ihya* (Informing the living about the mistakes of the *Ihya*), *Talbis Iblis, Kitab al-qussas*,[113] and his history *al-Muntazam fi tarikh al-muluk wa al-umam*.[114]

Ibn al-Jawzi's views were in part adopted by Ibn Taymiyya and his student Dhahabi. The basis of each of their positions was Ghazali's use of weak hadiths.[115] Their criticism is most

---

111 Taha Jaber al-Alwani, *Usul al-fiqh al-islami: Source Methodology in Islamic Jurisprudence*, ed. Yusuf Talal DeLorenzo (Herndon, VA: IIIT, 1411/1990) p. 50.
112 Nuh Keller, *Reliance of the Traveller* p. 1048.
113 Ibn al-Jawzi, *Kitab al-qussas wa al-mudhakkirin* p. 201.
114 Ibn al-Jawzi, *al-Muntazam* 9:169.
115 A list is provided by Taj al-Din al-Subki in his *Tabaqat*

likely an exaggeration, considering that both the *hafiz* al-Iraqi (d. 806) and the *hafiz* al-Zabidi (d. 1205) documented every hadith in the *Ihya* and never questioned its usefulness as a whole. Instead, they accepted the book's immense standing among Muslims, contributed to its embellishment, and helped to promote it as a reliable manual for spiritual advancement. As Subki stressed, Ghazali never excelled in the hadith.[116]

More importantly, the majority of hadith masters permit the use of weak hadiths in anything other than the derivation of legal rulings. It is permitted, therefore, by countless hadith scholars, and other scholars as well, to use weaker hadiths in the encouragement of good and the discouragement of evil (*al-targhib wa al-tarhib*), for example.[117] It must be understood that Ghazali incorporated all material that was useful in the accomplishment of his didactic goals. He chose his hadith on the bases of content rather than origin or chain of transmission. Most of the *Ihya* consists of quotations from Quran, hadith, and the sayings of other scholars, with Ghazali's own prose accounting for less than 35% of the work.[118] Finally, most of the very numerous hadiths cited by Ghazali are authentic in origin.

In conclusion, it is true, as al-Safadi says, that the *Ihya* ranks as a work of *targhib*, or ethics, and represents the principal business of *tasawwuf*. Criteria for the authentication of evidence cited in such works are less rigorous than for works of doctrine (*aqida*) and jurisprudence (*fiqh*), according to the majority of the scholars. To use the same criteria for works of *tasawwuf* is to compare apples and oranges. Therefore, also as al-Safadi correctly indicated, the criticism of *Ihya ulum al-din* on the basis of weak hadiths is not valid. Nor is it valid to criticize similar works, for example Dhahabi's criticism of Abu Talik al-Makki's *Qut al-qulub*, based on this one aspect. To cling to such criticism and ignore the greater endorsement of

116 Taj al-Din al-Subki, *Tabaqat al-Shafiiyya* 4:179-182.

117 See al-Hakim, *al-Madkhal li ilm al-hadith* (beginning), al-Bayhaqi, *Dalail al-nubuwwa* (introduction), Nawawi, *al-Tibyan fi ulum al-quran* p. 17. The latter says: "The scholars are in agreement on the legitimacy of using weak hadiths in the realm of virtuous works." Al-Sakhawi stated the view of the scholarly consensus on this question in the Epilogue of of his *al-Qawl al-badi fi al-salat ala al-habib al-shafi* (The admirable doctrine concerning the invocation of blessings upon the beloved intercessor) (Beirut: Dar al-kutub al-ilmiyya, 1407/ 1987) p. 245-246.

118 T.J. Winter, trans. Ghazali's *Remembrance of Death* (Cambridge: Islamic Texts Society, 1989), Introduction, p. xxix n. 63.

tasawwuf and the works that address it is to cling to something other than sound knowledge. Let al-Dhahabi's advice be remembered: "Do not hasten to judge, rather, keep the best opinion of Sufis";[119] or Imam Ghazali's advice: "Think good thoughts (about Sufis) and do not harbor doubts in your heart";[120] or Ibn Hajar al-Haytami's: "Bad thoughts about them (Sufis) is the death of the heart."[121] It is better to take the immense good that is in each of the Sufis' works in the proper manner, and to respect the masters of *tasawwuf*, the least among whom towers high above most people in their knowledge. It is better not to search out disagreements among scholars, and respect those who speak about Allah.

4.14.2. THE VALIDITY OF WEAK HADITH

To conclude the discussion on *Ihya ulum al-din*, following are statements on the permissibility of weak hadith from the hadith masters. Each of these helps to establish, as Imam al-Sakhawi stated, that "The majority of the scholars (*al-jumhur*) hold that weak hadith can be used as a basis for practicing good deeds and achieving good character but not for legal rulings."[122]

Ibn Hajar writes in *Hadi al-sari*:

> Malik and Bukhari have a different understanding of the validity of hadith. Malik does not consider interruption in the chain of transmission to be a defect in the hadith. For this reason he cites hadiths with interrupted chains of the types *mursal* and *munqati*, and chainless communications (*balaghat*) as part of the main object of his book (*al-Muwatta*), whereas Bukhari considers interruption to be a defect in the chain of transmission. Thus, he does not cite these hadiths except as something outside the main object of his book (*al-Jami al-sahih*), for example commentaries (*taliq*) and titles of chapters.[123]

Al-Hakim (d. 405) relates in his *Madkhal*, a manual on the science of hadith:

> I heard Abu Zakariyya al-Anbari say that

---

119 Al-Dhahabi, *Mizan al-itidal* 3:214, in his biographical notice on Ibn al-Farid.
120 Al-Ghazali, a*l-Munqidh min al-dalal* (Damascus 1956) p. 40.
121 Ibn Hajar al-Haytami, *Fatawa hadithiyya* (Cairo: al-Halabi, 1970) p. 331. *Fatwa* concerning critics of those who respect *tasawwuf* and believe in saints.
122 Imam al-Sakhawi, at the conclusion of his book *al-Qawl al-badi*.
123 Ibn Hajar, *Hadi al-sari*, ed. Ibrahim Atwa Awad (Cairo, 1963) p. 21.

> Muhammad ibn Ishaq ibn Ibrahim al-Hanzali told him that his father used to relate from Abd al-Rahman ibn Mahdi that he used to say, "We were accommodating concerning the *isnad* in what we transmitted regarding reward and punishment and virtuous actions, and were indulgent concerning the men (i.e. concerning their identity and reliability); but when we transmit about what is lawful and what is prohibited, we are strict about the *isnad*s and scrutinize the men."
>
> I heard Abu Zakariyya Yahya ibn Muhammad al-Anbari say that he heard Abu al-Abbas Ahmad ibn Muhammad al-Sijzi say that he heard al-Naufali say that he heard Ahmad ibn Hanbal say, "When we transmit from Allah's Messenger about what is lawful and what is prohibited, about usages and legal ordinances, we are strict; but when we transmit from the Prophet (ﷺ) about virtuous actions and what does not lay down or rescind a legal ordinance, we are accommodating about the *isnad*s."[124]

Here is the complete text of Sakhawi's *al-Qawl al-badi*:

> Shaykh al-Islam Abu Zakariyya al-Nawawi said in the *Adhkar*: The *ulama* among the experts in hadith and the experts in law and others have said: it is permissible and (also) recommended that the religious practice (*al-amal*) concerning good deeds and good character (*al-fadail*), encouragement to good and discouragement from evil (*al-targhib wa al-tarhib*) be based (even) on weak hadith as long as it is not forged. As for legal rulings (*ahkam*) such as what is permitted and what is forbidden, or the modalities of trade, marriage, divorce and other than that: one's practice is not based upon anything other than sound (*sahih*) or fair (*hasan*) hadith, except as a precaution in some matter related to one of the above, for example, if a weak hadith was cited about the reprehensibility (*karahat*) of certain kinds of sales or marriages. In such cases what is recommended (*mustahabb*) is to avoid such sales and marriages, but it is not obligatory.

124 Al-Hakim, *al-Madkhal ila marifat al-iklil*, ed. and trans. James Robson, *An Introduction to the Science of Tradition* (London: Royal Asiatic Society of Great Britain and Ireland, 1953) p. 11.

Disagreeing with this Ibn al-Arabi al-Maliki said, "Absolutely no practice is based on weak hadith."

I have heard my shaykh (Ibn Hajar al-Asqalani) insist on the following, and he put it to me in writing himself:

The conditions for religious practice based on weak hadith are three:

1 This is unanimously agreed upon: That the weakness must not be very strong. This excludes those hadith singly recorded by liars or those accused of lying, and those who make gross mistakes.

2 That there be a general legal basis for it. This excludes what is invented and has no legal basis to start with.

3 That one not think, while practicing on the basis of it, that it has been established as true. This is in order that no words which the Prophet (ﷺ) did not (verifiably) say be attributed to him.

The last two conditions are from Ibn Abd al-Salam and his companion Ibn Daqiq al-Id; Abu Said al-Alai reported unanimity over the first one.

I say: It has been reported from Imam Ahmad that one may practice on the basis of the weak hadith if there is no other hadith to that effect and also if there is no hadith that contradicts it. In one narration he is reported to say, "I like weak hadith better than men's opinions." Ibn Hazm has similarly mentioned that Hanafi scholars unanimously agree that the school of Abu Hanifa holds that weak hadith is preferable to opinion (*ray*) and analogy (*qiyas*). Ahmad was asked about someone finding himself in a country with, on the one hand, a possessor of hadith (*sahib hadith*) who does not know the sound from the unsound, and, on the other, a possessor of opinion (*sahib ray*): who should he consult? He replied, "Let him consult the possessor of hadith and not the possessor of opinion."

Abu Abd Allah Ibn Mandah reported from Abu Dawud, the author of the *Sunan* and a student of Imam Ahmad, that Abu Dawud used to cite the chain of transmission of a weak hadith if he did not find other than it under that particular heading (*bab*), and that he considered it stronger evidence than opinion.

What emerges from this is that there are three diverging views:

- No practice is based on weak hadith whatsoever
- Practice is categorically based upon it if no other evidence is found under the same heading
- The majority of the scholars (*al-jumhur*) hold that it can be used as a basis for practicing good deeds and achieving good character, but not for legal rulings. And Allah is the Granter of success.[125]

Some question the fact that Imam Ahmad allowed the use of weak hadith following Ibn Taymiyya's assertion that "The one who relates from Ahmad that he used to rely upon the weak hadith, which is not *sahih* or *hasan*, has erred."[126] This is true, in part, as Sakhawi writes that Imam Ahmad did not apply weak hadith to *ahkam*, or legal rulings. Thus the meaning of what Ibn Taymiyya says is "the one who relates from Ahmad that he used to rely upon the weak hadith in deriving rulings in Sharia . . ." Although he did not do so in the derivation of legal rulings, there is no doubt that Imam Ahmad accepted weak hadith. This is related by al-Hakim, as already quoted, confirmed by Ibn Arabi al-Maliki,[127] and even confirmed by Ibn Taymiyya elsewhere in his work:

> Ahmad ibn Hanbal and other scholars permitted the narration of hadith regarding the virtues as long as it is not known that it is a lie... as it is possible that the reward will be true, although none of the Imams have said that it is permissible to consider something required (*wajib*) or recommended (*mustahabb*) by way of a weak hadith, and whoever said so differed from the consensus.[128]

However, Ibn Taymiyya's claim that "none of the Imams have declared an action recommended by way of a weak hadith, and whoever said so differed from the consensus" is evidently

---

125 Al-Sakhawi, *al-Qawl al-badi fi al-salat ala al-habib al-shafi* (The admirable doctrine concerning the invocation upon the beloved intercessor) (Beirut: Dar al-kutub al-ilmiyya, 1407/1987) p. 245-246.

126 Ibn Taymiyya, *Qaida jalila* p. 82.

127 Ibn al-Arabi al-Maliki, *Aridat al-ahwadhi* 5:201.

128 Ibn Taymiyya, *Qaida fi al-tawassul wa al-wasila*, ed. Rabia ibn Hadi Umayr al-Mudkhali, p. 162 (#478).

incorrect, as proven by Sakhawi's unquestioned relation of Nawawi's words:

> The *ulama* among the experts in hadith and the experts in law and others have said . . . for example, if a weak hadith was cited about the reprehensibility (*karahat*) of certain kinds of sales or marriages . . . what is recommended (*mustahabb*) is to avoid such sales and marriages, but it is not obligatory.

4.15. ABU AL-WAFA IBN AQIL AL-HANBALI (D. 513 AH)

Like al-Harawi al-Ansari, Ibn Aqil was a *hafiz* and *faqih* of the Hanbali school who was an ardent defender of the *sunna* and of *tasawwuf*. He is considered a reviver of the school of Imam Ahmad, although he himself had a number of teachers from different schools. Like other Sufis of his school, such as Ibn Qudama (d. 620) and al-Tufi (d. 715), Ibn Aqil considered al-Hallaj a saint and never doubted his sincerity and right-eousness. Ibn al-Jawzi reported that he had in his own posses-sion the autograph copy of a treatise Ibn Aqil wrote in praise of al-Hallaj, entitled *Juz fi nasr karamat al-Hallaj* (Opuscule in praise of al-Hallaj's gifts). Ibn Aqil was a polymath and extremely prolific writer. His *Kitab al-funun* reportedly num-bered up to eight hundred volumes, of which only one is extant.[129]

4.16. IBN AL-JAWZI (D. 597 AH)

This hadith master and historian of the Hanbali school was a fierce enemy of innovators in his time. His writings against anthropomorphists have been quoted extensively in the first half of this book. "Salafis" often quote his *Talbis iblis* (Satan's delusion) in their quest to oppose *tasawwuf*, but the book was written only to criticize excesses that he saw in all groups of the Community, including scholars of all kinds and Sufis.

Talbis iblis is perhaps the most important single factor in sustaining the notion of Ibn al-Jawzi's hostility towards *tasawwuf*. In reality, this work was not written against

---

129 See George Makdisi's article in the *Encyclopedia of Islam*, 2nd ed., s.v. "Ibn Akil."

tasawwuf or Sufis at all. It is an indictment of all unorthodox doctrines and practices, regardless of their origins, including anything the author considered an unwarranted innovation in the rule of Sharia. The book was written against specific innovative practices within many groups, including the philosophers (*al-mutafalsifa*), the theologians (*al-mutakallimun*), hadith scholars (*ulama al-hadith*), jurists (*al-fuqaha*), preachers (*al-wuaz*), philologists (*al-nahawiyyun*), poets (*al-shuara*), and certain Sufis. It is in no way an indictment of the subjects they studied and taught, but rather of specific innovations in their respective disciplines and fields.

Ibn al-Jawzi actually wrote many books of *manaqib*, or "merits," about the early Sufis, including *Manaqib Rabia al-Adawiyya*, *Manaqib Maruf al-Karkhi*, *Manaqib Ibrahim ibn Adham*, *Manaqib Bishr al-Hafi*, and others. His *Sifat al-safwa* (The manners of the elite)[130] and his *Minhaj al-qasidin wa mufid al-sadiqin* (The road of the travellers to Allah and the instructor of the truthful) are considered pillars in the field of *tasawwuf*. He was motivated to write the latter following the success of Ghazali's *Ihya ulum al-din*. Indeed the *Minhaj* adopts much of the methodology and language of the *Ihya*, as well as treating the same subject-matter: self-purification and personal ethics.

The *Minhaj* was epitomized in one volume by Najm al-Din Abu al-Abbas Ahmad ibn Qudama (d. 742). Following are some of the chapter titles and excerpts most illustrative of Imam Ghazali's influence on Ibn al-Jawzi, and of Ibn al-Jawzi's adoption of Sufi terminology:

- *Fasl ilm ahwal al-qalb* (Section on the science of the states of the heart)
- *Fasl fi daqaiq al-adab al-batina fi al-zakat* (Section on the ethics of the hidden minutiae of *zakat*)
- *Fasl fi al-adab al-batina wa al-ishara ila adab al-hajj* (Section on the ethics of the secrets of the pilgrimage)
- *Kitab riyadat al-nafs wa tahdhib al-khuluq wa mualajat amrad al-qalb* (Book of the training of the ego, the upbringing of the character, and the treating of the diseases of the heart)

130 An abridgment of Abu Nuaym's *Hilyat al-awliya* (The adornment of the saints).

- *Fasl fi faidat shahawat al-nafs* (Section on the benefit of the appetites of the ego)
- *Bayan al-riya al-khafi al-ladhi huwa akhfa min dabib al-naml* (Exposition of the hidden self-display which is more concealed than the treading of the ant)
- *Fasl fi bayan ma yuhbitu al-amal min al-riya wa ma la yuhbit* (Section exposing the self-display which nullifies one's deeds and the self-display which doesn't)
- *Fasl fi dawa al-riya wa tariqatu mualajat al-qalbi fih* (Section on the remedy of self-display and the way to treat the heart from its ill)
- *Kitab al-mahabba wa al-shawqi wa al-unsi wa al-rida* (Book of love, passionate longing, familiarity, and good pleasure)
- *Fasl fi bayan mina al-shawq ila allahi taala* (Section exposing the meaning of passionate longing for Allah)
- *Bab fi al-muhasaba wa al-muraqaba* (Chapter on taking account of oneself and vigilance)

al-maqam al-awwal: al-musharata
(The first station: commitment)

al-maqam al-thani: al-muraqaba
(The second station: vigilance)

al-maqam al-thalith: al-muhasaba bada al-amal
(The third station: self-accounting after a deed)

al-maqam al-rabi: muaqabat al-nafs ala taqsiriha
(The fourth station: berating the ego for its shortcomings)

al-maqam al-khamis: al-mujahada
(The fifth station: struggling)

al-maqam al-sadis: fi muatabat al-nafs wa tawbikhiha
(The sixth station: castigating and chiding the ego)

Abu Bakr al-Siddiq said: "Whoever hates his ego for Allah's sake, Allah will protect Him against what He hates."

Anas said: I heard Umar say as he was alone behind a wall, "Bakh, bakh! Bravo, well done, O my ego! By Allah, you had better fear Allah, O little son of Khattab, or he will punish you!"

Al-Bakhtari ibn Haritha said, "I saw one of the devoted worshippers sitting in front of a fire which he had kindled as he was castigating his ego, and he did not stop castigating his ego until he died."

One of them said, "When the saints are mentioned, I say to

myself, Fie on you and fie on you again." Know that your worst enemy is the ego that lies between your two flanks. It has been created a tyrant commanding to evil, always pushing you towards it, and you have been ordered to straighten it, cleanse it *(tazkiyat)*, wean it from what it feeds on, and drag it in chains, subdued, to the worship of its Lord.[131]

4.17. SHAYKH ABD AL-QADIR AL-JILANI (D. 561 AH)

Eminent among the great saints, and nicknamed al-Ghawth al-Azam or the Arch-helper, Abd al-Qadir is also a prominent jurist of the Hanbali school. His ties to the Shafii school and to Imam Abu Hanifa have already been mentioned. He was the disciple of well-known saints, including Abu al-Khayr Hammad ibn Muslim al-Dabbas (d. 525) and Khwaja Abu Yusuf al-Hamadani (d. 535), who is second in line after Abu al-Hasan al-Kharqani (al-Harawi al-Ansari's shaykh) in the early Naqshbandi chain of authority.

The most famous of Shaykh Abd al-Qadir's works are:
- *Al-Ghunya li talibi tariq al-haqq* (Sufficient provision for seekers of the path of truth). It is one of the most concise presentations of the school of law of Imam Ahmad ibn Hanbal ever written, and includes the sound Sunni teaching on doctrine *(aqida)* and Sufism *(tasawwuf)*;
- *Al-Fath al-rabbani* (The Lord's opening), a collection of sermons for the student and the teacher in the Sufi path and all those attracted to perfection. True to its title, this book brings its reader immense profit and spiritual benefit;
- *Futuh al-ghayb* (Openings to the unseen), another collection of sermons more advanced than the previous one, and just as priceless. Both have been translated into English;

Due to his standing in the Hanbali school, Abd al-Qadir was greatly respected by Ibn Taymiyya, who, in his entire *Fatawa*, gives him alone the title "my Shaykh" *(shaykhuna)*. Ibn

---

131 Ibn Qudama, *Mukhtasar minhaj al-qasidin li Ibn al-Jawzi*, ed. M. Ahmad Hamdan and Abd al-Qadir Arnaut, 2nd. ed. (Damascus: Maktab al-shabab al-muslim wa al-maktab al-islami, 1380/1961) p. 426.

Taymiyya reserves the title "my Imam" (*imamuna*) for Ahmad ibn Hanbal and frequently cites Jilani and his shaykh al-Dabbas as among the best examples of latter-time Sufis.

Shaykh Abd al-Qadir's *karamat*, or miracles, are too many to number. One of them was his gift of guidance, which, through his speaking, led untold thousands to Islam or repentance. Al-Shattanawfi mentions many of Abd al-Qadir's miracles, and provides a chain of transmission for each.[132] Ibn Taymiyya verified the authenticity of these chains of transmission, but his student al-Dhahabi expressed his doubts about many of them, despite having expressed his general acceptance of Abd al-Qadir's miracles. Dhahabi's doubt appeared earlier in relation to the sound report of Imam Ahmad's admiration of al-Muhasibi. These are his words about Jilani:

> [#893] al-Shaykh Abd al-Qadir (Al-Jilani): The shaykh, the imam, the scholar, the *zahid*, the knower, the exemplar, Shaykh Al-Islam, the distinguished one among the saints . . . the Hanbali, the Shaykh of Baghdad . . . I say that there is no one among the great shaykhs who has more spiritual states and miracles (*karamat*) than Shaykh Abd al-Qadir, but a lot of it is untrue and some of those things are impossible.[133]

The following account of Jilani's first encounter with al-Hamadani is related by Haytami in his *Fatawa hadithiyya*:

> Abu Said Abd Allah ibn Abi Asrun (d. 585), the Imam of the School of Shafii, said, "When I began a search for religious knowledge I kept company with my friend, Ibn al-Saqa, who was a student in the Nizamiyya School, and it was our custom to visit the pious. We heard that there was in Baghdad a man named Yusuf al-Hamadani who was known as al-Ghawth, and that he was able to appear whenever he liked and was able to disappear whenever he liked. So I decided to visit him along with Ibn al-Saqa and Shaykh Abd al-Qadir al-Jilani, who was a young man at that time. Ibn al-Saqa said, "When we visit Shaykh

---

132 Al-Shattanawfi, *Bahjat al-asrar.*

133 Dhahabi, *Siyar alam al-nubala.* This all-too-subjective denial on Dhahabi's part is reminiscent of his authentication-cum-denial of the report of Imam Ahmad's behavior upon hearing al-Muhasibi for the first time.

Yusuf al-Hamadani I am going to ask him a question the answer to which he will not know." I said, "I am also going to ask him a question and I want to see what he is going to say." Shaykh Abd al-Qadir al-Jilani said, "O Allah, protect me from asking a saint like Yusuf Hamadani a question, but I will go into his presence asking for his *baraka*–blessing–and divine knowledge."

We entered his association. He kept himself veiled from us and we did not see him until after some time. He looked at Ibn al-Saqa angrily and said, without having been informed of his name, "O Ibn al-Saqa, how dare you ask me a question when your intention is to confound me? Your question is this and your answer is this!" Then he said, "I am seeing the fire of disbelief burning in your heart." He looked at me and said, "O Abd Allah, are you asking me a question and awaiting my answer? Your question is this and your answer is this. Let the people be sad for you because they are losing as a result of your disrespect for me." Then he looked at Shaykh Abd al-Qadir al-Jilani, made him sit next to him, and showed him honor. He said, "O Abd al-Qadir, you have satisfied Allah and His Prophet (ﷺ) with your proper respect for me. I see you in the future sitting on the highest place in Baghdad and speaking and guiding people and saying to them that your feet are on the neck of every saint And I almost see before me every saint of your time giving you precedence because of your great station and honor."

Ibn Abi Asrun continues, "Abd al-Qadir's fame became widespread and all that Shaykh al-Hamadani said about him came to pass. There came a time when he did say, "My feet are on the necks of all the saints," and he was a reference and a beacon guiding all people in his time to their destinations.

The fate of Ibn al-Saqa was something else. He was brilliant in his knowledge of the divine law. He preceded all the scholars in his time. He used to debate with the scholars of his time and overcome them, until the caliph called him to his association. One day the caliph sent him as a messenger to the King of Byzantium, who in his turn called all his priests and the scholars of the Christian religion to debate with him. Ibn al-Saqa was able to defeat all of them in debate. They were helpless to give answers in his presence. He was giving answers to them that made them look like children and mere students in his presence.

His brilliance made the King of Byzantium so fascinated with him that he invited him to his private family meeting. There he saw the daughter of the King. He immediately fell in love with her, and he asked her father, the King, for her hand in marriage. She refused except on condition that he accept her religion. He did, leaving Islam and accepting the Christian religion of the princess. After his marriage he became seriously ill. They threw him out of the palace. He became a town beggar, asking everyone for food, yet no one would provide for him. Darkness had come over his face.

One day he saw someone that had known him before. That person relates, "I asked him, What happened to you?" He replied: "There was a temptation and I fell into it." The man asked him, "Do you remember anything from the Holy Quran?" He replied, "I only remember, "*Again and again will those who disbelieve wish that they were Muslims*" (rubbama yawaddu al-ladhina kafaru law kanu muslimin) (15:2)."

He was trembling as if he was giving up his last breath. I turned him towards the Kabah, but he kept turning towards the East. Then I turned him back towards the Kabah, but he turned himself to the East. I turned him a third time, but he turned himself to the East. Then as his soul was passing from him, he said, "O Allah, that is the result of my disrespect to Your saint, Yusuf al-Hamadani."

Ibn Abi Asrun continues, "I went to Damascus and the king there, Nur al-Din al-Shahid, put me in control of the religious department, and I accepted. As a result, this world entered from every side: provision, sustenance, fame, money, position for the rest of my life. That is what the *ghawth* Yusuf al-Hamadani had predicted for me."[134]

---

134 Al-Haytami, *Fatawa hadithiyya* 315-316.

4.18. IMAM FAKHR AL-DIN RAZI (D. 606 AH)

"A Shafii scholar of genius and a *mujtahid imam* in tenets of faith, he was among the foremost figures of his time in mastery of rational and traditional Islamic sciences, and preserved the religion of mainstream Islam from the deviations of . . . . aberrant sects of his era."[135]

Imam Fakhr wrote in his *Itiqadat firaq al-muslimin wa al-mushrikin*:

> The summary of what the Sufis say is that the way to the knowledge of Allah is self-purification and renunciation of material attachments, and this is an excellent way . . . Sufis are a folk who work with reflection and the detaching of the self from materialistic trappings. They strive in order that their inner being be solely occupied with the remembrance of Allah in all of their occupations and their actions, and they are characterized by the perfection of their manners in dealing with Allah. Verily these are the best of all the sects of human beings. [136]

4.19. ABU AL-HASAN AL-SHADHILI (D. 656 AH)

One of the great saints of the Community, he said about *tasawwuf*:

> He who dies without having entered into this knowledge of ours dies insisting upon his grave sins (*kabair*) without realizing it.[137]

4.20. AL-IZZ IBN ABD AL-SALAM AL-SULAYM (D. 660)

His nickname is "Sultan of the Scholars." As the Shaykh al-Islam of his time, he took hadith from the hafiz al-Qasim ibn Ali ibn Asakir al-Dimashqi, and *tasawwuf* from the Shafii Shaykh al-Islam Shihab al-Din al-Suhrawardi (539-632),

---

135 Nuh Keller, *Reliance of the Traveller* p. 1046.
136 Fakhr al-Din al-Razi, *Itiqadat firaq al-muslimin* p. 72-73.
137 In Ibn Ajiba, *Iqaz al-himam* p. 8.

whom al-Dhahabi calls, "The shaykh, the imam, the scholar, the *zahid*, the knower, the *muhaddith*, Shaykh al-Islam, the Peerless One of the Sufis . . ."[138] Al-Izz ibn Abd al-Salam also studied under Abu al-Hasan al-Shadhili (d. 656) and his disciple al-Mursi. The author of *Miftah al-saada* and *al-Subki* relate that al-Izz would say, upon hearing al-Shadhili and al-Mursi speaking, "This is a kind of speech that is fresh from Allah."[139]

In his two-volume *Qawaid al-ahkam fi masalih al-anam* on *usul al-fiqh* al-Izz mentions that the Sufis are those meant by Allah's saying, *"Allah's party"* (5:56, 58:22), and he defines *tasawwuf* as "the betterment of hearts, through whose health bodies are healthy, and through whose disease bodies are diseased." He considers the knowledge of external legal rulings an understanding of the law in its generalities, while the knowledge of internal matters is an understanding of the law in its subtle details.[140]

Among Al-Izz ibn Abd al-Salam's books on *tasawwuf* are:

- *Shajarat al-maarif wa al-ahwal wa salih al-aqwal wa al-amal* (The tree of the gnostic sciences and states and pious sayings and deeds). The last seven chapters are devoted to the various branches of *ihsan* in one's religion.
- *Mukhtasar riayat al-Muhasibi*, an abridgment of al-Muhasibi's book on the Observance of the rights of Allah;
- *Masail al-tariqa fi ilm al-haqiqa* (Questions of the Sufi path concerning the knowledge of Reality) in which al-Izz answers sixty questions regarding *tasawwuf*;
- *Risala fi al-qutb wa al-abdal al-arbain* (Treatise on the Pole of saints and the forty substitutes);
- *Fawaid al-balwa wa al-mihan* (The benefits of trials and afflictions);
- *Nihayat al-rughba fi adab al-suhba* (The obtainment of wishes in the etiquette of companionship).

Due to his strictness in every matter, he is famous for his

---

138 Al-Dhahabi, *Siyar alam al-nubala* [#969].
139 *Miftah al-saada* 2:353; al-Subki, *Tabaqat al-shafiiyya* 8:214.
140 Al-Izz ibn Abd al-Salam, *Qawaid al-ahkam* (Dar al-sharq li al-tibaa, 1388/1968) 1:29, 2:212.

religious edict (*fatwa*) permitting *sama*, or poetry recitals, and movement or dancing that is associated with trances during the remembrance of Allah (*dhikr*). Imam Ahmad related in his *Musnad*:

> Ali said: I visited the Prophet (ﷺ) with Jafar (ibn Abi Talib and Zayd (ibn Haritha). The Prophet (ﷺ) said to Zayd, "You are my freedman" (*anta mawlay*), whereupon Zayd began to hop on one leg (*hajala*) around the Prophet (ﷺ). The Prophet (ﷺ) then said to Jafar, "You resemble me in my creation and my manners" (*anta ashbahta khalqi wa khuluqi*), whereupon Jafar began to hop behind Zayd. The Prophet (ﷺ) then said to me, "You pertain to me and I pertain to you" (*anta minni wa ana minka*) whereupon I began to hop behind Jafar.[141]

According to Shaykh al-Islam Ibn Hajar al-Haytami, some scholars have seen this as evidence for the permissibility of dancing (*al-raqs*) upon hearing a recital (*sama*) that lifts the spirit.[142] Al-Yafii concurs with him in *Mirat al-jinan*.[143] Both mention al-Izz ibn Abd al-Salam as their chief example, since it is authentically reported that he himself "attended the sama and danced in states of ecstasy" (*kana yahduru al-sama wa yarqusu wa yatawajadu*).[144]

This permission of dancing by the Imams and hadith masters precludes the prohibition of *sama* in general, and of the dancing that accompanies it. This is true regardless of Ibn Taymiyya's reservations about *sama*, which, in the mouths of today's "Salafis," become cut-and-dry prohibitions.

In cases where dancing is prohibited, the issue is a worldly kind of dancing that has nothing to do with the ecstasy of *sama* and *dhikr*. Al-Izz ibn Abd al-Salam differentiated the two in his religious edicts:

> Dancing is a *bida* or innovation which is not countenanced except by one deficient in his mind. It is

141 Ahmad, *Musnad* 1:108 (#860).
142 Al-Haytami, *Fatawa hadithiyya* p. 212.
143 Al-Yafii, *Mirat al-jinan* 4:154.
144 Ibn al-Imad, *Shadharat al-dhahab* 5:302; Ibn Shakir al-Kutabi, *Fawat al-wafayat* 1:595; al-Yafii, *Mirat al-jinan* 4:154; al-Nabahani, *Jami karamat al-awliya* 2:71; Abu al-Saadat, *Taj al-maarif* p. 250.

unfitting for other than women. As for the audition of poetry (*sama*) which stirs one towards states of purity (*ahwal saniyya*) which remind one of the hereafter: there is nothing wrong with it, nay, it is recommended (*bal yundabu ilayh*) for lukewarm and dry hearts. However, the one who harbors wrong desires in his heart is not allowed to attend the *sama*, for the *sama* stirs up whatever desire is already in the heart, both the detestable and the desirable.[145]

He also said in his *Qawaid al-ahkam*:

Dancing and clapping are a bad display resembling the display of women, which no one indulges except frivolous men or affected liars . . . whoever apprehends the greatness of Allah, it cannot be imagined that he will start dancing and clapping as these are not performed except by the crassly ignorant, not those who have merit and intelligence, and the proof of their ignorance is that the Sharia has not cited any evidence for their action in the Quran and the sunna, and none of the prophets or their notable followers ever did it.[146]

4.20.1. AL-IZZ ON THE SUPERIORITY OF THE RANK OF THE SAINTS (*AWLIYA*) OVER THAT OF THE RELIGIOUS SCHOLARS (*ULAMA*)

Al-Izz ibn Abd al-Salam was asked about the correctness of Qushayri's and Ghazali's saying that the highest level among Allah's servants after messengers and prophets was that of saints (*awliya*), and then that of the religious scholars (*ulama*). He replied:

Concerning the priority of the knowers of Allah over the knowers of Allah's rulings, the saying of the teacher Abu Hamid (al-Ghazali) is agreed upon. No reasonable person doubts that the knowers of Allah . . . are not only better than the knowers of Allah's rulings, but also better than those of the branches and the roots of the religion, because the rank of a science is according to its immediate object . . . Most of the

---

145 Al-Izz ibn Abd al-Salam, *Fatawa misriyya* p. 158.
146 Al-Izz ibn Abd al-Salam, *Qawaid al-ahkam* 2:220-221.

time scholars are veiled from their knowledge of Allah and His Attributes, otherwise they would be among the gnostics whose knowledge is continuous, as befits the demand of true virtue. And how could the gnostics and the jurists be the same, when Allah says, *"The noblest among you in Allah's sight are the most Godwary"* (49:13)? . . . and by the "erudite" (*ulama*) in His saying *"The erudite among His bondsmen fear Allah alone"* (35:28), He means those who know Him, His Attributes, and His Actions, not those who know His Rulings . . . A sign of the superiority of the gnostics over the jurists is that Allah effects miracles at the hands of the former, but never at the hands of the latter, except when they enter the path of the gnostics and acquire their characteristics.[147]

It is noteworthy that al-Izz did not need to include the scholars of hadith, since they are considered below the rank of the scholars of jurisprudence and are therefore included with them below the saints. Ibn Abi Zayd al-Maliki reports Sufyan ibn Uyayna as saying, "Hadith leads to misguidance except the religious scholars (*fuqaha*)," and Malik's companion Ibn Wahb as saying, "Any master of hadith who has no Imam in jurisprudence (*fiqh*) is misguided (*dall*).[148] If Allah had not saved us with Malik and al-Layth, we would have been misguided." Malik's warning that religion does not consist in the narration of many hadiths, but in a light that settles in the breast has already been mentioned.

4.21. Imam Nawawi (D. 676 AH)

One of the great Sufi scholars, strictest latter-time hadith masters, and most meticulous of jurists, Shaykh al-Islam Imam Muhyiddin Yahya ibn Sharaf al-Nawawi is the principal reference of the late Shafii school, along with al-Rafii. His books remain authoritative in the methodology of law, in Quranic commentary, and in hadith. His commentary on *Sahih Muslim* is second only to Ibn Hajar's commentary on *Sahih Bukhari*. His famous compilation of *Forty Hadith* received more circulation and fame than possibly any other book of

---

147 Al-Izz ibn Abd al-Salam, *Fatawa*, ed. Abd al-Rahman ibn Abd al-Fattah (Beirut: Dar al-marifa, 1406/1986) p. 138-142.
148 Ibn Abi Zayd, *al-Jami fi al-sunan* p. 118-119.

hadith. Nawawi and his work have been of immense benefit to the Community of Islam.

Nawawi was considered a Sufi and a saint, as is evident in the title of Sakhawi's biography: *Tarjamat shaykh al-islam, qutb al-awliya al-kiram, faqih al-anam, muhyi al-sunna wa mumit al-bida Abi Zakariyya Muhyi al-Din al-Nawawi* (The biography of the Shaykh of Islam, the Pole of Noble Saints, the Jurist of Mankind, the Reviver of the Sunna and the Slayer of Innovation . . . al-Nawawi).

Nawawi writes in a short treatise:

> The specifications of the Way of the Sufis are five:
> 1 To keep the Presence of Allah in your heart in public and in private;
> 2 To follow the *sunna* of the Prophet (ﷺ) by actions and speech;
> 3 To keep away from people and from asking them;
> 4 To be happy with what Allah gave you, even if it is less;
> 5 To always refer your matters to Allah.[149]

He died before he could complete his *Bustan al-arifin fi al-zuhd wa al-tasawwuf* (The garden of the gnostics in asceticism and self-purification), which is a precious collection of sayings of the early and late masters of *tasawwuf* that elaborates on some of the finer points of self-purification. The following is an excerpt:

> Al-Shafii said, may Allah have mercy on him, "Only the sincere one (*mukhlis*) knows hypocrisy (*riya*)." This means that it is impossible to know the reality of hypocrisy and see its hidden shades except for one who resolutely seeks (*arada*) sincerity. That one strives for a long time searching and meditating and examining at length within himself until he knows or knows something of what hypocrisy is. This does not happen for everyone. Indeed, this happens only with the special ones (*al-khawass*). But for a given individual to claim that he knows what hypocrisy is, this is real ignorance on his part.

---

149 Nawawi, *al-Maqasid fi al-tawhid wa al-ibada wa usul al-tasawwuf* (The purposes in oneness, worship, and the foundations of self-purification). Cf. Nuh Keller, *Al-Maqasid*: Imam Nawawi's *Manual of Islam* (Evanston: Sunna Books, 1994) p. 85-86.

I shall mention in this book a chapter, Allah will-
ing, in which you will see a type of wonder that will
cool your eyes. To illustrate the great extent of the
concealment of hypocrisy we only need relate the following from the Teacher and Imam Abu al-Qasim al-
Qushayri, may Allah have mercy on him, from his
Risala with our *isnad* previously mentioned.

He said, "I heard Muhammad ibn al-Husayn say:
I heard Ahmad ibn Ali ibn Jafar say: I heard al-Hasan
ibn Alawiyya say: Abu Yazid [al-Bistami], may Allah
be well pleased with him, said, I was for twelve years
the blacksmith of my ego (*haddadu nafsi*), then for
five years I became the mirror of my heart (*miratu
qalbi*), then for a year I looked at what lay between
the two of them and I saw around me a visible belt
[i.e. of *kufr* = the vestimentary sign of a non-Muslim
subject of the Islamic state]. So I strove to cut it for
twelve years and then looked again, and I saw around
me a hidden belt. So I worked to cut it for five years,
looking to see how to cut. Then it was unveiled for me
(*kushifa li*) and I looked at creation and saw that they
were all dead. So I recited the funeral prayer over
them."

I say: That hypocrisy should be as inscrutable as
this to the peerless master in this path [i.e. *tasawwuf*]
is enough to show how greatly hidden it lies. His
phrase, "I saw them dead," is the apex of worth and
beauty, and seldom do other than the Prophet's
words, blessings and peace be upon him, gather up
such wealth of meanings. I shall touch upon its meaning briefly. It means that after he had struggled long
and hard and his ego had been disciplined and his
heart illumined, and when he had conquered his ego
and subdued it and achieved complete mastery over
it, and it had subjected himself to him totally, at that
time he looked at all created beings and found that
they were dead and completely powerless:

They cannot harm nor can they benefit.
They cannot give nor can they withhold.
They cannot give life nor can they give death.
They cannot convey nor can they cut off.
They cannot bring near nor can they take away.
They cannot make happy nor can they make sad.
They cannot bestow nor can they deprive.
They possess for themselves neither benefit nor

harm, nor death, nor life, nor resurrection.

This, then, characterizes human beings as dead: they are considered dead in all of the above respects, they are neither feared nor entreated, what they have is not coveted, they are not shown off to nor fawned upon, one does not concern oneself with them, they are not envied nor disparaged, their defects are not mentioned nor their faults pursued and exposed, one is not jealous of them nor thinks much of whatever Allah-given favors they have received, and they are forgiven and excused for their shortcomings, although the legal punishments are applied to them according to the Law. But the application of such punishment does not preclude what we have mentioned before, nor does it preclude our endeavoring to cover up their faults without disparaging them in the least.

This is how the dead are viewed. And if someone mentions human beings in a dishonorable manner we forbid him from probing that subject in the same way that we would if he were going to examine a person who died. We do not do anything for their sake nor do we leave Him for them. And we no more stop ourselves from fulfilling an act of obedience to Allah on their account than we do on account of a dead person, and we do not over-praise them. And we neither love their own praise for us nor hate their insults, and we do not reciprocate them.

In sum, they are as it were non-existent in all the respects we have mentioned. They are under Allah's complete care and jurisdiction. Whoever deals with them in such a way, he has combined the good of the next world with that of the lower world. May Allah the Generous grant us success towards achieving this These few words are enough to touch upon an explanation for Abu Yazid al-Bistami's saying, may Allah be well pleased with him.[150]

AL-IZZ B. ABD AL-SALAM AL-MAQDISI (D. 678 AH)

This preacher (*waiz*) is mentioned because he is often confused with Izz al-Din ibn Abd al-Salam al-Sulami, and his small

---

[150] Al-Nawawi, *Bustan al-arifin* (Beirut: Dar al-kitab al-arabi, 1405/1985) p. 53-54.

work on *tasawwuf* is mistakenly attributed to the latter. In this work, entitled variously *Hall al-rumuz wa mafatih al-kunuz* and *Zabad khulasat al-tasawwuf*, al-Maqdisi divides the levels of *suluk* or spiritual wayfaring along three ways that correspond to the Prophet's definition of religion in the hadith of Gabriel:

> *Islam* is the first of the levels of religion, characterizing the common believers;
> *Iman* is the first of the stepping-stones of the heart and it characterizes the elite of the believers;
> *Ihsan* is the first of the stepping-stones of the spirit, and it characterizes the elite of those brought near.[151]

4.23. IBN TAYMIYYA (D. 728 AH)

His admirers cite this jurist and hadith master of the Hanbali school as an enemy of Sufis, and he is the principal authority in "Salafi" campaign that is responsible for creating the current movement toward ignorance regarding *tasawwuf*. Yet, Ibn Taymiyya was himself a Sufi. "Salafis" are careful never to show the Sufi Ibn Taymiyya, as he would severely impede the anti-Sufi campaign that they would have him direct.

Ibn Taymiyya's discourse on *tasawwuf* is riddled with contradictions and ambiguities. Even though he leveled all sorts of judgments at Sufis, he was unable to deny the greatness of *tasawwuf* as agreed upon by the Community long before he came along. As a result he is often witnessed slighting *tasawwuf*, questioning his Sufi contemporaries, and reducing the primacy of the elite of Muslims to ordinariness. At the same time, he boasts of being a Qadiri Sufi in direct line of succession to Shaykh Abd al-Qadir al-Jilani, as shown in the lines that follow.

It should be clear that the reason the following evidence is quoted is not because the author considers Ibn Taymiyya in any way representative of *tasawwuf*. Rather, he no more represents *tasawwuf* than he represents mainstream Islamic doctrine. His views are quoted only to demonstrate that his mis-

---

151 Al-Izz ibn Abd al-Salam [*al-Maqdisi*], *Hall al-rumuz wa mafatih al-kunuz* (Cairo: Matbaat nur al-amal) p. 7.

representation by orientalists and "Salafis" as an enemy of *tasawwuf* does not withstand scrutiny. Regardless of the feelings of any one group, the facts provide clear evidence that Ibn Taymiyya had no choice but to accept *tasawwuf* and its principles. Furthermore, the facts show that he not only claimed to be a Sufi, but also to have been adorned with the cloak (*khirqa*) of shaykhhood in the Qadiri Sufi Order.

As mentioned above, Ibn Taymiyya greatly admired Abd al-Qadir Jilani, to whom he gives the title "my Shaykh" (*shaykhuna*) and "my Master" (*sayyidi*) exclusively in his entire *Fatawa*. Ibn Taymiyya's Sufi inclinations and reverence for Abd al-Qadir Jilani can also be seen in his hundred-page commentary on *Futuh al-ghayb*. The commentary covers only five of the seventy-eight sermons of the book, but demonstrate that Ibn Taymiyya considered *tasawwuf* essential within the life of the Islamic community.[152]

In his commentary, Ibn Taymiyya stresses that the primacy of the Sharia forms the soundest tradition in *tasawwuf*. To argue this point he lists over a dozen early masters, as well as more contemporary shaykhs like his fellow Hanbalis, al-Ansari al-Harawi and Abd al-Qadir, and the latter's own shaykh, Hammad al-Dabbas:

> The upright among the followers of the Path-like the majority of the early shaykhs (*shuyukh al-salaf*) such as Fudayl ibn Iyad, Ibrahim ibn Adham, Maruf al-Karkhi, al-Sari al-Saqati, al-Junayd ibn Muhammad, and others of the early teachers, as well as Shaykh Abd al-Qadir, Shaykh Hammad, Shaykh Abu al-Bayan and others of the later masters–do not permit the followers of the Sufi path to depart from the divinely legislated command and prohibition, even were that person to have flown in the air or walked on water.[153]

Elsewhere, Ibn Taymiyya defends the Sufis as those who belong to the path of the *sunna* and represent it in their teachings and writings:

---

152 The commentary is found in volume 10:455-548 of the first Riyadh edition of the *Majmu fatawa Ibn Taymiyya*.

153 Ibn Taymiyya, *Majmu fatawa Ibn Taymiyya* 10:516.

The great shaykhs mentioned by Abu Abd al-Rahman al-Sulami in *Tabaqat al-sufiyya*, and Abu al-Qasim al-Qushayri in *al-Risala*, were adherents of the Sunni school and the school of the followers of the hadith, such as al-Fudayl ibn Iyad, al-Junayd ibn Muhammad, Sahl ibn Abd Allah al-Tustari, Amr ibn Uthman al-Makki, Abu Abd Allah Muhammad ibn Khafif al-Shirazi, and others, and their speech is found in the *sunna*, and they composed books about the *sunna*.[154]

In his treatise on the difference between the lawful and the innovative forms of worship,[155] Ibn Taymiyya unmistakably states that the lawful way is the method and way of "those who follow the Sufi path," or "the way of self-denial" (*zuhd*), and those who follow "what is called poverty and *tasawwuf*" (i.e. the *fuqara* and the Sufis):

> The lawful is that by which one approaches near to Allah. It is the way of Allah. It is righteousness, obedience, good deeds, charity, and fairness. It is the way of those on the Sufi path (*al-salikin*), and the method of those intending Allah and worshipping Him; it is that which is travelled by everyone who desires Allah and follows the way of self-denial (*zuhd*) and religious practice, and what is called poverty and *tasawwuf* and the like.[156]

Regarding Abd al-Qadir's teaching that the Sufi wayfarer (*salik*), should abstain from permitted desires, Ibn Taymiyya determines that Abd al-Qadir's intention is that one should give up permitted things that are not commanded, for there may be a danger in them. To what extent? If Islam is essentially learning and carrying out the divine command, then there must be a way for the striver on the path to determine the will of Allah in each particular situation. Ibn Taymiyya concedes that the Quran and *sunna* cannot cover every possible event in the life of every believer. Yet, if the goal of submission

---

154 Ibn Taymiyya, *al-Risala al-Safadiyya* (Riyad: matabi hanifa, 1396/1976) 1:267.

155 Ibn Taymiyya, *Risalat al-ibadat al-shariyya wal-farq baynaha wa bayn al-bidiyya*.

156 Ibn Taymiyya, *Majmuat al-rasail wa al-masail* (Beirut: Lajnat al-turath al-arabi) 5:83.

of will and desire to Allah is to be accomplished by those seeking Him, there must be a way for the striver to ascertain the Divine command in its particularity.

Ibn Taymiyya's answer is to apply the legal concept of *ijtihad* to the spiritual path, specifically to the notion of *ilham*, or inspiration. In his efforts to unite his will with Allah's, the true Sufi reaches a state where he desires nothing more than to discover the greater good, which is most pleasing and loveable to Allah. When external legal arguments cannot direct him in such matters, he can rely on the standard Sufi notions of private inspiration (*ilham*) and intuitive perception (*dhawq*):

> If the Sufi wayfarer has creatively employed his efforts to the external *shari* indications and sees no clear probability concerning his preferable action, he may then feel inspired, along with his goodness of intention and reverent fear of Allah, to choose one of two actions as superior to the other. This kind of inspiration (*ilham*) is an indication concerning the truth. It may be even a stronger indication than weak analogies, weak hadiths, weak literalist arguments (*zawahir*), and weak presumption of continuity (*istishab*) which are employed by many who delve into the principles, differences, and systematizing of *fiqh*.[157]

Ibn Taymiyya bases this view on the principle that Allah has put a natural disposition for the truth in mankind, and when this natural disposition has been grounded in the reality of faith and enlightened by Quranic teaching, and still the striver on the path is unable to determine the precise will of Allah in specific instances, then his heart will show him the preferred course of action. Such inspiration, he holds, is one of the strongest authorities possible in the situation. The striver will certainly sometimes err, falsely guided by his inspiration or intuitive perception of the situation, just as the *mujtahid* sometimes errs. However, Ibn Taymiyya says, even when the *mujtahid* or the inspired striver is in error, he is obedient.

Appealing to *ilham* and *dhawq* does not mean following

---

157 Ibn Taymiyya, *Majmu fatawa Ibn Taymiyya* 10:473-474.

one's own whims or personal preferences.[158] In his letter to Nasr al-Manbiji, Ibn Taymiyya qualifies this intuition as "faith-informed" (*al-dhawq al-imani*). His point is, as in the commentary on the *Futuh*, that inspirational experience is by nature ambiguous, and needs to be qualified and informed by the criteria of the Quran and the *sunna*. Nor can inspiration lead to certainty of the truth, in his view. What it can do is give the believer firm grounds for choosing the more probably correct course of action in a given instance and help him to conform his will, in the specific details of his life, to that of his Creator and Commander.[159]

Ibn Taymiyya's other works also abound in praise for Sufi teachings. For example, in his book *al-Ihtijaj bi al-qadar*, he defends the Sufis' emphasis on love of Allah and their voluntarist rather than intellectual approach to religion as being in agreement with the teachings of the Quran, the sound hadith, and the *imja al-salaf*:

> As for the Sufis, they affirm the love (of Allah), and this is more evident among them than all other issues. The basis of their Way is simply will and love. The affirmation of the love of Allah is well-known in the speech of their early and recent masters, just as it is affirmed in the Book and the *sunna* and in the agreement of the Salaf.[160]

Ibn Taymiyya is also notorious for his condemnation of Ibn Arabi. However, what he condemned was not Ibn Arabi, but a tiny book of his entitled *Fusus al-hikam*, which consists of a single slim volume. As for Ibn Arabi's *magnum opus*, *al-Futuhat al-makkiyya* (The Makkan Divine disclosures), Ibn Taymiyya was no less an admirer of this great work than everyone else in Islam who saw it. His feelings are expressed in a letter to Abu al-Fath Nasr al-Munayji (d. 709):

> I was one of those who, previously, used to hold the best opinion of Ibn Arabi and extol his praise, because of the benefits I saw in his books, such as what he said in many of his books, for example: *al-*

---

158 *Ibid.* 10:479.

159 Ibn Taymiyya, *Majmua al-rasail wal-masail* 1:162.

160 Ibn Taymiyya, *al-Ihtijaj bi al-qadar* (Cairo: al-Matbaa al-salafiyya, 1394/1974) p. 38.

Futuhat, al-Kanh, al-Muhkam al-marbut, al-Durra al-fakhira, Matali al-nujum, and other such works.[161]

Ibn Taymiyya goes on to say he that changed his opinions, not because of anything in these books, but only after he read the *Fusus*.

Let us now turn to the evidence of Ibn Taymiyya's affiliation with the Qadiri Sufi Way and his own acknowledgement of having received the Qadiri *khirqa*, or cloak, of authority from Abd al-Qadir al-Jilani through a chain of three shaykhs.[162] These are no other than the three Ibn Qudamas who are among the established authorities in jurisprudence in the Hanbali school.[163]

In a manuscript of Yusuf ibn Abd al-Hadi al-Hanbali, Ibn Taymiyya is listed within a Sufi spiritual genealogy with other well-known Hanbali scholars. The links in this genealogy are, in descending order:

1. Abd al-Qadir al-Jilani (d. 561 AH)
2.a. Abu Umar ibn Qudama (d. 607 AH)
2.b. Muwaffaq al-Din ibn Qudama (d. 620 AH)
3. Ibn Abi Umar ibn Qudama (d. 682 AH)
4. Ibn Taymiyya (d. 728 AH)
5. Ibn Qayyim al-Jawziyya (d. 751 AH)
6. Ibn Rajab (d. 795 AH)[164]

Both Abu Umar ibn Qudama and his brother Muwaffaq al-Din received the *khirqa* directly from Abd al-Qadir himself.

Ibn Taymiyya is then quoted by Ibn Abd al-Hadi as affirming his Sufi affiliation both in the Qadiri order and in other Sufi orders:

I have worn the Sufi cloak of a number of shaykhs

---

161 Ibn Taymiyya, *Tawhid al-rububiyya* in *Majmua al-Fatawa al-kubra* (Riyad, 1381) 2:464-465.

162 As related by his student Ibn Abd al-Hadi (d. 909).

163 This information was brought to light by George Makdisi in a series of articles published in the 1970s. George Makdisi, "*L'isnad initiatique soufi de Muwaffaq ad-Din ibn Qudama*," in Cahiers de l'Herne: Louis Massignon (Paris: Editions de l'Herne, 1970) p. 88-96; "Ibn Taimiya: A Sufi of the Qadiriya Order," in American Journal of Arabic Studies I (Leiden: E.J. Brill, 1974) p. 118-129; "The Hanbali School and Sufism," in Boletin de la Asociacion Espanola de Orientalistas 15 (Madrid, 1979) p. 115-126.

164 Yusuf ibn Abd al-Hanbali, *Bad al-ilqa bi labs al-khirqa* (The beginning of the shield in the wearing of the Sufi cloak).

belonging to various tariqas (*labistu khirqata at-tasawwuf min turuqi jamaatin min al-shuyukhi*), among them the shaykh Abd al-Qadir al-Jili [=Jilani], whose *tariqa* is the greatest of the well-known ones.

Further on he says:

> The greatest Sufi Way (*ajall al-turuq*) is that of my master (sayyidi) Abd al-Qadir al-Jili [=Jilani], may Allah have mercy on him.[165]

Further corroboration comes from Ibn Taymiyya in one of his own works:

> I wore the blessed Sufi cloak of Abd al-Qadir, there being between him and me two shaykhs (*labistu al-khirqata al-mubarakata li al-Shaykh Abd al-Qadir wa bayni wa baynahu ithan*)[166]

Ibn Taymiyya thus affirms that he was an assiduous reader of Ibn Arabi's *al-Futuhat al-makkiyya*, that he considers Abd al-Qadir al-Jilani his shaykh, and that he belongs to the Qadiriyya order and other Sufi orders. What does he say about *tasawwuf* and Sufis in general?[167]

In his essay entitled *al-Sufiyya wa al-fuqara* and his *Majmua fatawa Ibn Taymiyya al-Kubra*, he states:

> The word Sufi was not well-known in the first three centuries but its usage became well-known after that. More than a few imams and shaykhs spoke about it, such as Ahmad ibn Hanbal, Abu Sulayman al-Darani, and others. It has been related that Sufyan al-Thawri used it. Some have also mentioned that concerning Hasan al-Basri.[168]

165 Ibn Abd al-Hadi, *Bad al-ilqa bi labs al-khirqa*, ms. al-Hadi, Princeton Library Arabic Collection, fols. 154a, 169b, 171b-172a; and Damascus University, copy of original Arabic manuscript, 985H.; also mentioned in at-Talyani, manuscript Chester Beatty 3296 (8) in Dublin, fol. 67a.

166 As quoted in his *al-Masala at-tabriziyya*. Manuscript Damascus, Zahiriyya #1186 H.

167 Ibn Taymiyya even wrote a commentary on Ibn Arabi's *Futuh al-ghayb*.

168 Ibn Taymiyya, *Majmua al-fatawa al-kubra* 11:5. published in the eleventh volume (*al-Tasawwuf*).

Ibn Taymiyya then goes on to deduce that *tasawwuf* originated in Basra among the generations after the *tabiin*, because he finds that many of the early Sufis originated from there while he does not find evidence of it elsewhere. In this way he mistakenly reduces *tasawwuf* to a specific place and time, cutting it off from its links with the time of the Prophet (ﷺ) and the Companions. This is one of the aberrant conclusions which gives rise, among today's "Salafis," to questions such as, "Where in the Quran and the *sunna* is *tasawwuf* mentioned?" As Ibn Ajiba replied to such questioners:

> The founder of the science of *tasawwuf* is the Prophet (ﷺ) himself to whom Allah taught it by means of revelation and inspiration.[169]

By Allah's favor, we have put this issue to rest in our lengthy exposition on the proofs of *tasawwuf* in the pages above.

Ibn Taymiyya continues:

> *Tasawwuf* has realities (*haqaiq*) and states of experience (*ahwal*) which the Sufis mention in their science . . . Some say that the Sufi is he who purifies himself from anything which distracts him from the remembrance of Allah and who becomes full of reflection about the hereafter, to the point that gold and stones will be the same to him. Others say that *tasawwuf* is safeguarding of the precious meanings and leaving behind pretensions to fame and vanity, and the like. Thus the meaning of Sufi alludes to the meaning of *siddiq* or one who has reached complete truthfulness, because the best of human beings after prophets are the *siddiqin*, as Allah mentioned in the verse: *Whoever obeys Allah and the Messenger they are in the company of those on whom is the grace of Allah: of the prophets, the truthful saints, the martyrs and the righteous; ah, what a beautiful fellowship!* (4:69).
>
> They consider, therefore, that after the prophets there is no one more virtuous than the Sufi, and the Sufi is, in fact, among other kinds of truthful saints,

---

169 Ibn Ajiba, *Iqaz al-himam* p. 6.

only one kind, who specialized in asceticism and wor-ship (*al-Sufi huwa fi al-haqiqa nawun min al-sid-diqin fahuwa al-siddiq alladhi ikhtassa bi al-zuhdi wa al-ibada*). The Sufi is "the righteous man of the path," just as others are called "the righteous ones of the *ulama*" and "the righteous ones of the emirs" . .

Some people criticized the Sufis and said that they were innovators and out of the *sunna* . . . but the truth is that they are exercising *ijtihad* in view of obeying Allah just as others who are obedient to Allah have also done. So from them you will find the Foremost in Nearness (*al-sabiq al-muqarrab*) by virtue of his striving, while some of them are from the People of the Right Hand . . . and among those claim-ing affiliation with them, are those who are unjust to themselves, rebelling against their Lord. These are the sects of innovators and free-thinkers (*zindiq*) who claim affiliation to the Sufis but in the opinion of the genuine Sufis, they do not belong, for example, al-Hallaj.[170]

Tasawwuf has branched out and diversified and the Sufis have become known as three types:

1 *Sufiyyat al-haqaiq*: the Sufis of realities, and these are the ones we mentioned above;
2 *Sufiyyat al-arzaq*: the funded Sufis who live on the religious endowments of Sufi guest-houses and schools; it is not necessary for them to be among the people of true realities, as this is a very rare thing . . .
3 *Sufiyyat al-rasm*: the Sufis by appearance only, who are interested in bearing the name and the dress etc.[171]

About *fana*, a term used by Sufis literally signifying extinc-tion or self-extinction, and the *shatahat*, or sweeping state-

170 Here Ibn Taymiyya's inappropriate citing of al-Hallaj is more symptomatic of his own misunderstanding of *tasawwuf* than it illustrates the point he is trying to make. In reality, as Abd al-Qahir al-Baghdadi said of al-Hallaj, "His case (among the Sufis) is not clear, though Ibn Ata Allah, Ibn Khafif, and Abu al-Qasim al-Nasir Abadi approved of him." (Abd al-Qahir al-Baghdadi, *Usul al-din* p. 315-16.) Furthermore, as already mentioned, major scholars in Ibn Taymiyya's own school, such as Ibn Aqil and Ibn Qudama, rejected the charges leveled against al-Hallaj and even considered him a saint. Can it be that Ibn Taymiyya was unaware of the positions that invalidate his point?

171 Ibn Taymiyya, *Majmua al-fatawa al-kubra* 11:16-20.

ments made by Sufis, Ibn Taymiyya says:

> This state of love characterizes many of the People of Love of Allah and the People of Seeking (*ahl al-irada*). A person vanishes to himself in the object of his love—Allah—through the intensity of his love. He will recall Allah, not recalling himself, remember Allah and forget himself, take Allah to witness and not take himself to witness, exist in Allah, not to himself. When he reaches that stage, he no longer feels his own existence. That is why he may say in this state, *ana al-haqq* (I am the Truth), or *subhani* (Glory to Me!), and *ma fi al-jubba illa Allah* (There is nothing in this cloak except Allah), because he is drunk in the love of Allah and this is a kind of pleasure and happiness that he cannot control . . .
>
> This matter has in it both truth and falsehood. Yet when someone enters through his fervor a state of ecstatic love (*ishq*) for Allah, he will take leave of his mind, and when he enters that state of absentmindedness, he will find himself as if he is accepting the concept of *ittihad* (union with Allah). I do not consider this a sin, because that person is excused and no one may punish him as he is not aware of what he is doing. The pen does not condemn the crazed person except when he is restored to sanity (and commits the same act). However, when he is in that state and commits wrong, he will come under Allah's address: *O Our Lord, do not take us to task if we forget or make mistakes* (2:286). There is no blame on you if you unintentionally make a mistake.[172]
>
> The story is mentioned of two men whose mutual love was so strong that one day, as one of them fell in the sea, the other one threw himself in behind him. Then the first one asked, "What made you fall here like me?" His friend replied, "I vanished in you and no longer saw myself. I thought you were I and I was you" . . . Therefore, as long as one is not drunk through something that is prohibited, his action is accepted from him, but if he is drunk through something prohibited (i.e. the intention was bad) then he is not excused.[173]

172 *Op. cit.* 2:396-397.
173 *Op. cit.* 10:339.

The above excerpts show the true extent of Ibn Taymiyya's familiarity with the broad lines of *tasawwuf*. Such knowledge was but part of the education of anyone who claimed to have learning, in Ibn Taymiyya's day and before his time. *Tasawwuf* was not extraneous or foreign to the great corpus of the Islamic sciences. Yet, as in his relationship with *aqida* unraveled above, Ibn Taymiyya's misunderstanding of *tasawwuf* far outweighs his understanding of it. This point was brought to light with quasi-surgical precision by the great Sufi shaykh Ibn Ata Allah in the debate he held with Ibn Taymiyya in the mosque of al-Azhar in Cairo.

4.23.1. THE DEBATE BETWEEN IBN ATA ALLAH AL-ISKANDARI AND IBN TAYMIYYA

One of the great Sufi imams who was also known as a *muhaddith*, preacher and Maliki jurist, is Abu al-Fadl Ibn Ata Allah al-Iskandari (d. 709). He is the author of a number of important works, including:

- *al-Hikam* (Aphorisms)
- *Miftah al-falah* (The key to success)
- *al-Qasd al-mujarrad fi marifat al-ism al-mufrad* (The pure goal concerning knowledge of the Unique Name)
- *Taj al-arus al-hawi li tadhhib al-nufus* (The bride's crown containing the discipline of souls)
- *Unwan al-tawfiq fi adab al-tariq* (The sign of success concerning the discipline of the path)
- The biographical *al-Lataif fi manaqib Abi al-Abbas al-Murs wa shaykhihi Abi al-Hasan* (The subtle blessings in the saintly lives of Abu al-Abbas al-Mursi and his master Abu al-Hasan al-Shadhili), and others.

He was Abu al-Abbas al-Mursi's (d. 686 AH) student and the second successor of the Sufi founder, Imam Abu al-Hasan al-Shadhili.

Ibn Ata Allah confronted Ibn Taymiyya for his excesses in attacking Sufis with whom he disagreed. Although he never refers to Ibn Taymiyya by name, it is clearly of him that he speaks when he says, in his *Lataif*, that Allah has put the Sufis to the test through what he terms "the scholars of external learning."[174] The pages below contain the first English translation of an account of an historical event that took place between the two.

4.23.2. TEXT OF THE DEBATE FROM *USUL AL-WUSUL* BY MUHAMMAD ZAKI IBRAHIM

Ibn Kathir, Ibn al-Athir, and other authors of biographies and biographical dictionaries have transmitted this authentic historical debate.[175] This account gives an idea of the ethics of debate among people of learning. It documents the controversy between a pivotal personality in *tasawwuf*, Shaykh Ahmad Ibn Ata Allah al-Iskandari, and an equally important representative of the so-called "Salafi" movement, Shaykh Ahmad Ibn Abd al-Halim Ibn Taymiyya. The debate took place during the Mamluk era in Egypt under the reign of the Sultan Muhammad Ibn Qalawun (al-Malik al-Nasir).

4.23.2.1. THE TESTIMONY OF IBN TAYMIYYA TO IBN ATA ALLAH

Shaykh Ibn Taymiyya had been imprisoned in Alexandria. When the Sultan pardoned him, he came back to Cairo. At the time of the evening prayer he went to al-Azhar mosque where *salat al-maghrib* was being led by Shaykh Ahmad Ibn Ata Allah al-Iskandari. Following the prayer, Ibn Ata Allah was surprised to discover that Ibn Taymiyya had been praying behind him. Greeting him with a smile, the Sufi shaykh cordially welcomed Ibn Taymiyya's arrival to Cairo, saying, "*as-salamu alaykum.*" Then Ibn Ata Allah started to talk with the learned visitor.

Ibn Ata Allah: "Ordinarily, I pray the evening

---

174 Ibn Ata Allah, *Lataif al-minan fi manaqib Abi al-Abbas* on the margins of Sharani's *Lataif al-minan wa al-akhlaq* (Cairo, 1357) 2:17-18.
175 See Ibn al-Imad, *Shadharat al-dhahab* (1350/1931) 6:20f.; al-Zirikly, *al-Alam* (1405/1984) 1:221; Ibn Hajar, *al-Durar al-kamina* (1348/1929) 1:148-273; Al-Maqrizi, *Kitab al-suluk* (1934-1958) 2:40-94; Ibn Kathir, *al-Bidaya wa al-nihaya* (1351/1932) 14:45; Subki, *Tabaqat al-Shafiiyya* (1324/1906) 5:177f. and 9:23f.; Suyuti, *Husn al-muhadara fi akhbar misr wa al-qahira* (1299/) 1:301; al-Dawadari, *al-Durr al-fakhir fi sirat al-malik al-Nasir* (1960) p. 200f.; al-Yafii, *Mirat al-janan* (1337/1918) 4:246; Sharani, *al-Tabaqat al-kubra* (1355/1936) 2:19f.; al-Nabahani, *Jami karamat al-awliya* (1381/1962) 2:25f.

prayer in the Mosque of Imam Husayn and the night prayer here. But look how the divine plan works itself out! Allah has ordained that I should be the first one to greet you (after your return to Cairo). Tell me, O *faqih*, do you blame me for what happened?

Ibn Taymiyya: "I know you intended me no harm, but our differences of opinion still stand. In any case, whoever has harmed me in any way, from this day on I hereby exonerate and free him from any blame in the matter."

Ibn Ata Allah: "What is it you know about me, Shaykh Ibn Taymiyya?"

4.23.2.1.1. ON INTERCESSION (*TAWASSUL*)

Ibn Taymiyya: "I know you to be a man of scrupulous piety, abundant learning, integrity and truthfulness in speech. I bear witness that I have seen no one like you either in Egypt or Syria who loves Allah more nor who is more self-effacing in Him nor who is more obedient in carrying out what He has commanded and in refraining from what He has forbidden. Nevertheless, we have our differences. What do you know about me? Are you claiming that I am misguided when I deny the validity of calling on anyone save Allah for aid (*istighatha*)?"

Ibn Ata Allah: "Surely, my dear colleague, you know that *istighatha* or calling for help is the same as *tawassul* or seeking a means to Allah and asking for intercession (*shafaa*); and that the Messenger, on him be peace, is the one whose help is sought since he is our means and he the one whose intercession we seek."

Ibn Taymiyya: "In this matter, I follow what the Prophet's *sunna* has laid down in the sharia. For it has been transmitted in a sound hadith, "I have been granted the power of intercession."[176] I have also collected the sayings on the Quranic verse, "*It may be that thy Lord will raise thee (O Prophet) to a praised estate*" (17:79) to the effect that the "praised estate" is intercession. Moreover, when the mother of the Commander of the Faithful Ali died, the Prophet (ﷺ) prayed to Allah at her grave and said: O Allah who lives and never dies, who quickens and puts to death,

---

176 Bukhari and Muslim, hadith of Jabir: "I have been given five things which no prophet was given before me."

forgive the sins of my mother Fatima bint Asad, make wide the place wherein she enters through the intercession of me, Thy Prophet (ﷺ), and the prophets who came before me. For Thou art the most merciful of those capable of having mercy.[177]

"This is the intercession that belongs to the Prophet (ﷺ). As for seeking the help of someone other than Allah, it smacks of idolatry; for the Prophet (ﷺ) commanded his cousin Abd Allah ibn Abbas not to ask of anyone to help him other than Allah.[178]

Ibn Ata Allah: "May Allah cause you to prosper, O faqih! As for the advice which the Prophet (ﷺ) gave to his cousin Ibn Abbas, he wanted him to draw near to Allah not through his familial relationship to the Prophet (ﷺ) but through his knowledge.

"With regard to your understanding of *istighatha* as being seeking the aid of someone other than Allah which is idolatry, I ask you, Is there any Muslim possessed of real faith and believing in Allah and His Prophet (ﷺ) who thinks there is someone other than Allah who has autonomous power over events and who is able to carry out what He has willed with regard to them? Is there any true believer who believes that there is someone who can reward him for his good deeds and punish him for his bad ones other than Allah?

"Besides this, we must consider that there are expressions which should not be taken just in their literal sense. This is not because of fear of associating a partner with Allah and in order to block the means to idolatry. For whoever seeks help from the Prophet (ﷺ) only seeks his power of intercession with Allah as when you yourself say, 'This food satisfies my

---

177 Al-Tabarani relates it in *al-Kabir*. Ibn Hibban and al-Hakim declare it sound. Ibn Abi Shayba on the authority of Jabir relates a similar narrative. Similar also is what Ibn Abd Al-Barr on the authority of Ibn Abbas and Abu Nuaym in his *Hilya* on the authority of Anas Ibn Malik relate, as al-Hafiz al-Suyuti mentioned in the *Jami al-kabir*. Haythami says in *Majma al-zawaid*: "Tabarani's chain contains Rawh ibn Salah who has some weakness but Ibn Hibban and al-Hakim declared him trustworthy. The rest of its sub-narrators are the men of sound hadith." This Fatima is Ali's mother, who raised the Prophet.

178 Hadith: "O young man if you have need to ask, ask of Allah. If you must seek help, seek help from Allah..." (*ya ghulam ala uallimuka. . .*): Tirmidhi (#2516 *hasan sahih*); Bayhaqi in *Asma wa al-sifat* p. 75-76 and *Shuab al-iman* 2:27-28 (#1074-1075) and 7:203 (#10000); Ahmad 1:307; Tabarani; Ibn Hibban; Abu Dawud; al-Hakim; Nawawi included it in his *Forty Hadith* (#19) but Ibn al-Jawzi placed it among the forgeries.

appetite." Does the food itself satisfy your appetite? Or is it the case that it is Allah who satisfies your appetite through the food?

"As for your statement that Allah has forbidden Muslims to call upon anyone other than Himself in seeking help, have you actually seen any Muslim calling on someone other than Allah? The verse you cite from the Quran was revealed concerning the idolaters and those who used to call on their false gods and ignore Allah. Whereas, the only way Muslims seek the help of the Prophet (ﷺ) is in the sense of *tawassul* or seeking a means, by virtue of the privilege he has received from Allah (*bi haqqihi inda Allah),* and *tashaffu* or seeking intercession, by virtue of the power of intercession which Allah has bestowed on him.

"As for your pronouncement that *istighatha* or seeking help is forbidden in the Sharia because it can lead to idolatry, if this is the case, then we ought also to prohibit grapes because they are means to making wine, and to castrate unmarried men because not to do so leaves in the world a means to commit fornication and adultery."

At the latter comment both the shaykhs laughed. Ibn Ata Allah continued,

"I am acquainted with the all-inclusiveness and foresight of the legal school founded by your shaykh, Imam Ahmad, and know the comprehensiveness of your own legal theory and about its principle of blocking the means to evil (*sadd al-dharai*) as well as the sense of moral obligation a man of your proficiency in Islamic jurisprudence and integrity must feel. But I realize also that your knowledge of language demands that you search out the hidden meanings of words that are often shrouded behind their obvious senses.

"As for the Sufis, meaning for them is like a spirit, and the words themselves are like its body. You must penetrate deeply into what is behind the verbal body in order to seize the deeper reality of the word's spirit.

"Now you have found a basis in your ruling against Ibn Arabi in the *Fusus al-hikam*, the text of which has been tampered with by his opponents not only with things he did not say, but with statements he could not even have intended saying (given the character of his Islam). When Shaykh al-Islam al-Izz ibn Abd al-Salam understood what Shaykh Ibn Arabi had actually said and analyzed, grasped and compre-hended the real meaning of his symbolic utterances, he asked Allah's pardon for his former opinion about the Shaykh and acknowledged that Muhyiddin ibn Arabi was an Imam of Islam.

"As for the statement of al-Shadhili against Ibn Arabi, you should know that Abu al-Hasan al-Shadhili is not the person who said it but one of the students of the Shadhiliyya. Furthermore, in making this statement that student was talking about some of the followers of Shadhili. Thus, his words were taken in a fashion he himself never intended.

"What do you think about the Commander of the Faithful, Ali ibn Abi Talib, may Allah be pleased with him?"

Ibn Taymiyya: "In the hadith the Prophet (ﷺ) said, "I am the city of knowledge and Ali is its door."[179] Ali ibn Abi Talib is the one *mujahid* who never went out to battle except to return victoriously. What scholar or jurist who came after him struggled for the sake of Allah using tongue, pen and sword at the same time? He was a most accomplished Companion of the Prophet (ﷺ). His words are a radi-ant lamp which have illumined me during the entire course of my life after the Quran and *sunna*. Ah! One

---

179 From the *Reliance of the Traveller* p. 954-957: "(Ali Qari:) The Hadith 'I am the city of knowledge and Ali is its gate' was mentioned by Tirmidhi... [who] said it was unacknowledgeable. Bukhari also said this, and said that it was without legitimate claim to authenticity. Ibn Main said that it was a baseless lie, as did Abu Hatim and Yahya ibn Said. Ibn Jawzi recorded it in his book of Hadith forgeries, and was con-firmed by Dhahabi, and others in this. Ibn Daqiq al-Eid said, 'This Hadith is not con-firmed by scholars, and is held by some to be spurious.' Daraqutni stated that it was uncorroborated. Ibn Hajar Asqalani was asked about it and answered that it was well authenticated (*hasan*), not rigorously authenticated (*sahih*), as Hakim had said, but not a forgery (*mawdu*), as Ibn Jawzi had said. This was mentioned by Suyuti. The Hadith master (*hafiz*) Abu Said Alai said, 'The truth is that the Hadith is well authen-ticated (*hasan*), in view of its multiple means of transmission, being neither rigorous-ly authenticated (*sahih*) nor weak (*daif*), much less a forgery' (*Risala al-mawduat*, 26)."

who is ever short of provision and long in his journeying."

Ibn Ata Allah: "Now, did Imam Ali ask anyone to take his side in a faction? For this faction has claimed that the Angel Gabriel made a mistake and delivered the revelation to Muhammad–on him be peace instead of Ali! Or did he ask them to claim that Allah had become incarnate in his body and the Imam had become divine? Or did he not fight and slay them and give a *fatwa* (legal opinion) that they should be killed wherever they were found?"

Ibn Taymiyya: "On the basis of this very religious edict (*fatwa*), I went out to fight them in the mountains of Syria for more than ten years."

Ibn Ata Allah: "And Imam Ahmad–may Allah be pleased with him–questioned the actions of some of his own followers who were in the habit of going on patrols, breaking open casks of wine (in the shops of their Christian vendors or wherever they find them), spilling their contents on the floor, beating up singing girls, and confronting people in the street. All of this they did in the name of enjoining good and prohibiting what is forbidden. However, the Imam had not given any *fatwa* that they should censure or rebuke all those people. Consequently, these followers of his were flogged, thrown into jail, and paraded mounted on assback facing the tail.

"Now, is Imam Ahmad himself responsible for the bad behavior which the worst and most vicious Hanbalis continue to perpetrate right down to our own day, in the name of enjoining good and prohibiting what is forbidden?

"All this is to say that Shaykh Muhyiddin Ibn Arabi is innocent with respect to his followers who absolve people of legal and moral obligations set down by the religion and from committing deeds that are prohibited. Do you not see this?"

Ibn Taymiyya: "But where do they stand with respect to Allah? Among you Sufis are those who assert that when the Prophet (ﷺ) gave glad tidings to the poor and said that they would enter paradise before the rich, the poor fell into ecstasy and began to tear their garments into pieces; that at that moment the Angel Gabriel descended from heaven and said to the Prophet (ﷺ) that Allah had sought his rightful portion from among these torn garments; and that the Angel Gabriel carried one of them and hung it on Allah's throne. For this reason, they claim, Sufis wear patchworked garments and call themselves *fuqara* or the "poor"!"

Ibn Ata Allah: "Not all Sufis wear patchworked vests and clothing. Here I am before you: what do you disapprove of in my appearance?"

Ibn Taymiyya: "You are from the men of sharia and teach in al-Azhar."

Ibn Ata Allah: "Al-Ghazali was equally an Imam both in the divine law and *tasawwuf*. He treated legal rulings, the *sunna*, and the Sharia with the spirit of the Sufi. And by applying this method he was able to revive the religious sciences. We know that *tasawwuf* recognizes that what is sullied has no part in religion and that cleanliness is the character of faith. The true and sincere Sufi must cultivate in his heart the faith recognized by the Sunni Muslims.

"Two centuries ago the very phenomena of pseudo-Sufis appeared which you yourself criticize and reject. There were persons who sought to diminish the performance of worship and religious obligations, to lighten fasting and to belittle the five daily prayers. They ran wild into the vast arenas of sloth and heedlessness, claiming that they had been liberated from the shackles of the slavery of Divine worship. Not satisfied with their own vile deeds until they had claimed intimations of the most extravagant realities and mystical states just as Imam al-Qushayri himself described in his well-known *Risala*, which he directed against them. He also set down in detail what constituted the true path to Allah, which consists in taking a firm hold upon the Quran and the *sunna*.

"The Imams of *tasawwuf* desire to arrive at the true reality not only by means of rational evidences thought up by the human mind which are capable of being false as well as true, but by means of purifying the heart and purging the ego through a series of spiritual exercises. They cast aside concerns for the life of this world inasmuch as the true servant of Allah does not busy himself with anything else except love of Allah and His Prophet (ﷺ). This is a high order of business and one that makes a servant pious and healthy and prosperous. It is an occupation that

reforms those things that corrupt the human creature, such as love of money and ambition for personal
standing in society. However, it is an order of business
which is constituted by nothing less than spiritual
warfare for the sake of Allah.

"My learned friend, interpreting texts according
to their literal meanings can sometimes land a person
in error. Literalism is what has caused your judgments about Ibn Arabi who is one of the Imams of our
faith known for his scrupulous piety. You have understood what he wrote in a superficial fashion; whereas
Sufis are masters of literary figures which intimate
much deeper meanings, hyperbolic language that
indicates heightened spiritual awareness and words
which convey secrets concerning the realm of the
unseen."

Ibn Taymiyya: "This argument goes against you,
not in your favor. For when Imam al-Qushayri saw
his followers deviating from the path to Allah he took
steps to improve them. What do the Sufi shaykhs in
our day do? I only ask that Sufis follow the path of the
sunna of these great and pious predecessors of our
faith (Salaf): the ascetics (*zuhhad*) among the
Companions, the generation which succeeded them,
and the generation that followed in their footsteps to
their best!

"Whoever acts in this way I esteem him highly
and consider him to be an imam of the religion. As for
unwarranted innovation and the insertion of the
ideas of idolaters such as the Greek philosophers and
the Indian Buddhists, or like the idea that man can
incarnate Allah (*hulul*) or attain unity with Him (*ittihad*), or the theory that all existence is one in being
(*wahdat al-wujud*) and other such things to which
your shaykh summons—people: this is clearly god-
lessness and unbelief."

Ibn Ata Allah: "Ibn Arabi was one of the greatest
of the jurists who followed the school of Dawud al-
Zahiri after Ibn Hazm al-Andalusi, who is close to
your methodology in Islamic law, O Hanbalis! But
although Ibn Arabi was a Zahiri (i.e. a literalist in
matters of Islamic law), the method he applied to
understand ultimate reality (*al-haqiqa*) was to search

out the hidden, spiritual meaning (*tariq al-batin*), that is, to purify the inward self (*tathir al-batin*).[180] However, not all followers of the hidden are alike.

"In order that you not err or forget, repeat your reading of Ibn Arabi with fresh understanding of his symbols and inspirations. You will find him to be very much like al-Qushayri. He has taken his path in *tasawwuf* under the umbrella of the Quran and *sunna* just like the Proof of Islam, Shaykh al-Ghazali, who carried on debates about doctrinal differences in matters of creed and issues of worship but considered them occupations lacking in real value and benefit. He invited people to see that the love of Allah is the way of a proper servant of Allah with respect to faith.

"Do you have anything to object to in this, O *faqih*? Or do you love the disputations of Islamic jurists? Imam Malik, may Allah be pleased with him, exercised extreme caution about such wrangling in matters of creed and used to say, 'Whenever a man enters into arguing about issues of creed it diminishes his faith.' Similarly al-Ghazali said: The quickest means of drawing near to Allah is through the heart, not the body. I do not mean by heart this fleshy thing palpable to seeing, hearing, sight and touch. Rather, I have in mind the inner most secret of Allah himself the Exalted and Great which is imperceptible to sight or touch.

"Indeed, Sunnis are the very ones who named the Sufi shaykh al-Ghazali 'the Proof of Islam,'[181] and there is no-one to gainsay his opinions even if one of the scholars has been excessive in praising his book when he said, "The *Ihya ulum al-din* was almost a Quran."[182]

"The carrying out of a religious obligation (*taklif*)

---

180 This is a key equivalence in Ibn Ata Allah's Hikam, for example #205: "Sometimes lights come upon you and find the heart stuffed with forms of created things, so they go back from whence they descended." Ibn Ata Allah, *Sufi Aphorisms* (*Kitab al-hikam*), trans. Victor Danner (Leiden: E.J. Brill, 1984) p. 53.

181 As illustrated by Salah al-Din al-Safadi for Ghazali's entry in his biographical dictionary: "Muhammad ibn Muhammad ibn Muhammad ibn Ahmad, the Proof of Islam, the Ornament of the Faith, Abu Hamid al-Tusi." al-Safadi, *al-Wafi bi al-wafayat* 1:274.

182 Ironically, a similar kind of praise on Ibn Ata Allah's own book *al-Hikam* is related on the authority of the great shaykh Mawlay al-Arabi al-Darqawi by Ibn Ajiba in *Iqaz al-himam* (p. 3-4): "I heard the jurist al-Bannani say: "The *Hikam* of Ibn Ata is almost a revelation (*wahy*). Were it permitted to recite the daily prayer without the Quran, the words of the *Hikam* would be allowed." He meant by this that there is nothing in the Hikam except what proceeds from the Quran and points back to it again, and Allah knows best.

in the view of Ibn Arabi and Ibn al-Farid is a worship whose *mihrab*, or prayer-niche indicating the orientation of prayer, is its inward aspect, not merely its external ritual. For what is the good of you standing and sitting in prayer if your heart is preoccupied with something other than Allah. Allah praises people when He says in the Quran, *"Those who are humble in their prayer"* (23:2) and He blames people when He says, *"Those who are heedless in their prayer"* (107:5). This is what Ibn Arabi means when he says, "Worship is the *mihrab* of the heart, that is, the inward aspect of prayer not the outward."

"The Muslim is unable to arrive at the knowledge of certitude (*ilm al-yaqin*) nor at certitude itself (*ayn al-yaqin*) of which the Quran speaks unless he empties his heart from whatever distracts it in the way of worldly cravings and center himself on inward contemplation. Then the outpourings of divine Reality will fill his heart, and from there will spring his sustenance.

"The real Sufi is not the one who derives his sustenance from asking and begging people for alms. The only one who is sincere is he who rouses his heart and spirit to self-obliteration in Allah by obedience to Allah. Perhaps Ibn Arabi caused the jurists to rise up against him because of his contempt of their preoccupation with arguing and wrangling about credal matters, actual legal cases, and hypothetical legal situations, since he saw how much it distracted them from purifying the heart. He named them 'the jurists of women's menses.' May Allah grant you refuge from being among them! Have you read Ibn Arabi's statement: 'Whoever builds his faith exclusively on demonstrative proofs and deductive arguments, builds a faith on which it is impossible to rely, for he is affected by the negativities of constant objections. Certainty (*al-yaqin*) does not derive from the evidences of the mind but pours out from the depths of the heart.' Have you ever read talk as pure and sweet as this?"

Ibn Taymiyya: "You have spoken well if only your

master were as you say, for he would then be as far as possible from unbelief. But what he has said cannot sustain the meanings that you have given in my view."[183]

4.24. TAJ AL-DIN AL-SUBKI (D. 771 AH)

Shaykh al-Islam Taj al-Din al-Subki, the son of Shaykh al-Islam *al-hafiz* Taqi al-Din al-Subki (d. 756) who was a student of Ibn Ata Allah, mentioned:

May Allah give them life and greet them (Sufis), and may He place us with them in Paradise. Too many things have been said about them and too many ignorant people have said things which are not related to them . . . The truth is that those people left the world and were busy with worship.

Shaykh Abu Muhammad al-Juwayni (Imam al-Haramayn's father) said, They are among Allah's people and His elite. His mercy is sought through their remembrance of Allah, and rain descends with their invocation. May Allah be pleased with them and may Allah be pleased with us for their sake.[184]

4.25. IMAM ABU ISHAQ AL-SHATIBI AL-MALIKI (D. 790 AH)

Imam Abu Ishaq al-Shatibi al-Maliki is one of the foundational scholars of *Usul al-fiqh*, or methodology of the law, whose books, like al-Ghazali's, are required reading in that field. He laid great emphasis on the requirement of complete knowledge and erudition in the Arabic language—not merely correct understanding—for those who practice *ijtihad*. In his book *al-Muwafaqat fi usul al-sharia* (The congruences of the sources of the divine law), he held that the language of the Quran and the *sunna* is the key to understanding the scholars, and that the *ijtihad* of anyone deficient in their understanding of Arabic was unacceptable. Since the opinion of the *mujtahid* is a *hujja*, or proof, for the common person, this degree of authority necessitates direct access to the sources and full competence in Arabic.[185]

183 In Muhammad Zaki Ibrahim, *Usul al-wusul* (Cairo: 1404/ 1984) 299-310.
184 Al-Subki, *Muid al-niam wa mubid al-niqam* p. 190. In a chapter entitled "Tasawwuf."
185 Al-Shatibi, *al-Muwafaqa fi usul al-sharia* (Cairo:al-Maktaba al-tijariyya al-kubra, 1975) 4:60.

He writes in *al-Itisam*:

> Many of the ignorant think that the Sufis are lax
> in conforming to sharia. Far be it from them to be
> attributed such a belief! The very first foundation of
> their path is the *sunna* and the avoidance of what
> contravenes it!

Their chief spokesman and the master of their ways and
pillar of their group, Abu al-Qasim al-Qushayri, declared that
they acquired the name of *tasawwuf* in order to dissociate
themselves from the People of Innovation. He mentioned that
the most honorable of Muslims after the Prophet (ﷺ) did not
give themselves, in their time, any other title than
Companions, as there is no merit above that of being a
Companion– then those who followed them were called the
Successors. After that the people differed and the disparity of
level among them became more apparent. The elite among
whom prudence in belief was seen to be intense were then
called *zuhhad* and *ubbad*. Subsequently all kinds of innovations made their appearance, and the elite of the mainstream
Islamic scholars who observed their obligations with Allah, and
preserved their hearts from heedlessness became unique in
their kind under the name of *tasawwuf*. Consider this, you will
gain thereby. And Allah knows best.[186]

4.26. IBN KHALDUN (D. 808 AH)
Ibn Khaldun said in his famous *Muqaddima*:

> *Tasawwuf* is one of the latter-day sciences of the
> law in the Islamic Community. The foundation of
> *tasawwuf*, however, is (more ancient, as seen in the
> fact) that these folk and their way have always been
> present among the Salaf and among the most senior
> of the Companions and the Successors, and their way
> is the way of truth and guidance.
> The foundation of the way of the Sufis is self-
> restraint in the world and utter dependence on Allah;
> shunning of the adornment and beauty of the world;
> self-deprivation of pleasure, money, and title in the

---

186 Al-Shatibi, *al-Itisam min al-kutub*, quoted in al-Muslim: Majallat al-ashira al-
muhammadiyya (Dhu al-qida 1373).

manner agreed upon by the vast majority of the scholars; and isolation from creatures in seclusion and devotion to worship.

All these aspects were widespread among the Companions and the Salaf, but with the pervasiveness of worldliness in the second century and the next, and the general inclination of the people towards the world, those who remained attached to worship became known under the name of Sufis. [187]

4.27. IMAM AL-SAKHAWI (D. 902 AH)

He was the foremost student of Ibn Hajar al-Asqalani and a great jurist, historian, and hadith master. Shams al-Din Muhammad ibn Abd al-Rahman al-Sakhawi, like Taqi al-Din al-Subki and al-Suyuti, belonged to the Shadhili order founded by Abu al-Hasan al-Shadhili, as represented by the great Maliki Master Ibn Ata Allah. He transmitted five of Ibn Ata Allah's works to posterity, including the *Hikam*, from the Shadhili commentator Ahmad Zarruq (d. 899).

In his biography of the famous men of his time, entitled *al-Daw al-lami*, al-Sakhawi reveals that his father, Zayn al-Din Abd al-Rahman ibn Muhammad (d. 874), was a Cairo-born Sufi of great piety, and a member of the Baybarsiyya Sufi community where Ibn Hajar, Sakhawi's teacher, taught for forty years.[188]

In the section of his *al-Jawahir al-mukallala fi al-akhbar al-musalsala* devoted to the transmission of hadith through chains formed exclusively of Sufi narrators, Sakhawi states that he himself had received the Sufi path from Zayn al-Din Ridwan al-Muqri in Cairo.[189] In the same work Sakhawi also mentions several of his teachers and students of hadith who were Sufis. Following are some of their names, accompanied by the words used by Sakhawi to describe them:

• Abu Bakr ibn Muhammad al-Hishi al-Halabi Al-Shafii (b. 848) the head of the Bistamiyya Sufis in Aleppo, the mother trunk of the Naqshbandi Sufi order affiliated with Abu Yazid al-Bistami. He spent

187 *Muqaddimat ibn Khaldun*, p. 328.
188 Al-Sakhawi, *al-Daw al-lami* (Beirut: Dar maktabat al-hayat, 1966) 4:124-125.
189 A.J. Arberry, *Sakhawiana: A Study Based on the Chester Beatty Ms. Arab.* 773 (London: Emery Walker Ltd., 1951) p. 35.

two years in Makka with Sakhawi, who certified (*ijaza*) him to teach. In this *ijaza* Sakhawi calls him:

Our master, the masterful imam of merits and guidance, the Educator of *murid*s (students in the Sufi path), the Mainstay of Wayfarers in the Sufi path, the Noble Abu Bakr al-Hishi al-Halabi, may Allah preserve him and have mercy on his gracious predecessors (i.e. the chain of his shaykhs in the Sufi path), and may Allah grant us and all Muslims their benefits.[190]

• Badr al-Din Hussayn ibn Siddiq al-Yamani al-Ahdal (d. 903). Al-Sakhawi gave him a comprehensive *ijaza* granting him permission to teach all of his books. [191]

• Abu al-Fath Muhammad ibn Abi Bakr al-Madani al-Maraghi (d. 859). Sakhawi took hadith from him. He was head of two Sufi *khaniqa*s in Cairo, the Zamamiyya and the Jamaliyya. He led a life of seclusion for the most part, wrote a commentary on Nawawi's manual of law *Minhaj al-talibin*, and an epitome of Ibn Hajar's *Fath al-bari*. Due to his defense of Ibn Arabi, he was murdered in front of the Kabah by a fanatic.[192]

Taqi al-Din Abu Bakr ibn Muhammad al-Qalqashandi (d. 867), also called Abd Allah. He received the Sufi cloak (*khirqa*) of authority in Cairo. He is said to have read the whole of *Sahih al-Bukhari* in three days while in Makka. He lived in al-Quds, where al-Sakhawi met him and studied hadith with him.[193]

• Thiqat al-Din Abu al-Abbas Ahmad ibn Muhammad al-Uqbi (d. 861). He taught hadith and *tajwid* in Makka, where Sakhawi studied under him.[194]

• Kamal al-Din Muhammad ibn Abd al-Wahid al-Sikandari al-Siwasi (d. 861). He was a master of all sciences and taught at the Madrasa al-Ashrafiyya in Cairo, after which he headed the Shaykhuni Sufi *khaniqa*. He authored many books.[195]

• Abu Abd Allah Muhammad ibn Ali al-Husayni

---

190 Al-Sakhawi, *al-Daw al-lami* 11:96-97, 74-75.
191 *Ibid*. 3:144-145.
192 *Ibid*. 7:162-165.
193 *Ibid*. 11:69-71.
194 *Ibid*. 2:212-213.
195 *Ibid*. 8:127-132.

al-Qahiri Al-Shafii al-Sufi (d. 876). Munawi's deputy judge in Cairo, a student of Izz al-Din ibn Jamaa, Jalal al-Din al-Bulqini and many others, and a student and friend of Sakhawi's teacher Ibn Hajar whose work *Fath al-bari* he copied twice. A teacher of jurisprudence and hadith, he wrote an epitome of Ibn al-Athir's *Kitab al-ansab*. He was an old acquaintance of Sakhawi's father, and consequently treated Sakhawi himself "with indescribable respect." He was one of the ten students to whom Ibn Hajar gave his authority in teaching hadith after him.[196]

*Abu Khalid Muhammad ibn Abi Bakr al-Jibrini (d. 860). He was a writer, archer, horseman, and Sufi shaykh at the *zawiya* (alcove-mosque) of Jibrin, where al-Sakhawi met him and received certification in hadith from him. Sakhawi says of him, "He was handsome, modest, generous, courageous, and endowed with spiritual strength and virility after the shaykhs of true majesty."[197]

*Zaki al-Din Abu al-Abbas Ahmad ibn Muhammad al-Ansari al-Khazraji al-Sadi al-Muqri al-Sufi (d. 875). An associate of Ibn Hajar and a prolific writer, he wrote an autobiography in more than fifty volumes, although Sakhawi said he was unaffected, congenial, readily given to tears, and quick of repartee.[198]

*Thiqat al-Din Abu Ali Mahmud ibn Ali al-Sufi al-Khaniki (d. 865). Born and raised in Cairo's *khaniqa al-siryaqusiyya* where he taught late in life. He died while in Makka for the pilgrimage.[199]

*Abu al-Faraj Abd al-Rahman ibn Khalil al-Dimashqi al-Sufi (d. 869). He was a *muhaddith*. Al-Sakhawi studied under him in Cairo and at the Umayyad Mosque in Damascus. [200]

4.28 JALAL AL-DIN AL-SUYUTI (D. 911 AH)

Shaykh al-Islam al-Suyuti, the Renewer of the Eighth Islamic century and *mujtahid imam*, said in his book on *tasawwuf*:

Tasawwuf in itself is a most honorable knowledge.

196 *Ibid.* 8:176-178.
197 *Ibid.* 7:197.
198 *Ibid.* 2:146-149.
199 *Ibid.* 10:140-141.
200 *Ibid.* 4:76.

It explains how to follow the *sunna* of the Prophet (ﷺ) and to leave innovation, how to purify the ego . . . and submit to Allah truly . . .

I have looked at the matters which the imams of sharia have criticized in Sufis, and I did not see a single true Sufi holding such positions. Rather, they are held by the people of innovation and the extremists who have claimed for themselves the title of Sufi while in reality they are not . . .

Pursuit of the science of the hearts, knowledge of its diseases such as jealousy, arrogance and pride, and leaving them are an obligation on every Muslim. [201]

4.29 ZAKARIYYA IBN MUHAMMAD ANSARI (D. 926 AH)

Shaykh al-Islam Zakariyya Ansari was known as the Shaykh of shaykhs. He was a hadith master, judge, and exegete of Quran. He was Shaykh al-Islam Ibn Hajar al-Haytami's teacher and authored many books on *tasawwuf*, including a commentary on Qushayri's *Risala* that underwent several editions.

In his commentary on Qushayri, Ansari gives the following definitions for *tasawwuf*:

> *Tasawwuf* is the abandonment of deliberation. It is also said: It is the guarding of your senses and the mindfulness of your every breath; also: it is complete earnestness in the progression towards the King of all kings; also: it is the devotion to works of good and the avoidance of defects; and other explanations . . . The Sufiyya or Sufis are called thus because the Truth–Allah–has made them pure (*safahum*) and has favored them unreservedly (*akhlasa lahum al-niam*) through what He has allowed them to look upon. [202]

201 Al-Suyuti, *Tayid al-haqiqa al-aliyya wa-tashyid al-tariqa al-shadhiliyya*, (The upholding of the lofty truth and the buttressing of the Shadhili path) ed. Abd Allah ibn Muhammad ibn al-Siddiq al-Ghumari al-Hasani (Cairo: al-Matbaa al-islamiyya, 1934), p. 56-57.

202 Zakariyya al-Ansari, *Sharh al-risala al-qushayriyya* (Cairo: Dar al-kutub al-arabiyya al-kubra, 1330/1912) p. 126.

4.30. IBN HAJAR AL-HAYTAMI (D. 974 AH)

Shaykh al-Islam Ibn Hajar al-Haytami was a student of Zakariyya al-Ansari. As mentioned before, he represents the foremost source of legal opinion (*fatwa*) in the entire late Shafii school. He was once asked about the legal status of those who criticized Sufis, "Is there an excuse for such critics?" He replies in his *Fatawa hadithiyya*:

> It is incumbent upon every person endowed with mind and religion not to fall into the trap of criticizing these folk (Sufis), for it is a mortal poison, as has been witnessed of old and recently.[203]

As many others have on the same topic, he gave an important *fatwa* entitled, "Whoever denies, rejects, or disapproves of the Sufis, Allah will not make his knowledge beneficial." It is transcribed below in full:

> Our shaykh, the gnostic (*arif*) scholar Abu al-Hasan al-Bakri (d. 952) told me, on the authority of the shaykh and scholar Jamal al-Din al-Sabi verbatim—and he is one of the most distinguished students of our shaykh, Zakaria al-Sabiq (al-Ansari), that al-Sabi used to reject and criticize the way of the honorable Ibn al-Farid. One time al-Sabi saw in a dream that it was the Day of Judgment, and he was carrying a load which made him exhausted, then he heard a caller saying, "Where is the group of Ibn al-Farid?" He said:
>
> I came forward in order to enter with them, but I was told, "You are not one of them, so go back." When I woke up I was in extreme fear, and felt regret and sorrow, so I repented to Allah from rejecting the way of Ibn al-Farid, and renewed my commitment to Allah, and returned to believing that he is one of the saints and friends of Allah. The following year on the same night, I had the same dream. I heard the caller saying, "Where are the group of Ibn al-Farid? Let them enter paradise." So I went with them and I was told, "Come in, for now you are one of them."
>
> Examine this matter carefully as it come from a

---

203 Ibn Hajar al-Haytami, *Fatawa hadithiyya* (Cairo: al-Halabi, 1970) p. 331.

man of knowledge in Islam. It appears–and Allah knows best–that it is because of the blessing (*baraka*) of his shaykh Zakariyya al-Ansari that he has seen the dream which made him change his mind. Otherwise, how many of their deniers they have left to their blindness, until they found themselves in loss and destruction!

If you ask: Some eminent scholars, like al-Bulqini and others, the latest being al-Biqai and his students, and others under whom you yourself (i.e. al-Haytami) have studied, have disapproved of the Sufis, so why did you prefer this way over another?

I answer: I have preferred this way for a number of reasons, among them:

*What our shaykh has mentioned in *Sharh al-rawd* on the authority of Sad al-Din al-Taftazani (d. 791),[204] the truthfinder of Islam, the knight of his field, the remover of the proofs of darkness . . . that the latter said, responding to Ibn al-Muqri's statement, "Whoever doubts in the disbelief (*kufr*) of Ibn al-Arabi's group, he himself is a disbeliever." The truth is that Ibn al-Arabi and his group are the elite of the *umma*, and al-Yafii, Ibn Ata Allah, and others have clearly declared they considered Ibn Arabi a saint, and that the language which Sufis use is true among the experts in its usage, and that the gnostic (*arif*), when he becomes completely absorbed in the oceans of Unity, might make some statements that are liable to be misconstrued as incarnation (*hulul*) and union (*ittihad*), while in reality there is neither incarnation nor union.

*It has been clearly stated by our Imams, such as al-Rafii in his book a-Aziz, and al-Nawawi in *al-Rawda, al-Majmu*, and others, "When a *mufti* is being asked about a certain phrase that can be construed as disbelief, he should not immediately say that the speaker should be put to death nor make permissible the shedding of his blood. Rather let him say, 'The speaker must be asked about what he meant by his statement, and he should hear his explanation, then act accordingly.'

Look at these guidelines–may Allah guide

---

204 Sad al-Din Masud ibn Umar al-Taftazani, one of the great *mujtahid* polymaths of the Shafii school, he authored books in *tafsir, kalam, usul, fiqh, ilm al-mantiq* (logic), grammar, rhetoric, and philology.

you!–and you will find that the deniers who assault this great man (Ibn Arabi) and positively assert his disbelief, ride upon blind mounts, and stumble about like a camel affected with troubled vision. Verily Allah has removed their sight and their hearing from perceiving this, until they fell into whatever they fell into, which caused them to be despised, and made their knowledge of no benefit.

*Their great knowledge and utter renunciation of this world and of anything other than Allah testify to their innocence from these terrible accusations, therefore we preferred to dismiss such accusations, because their statements are true realities in the way they expressed them. Their way cannot be denied without knowing the meaning of their statements and the expressions they use, and then turning to apply the expression to the meaning and see if they match or not. We thank Allah that all of their deniers are ignorant in that kind of knowledge, as not one of them has mastered the sciences of unveilings (*mukashafat*), or even smelled them from a distance; nor has anyone of them sincerely followed any of the saints, so that he could master their terminology.

If you object saying: I disagree that their expressions refer to a reality rather than being metaphorical phrases, therefore show me something clearer than the explanations that have been given?

I say: Rejecting that is stubborness. Let us assume that you disagree with what I have said, but the correct way of stating the objection is to say, "This statement could be interpreted in several ways," and proceed to explain them; do not say: "If it meant this, then . . . and if it meant that, then . . ."[205] and state from the start 'This is *kufr*!' That is ignorance and goes beyond the scope of good advice (*nasiha*) that is being claimed by the critic.

Don't you see that if Ibn al-Muqri's real motivation were good advice, he would not have exaggerated by saying, "Whoever has a doubt in the disbelief of the group of Ibn al-Arabi, he himself is a disbeliever?" So he extended his judgment that Ibn al-Arabi's followers were disbelievers, to everyone who had a doubt as

---

205 An allusion to Ibn Taymiyya, who predicated his judgment of Ibn Arabi on the erroneous assumption that he understood his terminology and meanings.

to their disbelief. Look at this fanaticism that exceeds all bounds and departs from the consensus of the imams, and goes so far as to accuse anyone who doubts their *kufr*. "*Glorified are You, this is awful calumny!*" (24:16) *When you welcomed it with your tongues, and uttered with your mouths that whereof you had no knowledge, you counted it a trifle. In the sight of Allah, it is very great.*" (24:15)

Notice also what his statement suggests that it is an obligation on the whole Community to believe that Ibn Arabi and his followers are disbelievers, otherwise they will all be declared disbelievers–and no one thinks likes this. As a matter of fact, it might well lead into something forbidden which he himself has stated clearly in his book *al-Rawd* when he said, 'Whoever accuses a Muslim of being a disbeliever based on a sin committed by him, and without an attempt to interpret it favorably, he himself commits disbelief.' Yet here he is accusing an entire group of Muslims of disbelief. Moreover, no consideration should be paid to his interpretation, because he only gives the kind of interpretation that goes against those he is criticizing, for that is all that their words have impressed upon him.

As for those who did not think of of the words of Ibn Arabi and the Sufis except as a pure light in front of them, and believed in their sainthood–then how can a Muslim attack them by accusing them of disbelief? No one would dare to do so unless he is accepting the possibility to be himself called a disbeliever. This judgment reflects a great deal of fanaticism, and an assault on most of the Muslims. We ask Allah, through His Mercy, to forgive the one who uttered it.

It has been narrated through more than one source and has become well-known to every one that whoever opposes the Sufis, Allah will not make His Knowledge beneficial, and will be inflicted with the worst and ugliest (diseases/illnesses), and we have witnessed that happening to many deniers. For example, al-Biqai (d. 885) may Allah forgive him, used to be one of the most distinguished scholars, with numerous acts of worship, an exceptional intelligence, and an excellent memory in all kinds of knowledge, especially in the sciences of exegesis and hadith, and he wrote numerous books, but Allah did not allow them to be of any kind of benefit to anyone. He also authored a book on *Munasabat al-Quran* in about ten volumes, about which no one knows except the elite, and as for the rest, they have never heard about it. If this book had been written by our Shaykh Zakariyya, or by anyone who believes (in *awliya*), it would have been written with gold, because, as a matter of fact, it has no equal: for *'Of the bounties of thy Lord We bestow freely on all, these as well as those: the bounties of thy Lord are not closed to anyone'* (17:20). [206]

Al-Biqai went to an extreme in his denial, and wrote books about the subject, all of them clearly and excessively fanatical and deviating from the straight path. But then he paid for it fully and even more than that, for he was caught in the act on several occasions and was judged a disbeliever (*kafir*). It was ruled that his blood be shed and he was about to get killed, but he asked the help and protection of some influential people who got him out of it, and he was made to repent in Salihiyya, Egypt, and renew his Islam. On the latter occasion he was asked "What exactly do you disapprove of in Shaykh Muhiyyiddin (Ibn Arabi)?" He said, "I disagree with him on certain passages, fifteen or less, in his book *al-Futuhat.*"

Consider well this individual who contradicts his own books, where he mentions that he opposes many parts of *al-Futuhat* and other books and declares that they constitute disbelief; is there any reason to this other than fanaticism? He had some distinguished students who listened to his words and believed in them, among them some of my shaykhs, but they did not gain any kind of true knowledge from it, because some of them did not succeed in writing any books, while some wrote books on the art of *fiqh* equal to the books of Sad al Din al-Taftazani and others in their eloquence, the beauty of their style and the excellence of their diction, but no one paid any attention to them or even noticed them, on the contrary, people ignored them.

It happened to me with one of those, that while I

206 Al-Biqai is the author, among others, of a vicious attack on *tasawwuf* and Sufis entitled *Masra al-tasawwuf aw tanbih al-ghabi ila takfir Ibn Arabi wa-tahdir al-ibad min ahl al-inad* (The destruction of *tasawwuf*, or: The warning of the ignoramus concerning the declaration of Ibn Arabi's disbelief, and the cautioning of Allah's servants against the People of Stubbornness).

was studying under him, he started to have difficulties breathing, and I did not know at that time that he opposed the Sufis. In one of his sessions, the name of Shaykh Umar Ibn al-Farid, may Allah sanctify his secret, was mentioned, and he was asked, 'What do you think about him?' He said, 'He is a great poet;' then he was asked, 'and what else after that?' He said 'He is a *kafir*.' Then I had to leave, then I came back later to read something to him and I examined carefully to see if he had repented, but I found him seriously ill and oppressed in his breathing to the point that he was almost dying. I said to him, 'If you believe in Ibn al-Farid (i.e. in his Friendship with Allah), I guarantee that Allah will cure you of your illness.' He said, 'I have had this condition for years.' I said, 'Even so.' He said, 'All right, then I will,' after which he began to feel better and better. One day, while I was walking with him, trying to correct his doctrine *(aqida)*, he said to me, 'As far as that man is concerned, I do not judge him to be a *kafir*, but as far as his discourses are concerned, they do include *kufr*.' I said, 'One evil deed out of two,' after which I quit studying under him, and that illness stayed with him, but relatively better than before.

One of the students of al-Biqai, the scholar Shaykh Nur al-Din Al-Mahalli, also used to say 'As far as the man is concerned, I don't judge him to be a *kafir*, but as far as his discourses are concerned, they do include *kufr*.'[207]

If you ask: Has not Allah made the knowledge of some of the deniers of Sufis beneficial?

I say: There are two groups of deniers: in the case of those we mentioned, their intention was not to show pure good counsel to Muslims, but pure fanaticism, which is why they believed whatever they believed. They were overcome by a kind of envy and the desire to be different from others in their time, in order to be distinguished from them by means of these unusual things and to gain the reputation that they disapprove of any reprehensible matter without

207 This resort to "one evil out of two" is characteristic of many of today's "Salafis," who do not hesitate to brand Sufis with disbelief, both on the whole and individually. When they are admonished for their reprehensible act, they answer, "I do not judge them to be *kafir*, but their words do include *kufr*"! As Haytami said, criticizing the Sufis is a mortal poison and a pitfall from which one does irremediable damage to one's belief.

fearing anyone, and the like of such corrupted intentions which contains not the slightest portion of sincerity. [208]

4.31. ABD AL-WAHHAB AL-SHARANI (D. 973 AH)

Abd al-Wahhab was a Hanafi scholar of comparative *fiqh* and an author of numerous works on Law and *tasawwuf*. In *al-Tabaqat al-kubra*, for example, he writes:

> The path of the Sufis is built on the Koran and *sunna*, and is based upon living according to the morals of the prophets and purified ones. It may not be blamed unless it violates an explicit statement from the Koran, *sunna*, or scholarly consensus, exclusively. If it does not contravene one of these, the very most that one may say of it is that it is an understanding a Muslim man has been given, so let whoever wishes act upon it, and whoever does not refrain, this being as true of works as of understanding. So no pretext remains for condemning it except one's own low opinion of others, or interpreting what they do as ostentation, which is unlawful.
>
> Whoever carefully examines the branches of knowledge of the Folk of Allah Most High will find that none of them are beyond the pale of the Sacred Law. How should they lie beyond the pale of the Sacred Law when it is the law that connects the Sufis to Allah at every moment? Rather, the reason for the doubts of someone unfamiliar with the way of the Sufis that it is of the very essence of the sacred law is the fact that such a person has not thoroughly mastered the knowledge of the law. This is why Junayd (May Allah Most High have mercy on him) said, "This knowledge of ours is built of the Koran and *sunna*," in reply to those of his time or any other who imagine that it is beyond the pale of the Koran and *sunna*.
>
> The Folk unanimously concur that none is fit to teach in the path of Allah Mighty and Majestic save someone with comprehensive mastery of the sacred law, who knows its explicit and implicit rulings, which of them are of general applicability and which are

208 Al-Haytami, *Fatawa hadithiyya* p. 52-54.

particular, which supersede others and which are superseded. He must also have a thorough grounding in Arabic, be familiar with its figurative modes and similes, and so forth. So every true Sufi is a scholar in Sacred Law, though the reverse is not necessarily true.

To summarize, no one denies the states of the Sufis except someone ignorant of the way they are. Qushayri says, "No era of the Islamic period has had a true shaykh of this group, save that the imams of the scholars of that time deferred to him, showed humility towards him, and visited him for the benefit of his spiritual grace (*baraka*). If the Folk had no superiority or election, the matter would have been the other way around.[209]

4.32. MULLA ALI AL-QARI (D. 1014 AH)

One of the great Hanafi masters of hadith and jurist, Quranic commentary, language, history and *tasawwuf*, al-Qari authored several great commentaries. These include *al-Mirqat* on *Mishkat al-masabih* in several volumes, a two-volume commentary on Qadi Iyad's *al-Shifa*, and a two-volume commentary on Ghazali's abridgment of the *Ihya* entitled *Ayn al-ilm wa zayn al-hilm* (The spring of knowledge and the adornment of understanding). His book of prophetic invocations, *al-Hizb al-azam* (The supreme daily *dhikr*), forms the basis of Imam al-Jazuli's celebrated manual of *dhikr, Dalail al-khayrat*, which is recited daily along with the Quran by many pious Muslims around the world.

He writes in the foreword to his commentary on Ghazali:

> I wrote this commentary on the abridgment of *Ihya ulum al-din* by the Proof of Islam and the Confirmation of Creatures hoping to receive some of the outpouring of blessings from the words of the most pure knowers of Allah, and to benefit from the gifts that exude from the pages of the shaykhs and the saints, so that I may be mentioned in their number and be raised in their throng, even if I fell short in their following and their service, for I rely on my

---

209 Abd al-Wahhab, *Al-Tabaqat al-kubra al-musamma bi lawaqih al-anwar fi tabaqat al-akhyar* (1374/1954) (Reprint, Beirut: dar al-fikr, n.d.) 1:4. In *Reliance of the Traveller* p. 863-864.

love for them and content myself with my longing for them.[210]

On the obligation to seek purification of the heart he writes:

The greatest of the great (al-akabir) have striven to pray only two rakat without conversing with their ego about this world in the midst of their prayer, and they were unable to do this. Therefore there is not any such ambition for us of ever achieving this. Would that one saves only half of his prayer, or only a third, from the whisperings and the passing thoughts turning over in the mind. He is like him who mixes good and bad, like a glass full of vinegar into which water is poured: inevitably vinegar is spilled in proportion to the water poured and the two amounts never coexist. We ask for Allah's help![211]

The last chapter of Qari's commentary on Ghazali, which is perhaps the most valuable of the entire work, is devoted to both of their explanations of the verse *"If you love Allah, follow me, and Allah will love you!"* (3:31).[212] In this chapter Qari cites al-Hasan al-Basri as saying, "Whoever (truly) knows his Lord loves Him, and whoever (truly) knows the world does without it." Qari begins the chapter with a warning that the various spiritual states of love for Allah described by Sufis all proceed from the same Quranic source and that it is not permitted to deny them unless one denies the source itself:

Love and the discipline of the path (al-mahabba wa al-suluk) mean the path of love and longing, and whoever does not scoop his drink from the ocean of gnosticism does not know the reality of love, even if the genus, examples, and terminology are different. Love has no other meaning than the exhortation to obedience, and whoever denies love denies familiarity (uns) and passion (shawq) and taste (dhawq) and effacement (mahu) and clarity (sahu) and extinction (fana) and subsistence (baqa) and contraction (qabd) and expansion (bast) and all the rest of the necessary

---

210 Al-Qari, *Sharh ayn al-ilm wa zayn al-hilm* 1:1.
211 *Ibid.* 1:78.
212 Qari's work is reminiscent of al-Harawi's *Kitab sad maydan* on the same topic.

characteristics of love and longing, and the rest of the stations of the People of Gnosis.[213]

4.33. IBN ABIDIN (D. 1252 AH)

Nicknamed the Seal of Self-Realized Scholars (khatimat al-muhaqqiqin), Ibn Abidin was a great scholar and faqih. He said in his fatwa on the permissibility of loud dhikr in assembly:

> The imam of the Two Groups (Sufis and fuqaha) our master al-Junayd was asked, 'A certain people indulge in wajd or ecstatic behavior, and sway with their bodies?' He replied, "Leave them to their happiness with Allah. They are the ones whose affections have been smashed by the path and whose breasts have been torn apart by effort, and who are unable to bear it. There is no blame on them if they breathe awhile as a remedy for their intense state. If you tasted what they taste, you would excuse their shouting' . . .
>
> The Seekers in this Way don't hear except from the Divine Presence and they don't love any but Him. If they remember Him they cry, and if they thank Him they are happy; if they find Him they cry out, and if they witness Him they rest; if they walk in His divine presence, they melt . . . some of them they are drunk with His Blessings and lose sight of themselves . . .
>
> Their assemblies for dhikr and recital (sama) give fruit to Divine knowledge and spiritual realities, which only takes place upon hearing the description of Allah, exhortations to wisdom, and praises of the Prophet (ﷺ). Nor do we have one word of reproach to those who follow them in their method and find in themselves the expressions of passionate longing (ishq) for Allah characteristic of some of their states.[214]

4.39. ABU AL-ALA MAWDUDI (D. 1399 AH)

The most famous contemporary Islamic thinker of the Indian subcontinent and author of a Quranic commentary in Urdu and English, he wrote:

---

213 Ibid. 2:354-355.

214 Ibn Abidin, Seventh Letter in Shifa al-alil wa ball al-ghalil fi hukm al-wasiyya bi al-khatamat wa al-tahalil p. 172-173.

Jurisprudence addresses only external actions: did you perform them according to what is required? The condition of your heart is not taken under consideration. As for the science that investigates the states of the heart and its conditions: this is *tasawwuf*. The questions asked by *fiqh* are: Did you complete your ablution correctly? Did you pray towards the *qibla*? Did you fulfill the pillars of prayer? If you did all this your prayer is correct according to the ruling of jurisprudence. As for *tasawwuf*, it asks questions about your heart: Did you repent and turn to your Lord in your prayer? Did you empty your heart of the preoccupations of the world in your prayer? Did you pray in fear of Allah and knowing that He sees and hears you? . . . If you did all this and other things, then your prayer is correct according to *tasawwuf*, otherwise it is defective . . . *Tasawwuf* is the establishment of the law of Islam to the utmost point of sincerity, clarity of intention, and purity of heart.[215]

215 Abul Ala al-Mawdudi *Mabadi al-Islam* p. 114-117.

5. MORE ON THE HISTORY AND MEANING OF *TASAWWUF*

The topic of *tasawwuf* has been addressed at length in the preceding pages. Let us now address specific questions by way of a recapitulation.

Tasawwuf is linked historically to *zuhd* (asceticism), lexically to *suf* (wool), and semantically to *tazkiya al-nafs* (purifying one's soul and manners).

1. Briefly put, Sufi is a second-century name applied to a type of Muslim earlier known as *zahid* (ascetic, one who renounces and does without). The lexical root of Sufi is traced, among other roots, to:

suf = wool
safa = purity

While the first is more likely, the second is given preference. The two were nicely combined by Abu Ali al-Rudhabari (d. 322), who said:

> The Sufi is the one who wears wool (*suf*) on top of purity (*safa*) (*al-sufi man labisa al-sufa ala al-safa*).[1]

These are the more likely etymologies mentioned by al-Qushayri, al-Huwjiri, Ibn Taymiyya, al-Shatibi, and many others.

---

1 Suyuti, *Tayid al-haqiqa al-aliyya.*

It is established that the wearing of wool is a *sunna* of the Prophet (ﷺ):

> Al-Mughira ibn Shuba said: "[The Prophet] washed his face and hands while wearing a cloak of wool (*jubbatun min al-suf*)."[2]

Anas said: "Allah's Messenger wore wool (*labisa al-suf*)."[3]

Ibn Rajab al-Hanbali said in his book on love of Allah and love of the Prophet (ﷺ):[4]

> Love for the Prophet (ﷺ) is on two levels . . . The second level is superior. This type of love requires following his example in an excellent way and adhering to his *sunna* with respect to his behavior, manners, voluntary deeds, supererogatory actions, eating, drinking, dressing, excellent behavior with his wives and other aspects of his perfect manners and pure behavior.

In his major work on the definition of *bida* (innovation), Al-Shatibi (d. 790) categorically and meticulously rejected the ascription of Sufis and *tasawwuf* to innovation in Islam.[5]

A third etymology for *tasawwuf* is in the name of the poorer Companions who lived in the mosque of the Prophet (ﷺ) and who were called *ashab al-suffa*, the Companions of the Porch. Indeed they are the earliest Sufis in Islam, being literally *fuqara*, or dependent ones, a word which like *zahid* is an early synonym of Sufi.

> Fadala ibn Ubayd said that when the Prophet (ﷺ) used to pray among the people, some of the men would collapse during prayer due to the length of their prayer and due to their indigence. They were the Companions of the Porch (*ashab al-suffa*). It reached the point when the bedouins of the Arabs would say, 'These are possessed madmen.' (One day) after the

---

2 Bukhari narrated it in his *Sahih*.

3 Ibn Majah narrated it in the *Sunan* with two weak chains, but the narrations are confirmed by Bukhari's narrations in the three chapters of wearing wool in his Book of Vestments (*Kitab al-libas*).

4 Ibn Rajab al-Hanbali, *Istinshaq nasim al-uns min nafahat riyad al-quds* (Inhaling the breeze of intimacy from the whiffs of the gardens of sanctity).

5 Al-Shatibi, *al-Itisam*.

Prophet (ﷺ) prayed he walked over to them and say, 'If you knew how much you own in Allah's presence, you would dearly wish to increase in poverty and need.' Fadala added, 'That day I was with Allah's Messenger.'[6]

Ahl al-suffa was a term applied to a group of over ninety poor refugees and homeless people who were supported by Muslim charity. They were lodged in the *suffa* of the Prophet's mosque in Madina, which was a *saqifa*, or roof or covering for shade, made of palm-sticks and leaves. *Lisan al-arab* defines it as *mawdi muzallal min al-masjid kana yawi ilayhi al-masakin*, "a shaded spot of the mosque to which the poor sought shelter.[7]

2. As for the term *zahid*, Imam Ahmad (d. 241) established that it applies first and foremost to the Prophet (ﷺ) and his eminent Companions, may Allah be well pleased with them. It also applies to all of the prophets of Allah.

Abd al-Qadir al-Baghdadi (d. 429) mentioned the terms *zahid* and Sufi interchangeably in his classifications of the groups that belong to mainstream Islam:

> Know that Sunnis are divided in eight groups of people . . . the sixth group being the Sufi Ascetics (*al-zuhhad al-sufiyya*), who have seen things for what they are and therefore have abstained, who have known by experience and therefore have taken heed truly, who have accepted Allah's allotment and contented themselves with what is within reach.[8]

3. The term Sufi has been used in contrast with *faqih* (jurist) by the great Imams of jurisprudence and usul to signify the inner and outward practices of religion, respectively.

---

6 Tirmidhi narrates it with a strong chain in his *Sunan*, Book of *zuhd*, and he said: "This is a sound (*sahih*) narration."

7 Suyuti, *Tayid al-haqiqa al-aliyya* (Cairo: al-matbaa al-islamiyya, 1352/1934) p. 15; Qushayri, *al-Risala*, introduction and chapter on *tasawwuf* and their commentary by Shaykh al-Islam Zakariyya al-Ansari, also Qushayri's short treatise *Tartib al-suluk fi tariq Allah*; Huwjiri, *Kashf al-mahjub*, Introduction; Ibn Taymiyya, see reference below; al-Shatibi, *al-Itisam* (Beirut: Dar al-kutub al-ilmiyya, 1415/1995) p. 150-159; Ibn Manzur, *Lisan al-arab* 3:451.

8 Ahmad ibn Hanbal, *al-Zuhd*, 2nd. ed. (Beirut: Dar al-kutub al-ilmiyya, 1414/1994); Abd al-Qahir al-Baghdadi, *al-Farq bayn al-firaq* (Beirut: Dar al-kutub al-ilmiyya, n.d.) 242-243.

Imam Al-Shafii said:

(Be both) a jurist (*faqih*) and a Sufi: do not be only one
of them,
Verily, by Allah's truth, I am advising you sincerely.
(*faqihan wa Sufiyyan fa kun laysa wahidan
fa inni wa haqqillahi iyyaka ansahu*)[9]

Imam Malik said:

> He who practices *tasawwuf* without learning
> Sacred Law corrupts his faith, while he who learns
> Sacred Law without practicing tasawwuf corrupts
> himself. Only he who combines the two proves true
> (*man tasawwafa wa lam yatafaqqah fa qad tazan-
> daqa wa man tafaqqaha wa lam yatasawwaf fa qad
> tafassaqa wa man jamaa bayn al-ithnayn fa qad
> tahaqqaqa*).

> 4. The hafiz Ibn al-Jawzi wrote a 100-page book
> on al-Hasan al-Basri's life and personality entitled
> *Adab al-Shaykh al-Hasan ibn Abi al-Hasan al-Basri*.
> Ibn al-Jawzi also mentions a report that al-Hasan left
> behind a white cloak (*jubba*) made of wool (*suf*) which
> he had worn exclusively of any other for the past
> twenty years, winter and summer, and that when he
> died it was in a state of immaculate beauty, cleanness,
> and quality.[10]

As to when the Sufis formally appeared, the earliest date
that can be established is based on Hasan al-Basri's student,
Abd al-Wahid ibn Zayd's (d. 177) construction of the first Sufi

---

9 Al-Shafii, *Diwan*, (Beirut and Damascus: Dar al-fikr) p. 47; Imam Malik: see Ali
al-Qari, *Sharh ayn al-ilm wa-zayn al-hilm* (Cairo: Maktabat al-thaqafa al-diniyya,
1989) 1:33 and *Mirqat al-mafatih sharh mishkat al-masabih* 1:256; Ahmad Zarruq,
Qawaid al-tasawwuf (Cairo, 1310); Ali al-Adawi, *Hashiyat al-adawi ala sharh Abi al-
Hasan li-risalat* Ibn Abi Zayd *al-Musammat kifayat al-talib al-rabbani li-risalat Ibn
Abi Zayd al-Qayrawani fi madhhab Malik* (Beirut?: Dar ihya al-kutub al-arabiyah,
<n.d.>) 2:195; Ibn Ajiba, *Iqaz al-himam fi sharh al-hikam* (Cairo: Halabi, 1392/1972)
p. 5-6. See also Sufyan al-Thawri's saying on the best of people being the Sufi who is
versed in *fiqh*, cited below.
10 In his chapter on al-Hasan in his compendium of the saints entitled *Sifat al-
safwa*–based on Abu Nuaym's *Hilyat al-awliya*.

khaniqa, or guest-house and school, at Abadan on the present-day border of Iran with Iraq.[11] The *hafiz* al-Harawi al-Ansari (d. 481) says, in his biographies of the Sufi masters, that the first person to be actually named "Sufi" was Abu Hashim al-Sufi (d. 150?), a contemporary of Imam Sufyan al-Thawri (d. 165). Al-Thawri said:

> If it were not for Abu Hashim al-Sufi I would have never perceived the presence of the subtlest forms of hypocrisy in the self . . . Among the best of people is the Sufi learned in jurisprudence.[12]

Sufyan al-Thawri's remark highlights the need for a master of self-purification. Shaykh Abd al-Qadir al-Jilani said:

> Let it be fully realized that Allah Almighty has made it the customary practice that there be on the earth the shaykh and the *murid,* the companion and the one whose company is kept, the follower and the one who is followed. This has held since the time of Adam and will hold until the rising of the Hour (*wa liyatahaqqaq bi annallaha azza wa jall ajra al-ada bian yakuna fi al-ardi shaykhun wa murid sahibun wa mashub tabi wa matbu min ladun adam ila an taquma al-saa*).

The famous student of the Khwaja Ubayd Allah Ahrar, Abd al-Rahman Jami, said in his book *Nafahat al-uns:*

> All the prophets have come in order to open people's eyes to see their own faults and Allah's perfection, their own weakness and Allah's power, their own injustice and Allah's justice . . . And the shaykh is also there for the purpose of opening the eyes of his disciples. *"For Allah the worst of all beasts are the deaf and dumb human beings who understand not"* (8:22).

---

11 This is related by the *hafiz* Abu Nuaym (d. 430) and confirmed by Ibn Taymiyya.

12 Abu Nuaym narrated in *Hilyat al-awliya* and al-Ansari in his *Tabaqat,* while Ibn al-Jawzi, who dislikes the word "Sufi," names him Abu Hashim al-Zahid in his *Sifat al-safwa.*

Ali ibn Abi Talib, may Allah be well pleased with him, said:

> Thus does knowledge die: when those who possess
> it die. By Allah I do swear it: the earth will never be
> empty of one who establishes the proofs of Allah so
> that His proofs and signs never cease. They are the
> fewest in number, but the greatest in rank before
> Allah. Through them Allah preserves His proofs until
> they bequeath it to those like them (before passing on)
> and plant it firmly in their hearts. By them knowl-
> edge has taken by assault the reality of things, so that
> they found easy what those given to comfort found
> hard, and found intimacy in what the ignorant found
> desolate. They accompanied the world with bodies
> whose spirits were attached to the highest regard (al-
> mahall al-ala). Ah, ah! how one yearns to see them![13]

It is the notion of "yearning to see" those who possess and bequeath knowledge that is prevalent in the Prophet's hadiths that pertain to the shaykh and the student, such as the following:

> Abu Hurayra said that the Prophet (ﷺ) said, "The
> earth and everything in it is cursed, except for *dhikr*
> and what attends *dhikr*, and the teacher and the stu-
> dent."[14]

The above hadith of the Prophet (ﷺ) stresses the importance of following a teacher of knowledge in order to earn blessings instead of a curse. This is what Abu Yazid al-Bistami
meant when he said, "Whoever has no shaykh, his shaykh is
satan." It is confirmed by two other hadiths of the Prophet (ﷺ):

> Abu Bakrah said: I heard the Prophet (ﷺ) say,

---

13 Ibn al-Jawzi, *Sifat al-safwa* 2(4):10 (#570) and 1(2):203 (#254); Abu Nuaym,
Hilyat al-awliya 6:155 and s.v. "Abu Hashim"; Ibn Taymiyya, *al-Sufiyya wa al-fuqara*,
beginning of volume 11 of his *Majmua al-fatawa al-kubra* entitled *al-Tasawwuf*; al-
Harawi al-Ansari, *Tabaqat al-Sufiyya*, Mawlayi ed. (1983) p. 1, p. 159; Shaykh Abd al-
Qadir al-Jilani, *al-Ghunya li talibi tariq al-haqq* (p. 840); Abd al-Rahman Jami,
Nafahat al-uns, ed. M. Tauhidipur, 1336/1957 (p. 441).
14 Narrated by Tirmidhi who said it is *hasan*, Ibn Majah who said the same,
Bayhaqi, and others. Suyuti cites it in *al-Jami al-saghir* from al-Bazzar's similar narration from Ibn Masud and he declared it *sahih*. Tabarani also narrated it in *al-Awsat*
from Abu al-Darda.

'Become a learned person (*alim*), or a student of knowledge (*mutaallim*), or an auditor of knowledge (*mustami*), or an amateur of knowledge (*muhibb*), but do not be the fifth one for you will perish.'

Al-Haythami said, "Tabarani narrated it in *al-Mujam al-saghir* (2:9), *al-Mujam al-awsat*, and *al-Mujam al-kabir*, also al-Bazzar [in his *Musnad*], and its narrators are considered trustworthy."[15] Sakhawi said,[16]

Ibn Abd al-Barr said, The fifth one is enmity towards the scholars and contempt of them, and whoever does not love them shows contempt for them or is on the brink of having contempt for them, and there lies destruction.[17]

The second hadith reads:

The Prophet (ﷺ) said: "Blessing is with your elders" (*al-baraka ma akabirikum*).

This is narrated by Ibn Hibban in his *Sahih*, al-Hakim who said it is *sahih*, and Ibn Daqiq al-Eid confirmed him. Another narration has, "When the young teach the old, then blessing has been lifted."[18]

Most importantly, the Prophet (ﷺ) said, "The scholars of knowledge are the inheritors of the prophets." Ibn Khaldun has mentioned this as one of the proofs for the necessity of following a shaykh in the sciences of *tasawwuf*.[19] He says, "To be in no need of the heir amounts to being in no need of the Prophet (ﷺ)."

5. The derogatory remarks about *tasawwuf* that are attributed to Imam Al-Shafii and are being quoted today must be understood in light of the imam's disavowal of certain people who called themselves Muslims or Sufis when in reality they were nothing more than hypocrites, free-thinkers, and dis-

15 Al-Haythami, in *Majma al-zawaid* (1:122). It is also narrated by Abu Nuaym in *Hilyat al-awliya* (7:237) and al-Khatib in *Tarikh Baghdad* (12:295).
16 Sakhawi, in *al-Maqasid al-hasana* (p. 88 #134).
17 See Ibn Abd al-Barr's *Jami bayan al-ilm wa fadlih* (1:30).
18 See Sakhawi's *al-Maqasid al-hasana* (p. 158-159 #290).
19 Ibn Khaldun, in the sixth chapter of his book *Shifa al-sail li tahdhib al-masail* (Chapter on following a sufi shaykh).

solute people. This should be born in mind by anyone who is approached by "Salafis" who use narrations from Ibn al-Jawzi's *Talbis Iblis* to attribute sweeping disapproval of *tasawwuf* to Imam Shafii. How can Imam Shafii disapprove of *tasawwuf* and at the same time advise the *fuqaha* to be Sufis, as quoted above?

The *muhaddith* al-Ajluni also relates that Imam Shafii said:[20]

> Three things in this world have been made lovely to me: avoiding affectation, treating people kindly, and following the way of *tasawwuf*.

Ibn al-Qayyim and al-Suyuti also relate that Imam Al-Shafii said:

> I accompanied the Sufis and received from them but three statements: their statement that time is a sword; if you do not cut it, it cuts you; their statement that if you do not keep your ego busy with truth it will keep you busy with falsehood; their statement that deprivation is immunity.[21]

The Maliki shaykh Ahmad al-Alawi said:

> Reflect on the sincerity of this great imam [Shafii] and how he became a witness for the Sufis, and confirmed their seriousness and struggle. Shaykh Sharani, may Allah be pleased with him, said: Reflect on how Shafii has taken this from the Sufis and not from others. It is by this that you know their superiority over others, the men of outward knowledge, the ones from whom he once learned.[22]

An authority whom the "Salafis" would claim as their own is Ibn Qayyim al-Jawziyya. However, Ibn Qayyim made many statements that contravene what "Salafis" claim. He said:[23]

---

20 Al-Ajluni, in his book *Kashf al-khafa wa muzil al-albas* (1:341 #1089).

21 Ibn al-Qayyim, *Madarij al-salikin* (3:128) and Al-Suyuti, *Tayid al-haqiqa al-aliyya* (p. 15).

22 Ahmad al-Alawi, as cited in the translation from his work entitled *Knowledge of God* (p. xxi).

23 Ibn Qayyim, *Madarij al-salikin* (2:307).

> Religion consists entirely of good character (*al-dinu kulluhu khuluq*). Whoever surpasses you in good character surpasses you in religion, and the same is true of *tasawwuf*. Al-Kattani said, "*Tasawwuf* is good character (*al-tasawwuf khuluq*). Whoever surpasses you in good character surpasses you in *tasawwuf*."

It may be asked whether the "Salafis" know the position of Ibn Abd al-Wahhab on *tasawwuf*. It is evident that the majority of them are unaware that Ibn Abd al-Wahhab accepted the attribution of *tasawwuf* to the Prophet (ﷺ) himself. Ibn Abd al-Wahhab said:

> Know–may Allah guide you–that Allah Almighty has sent Muhammad, blessings and peace upon him, with right guidance, consisting in beneficial knowledge, and with true religion consisting in righteous action. The adherents of religion are as follows: among them are those who concern themselves with learning and *fiqh*, and discourse about it, such as the jurists; and among them are those who concern themselves with worship and the pursuit of the hereafter, such as the Sufis. Allah has sent His Prophet (ﷺ) with this religion which encompasses both kinds, that is: jurisprudence and self-purification (*tasawwuf*).[24]

Those who would discredit the Sufis also invoke Ibn al-Jawzi's exhortative work *Talbis iblis*, in which he attributes to Al-Shafii sayings that are detrimental to Sufis, or sayings of Imam Ahmad detrimental to Imam al-Harith al-Muhasibi. However, as Dhahabi said, "We call Ibn al-Jawzi *hafiz* (hadith memorizer) in deference to the profusion of his writings, not to his scholarliness." That is, he was not reliable when it came to reporting narrations.

The following remarks are by the late *muhaddith* of Syria Shaykh Abd al-Fattah Abu Ghudda:

> Our reliance is on Allah! Ibn al-Jawzi composed a great big book on hadith forgeries so that jurists, preachers, and others may avoid them, then you will

---

24 Ibn Abd al-Wahhab, in the third volume of his complete works published by Ibn Saud University, on page 31 of the *Fatawa wa rasail*, Fifth Question.

see him cite in his exhortative works forged hadiths
and rejected stories without head nor tail, without
shame or second thought. In the end one feels that
"Ibn al-Jawzi" is two people and not one! . . . For this
reason Ibn al-Athir blamed him in his history entitled
al-Kamil (10:228), with the words:
    Ibn al-Jawzi blamed him [Ghazali] for many
    things, among them his narration of unsound hadiths
    in his exhortations. O wonder that Ibn al-Jawzi
    should criticize him for that! For his own books and
    exhortative works are crammed full with them
    (*mahshuw bihi wa mamlu minh*)!
    And the hadith master al-Sakhawi said in *Sharh
    al-alfiyya* (p. 107): Ibn al-Jawzi cited forgeries and
    their likes in high abundance in his exhortative
    works![25]

Besides the above, there is Imam Taj al-Din al-Subki's
advice for serious students of the Islamic sciences, also quoted
above:

    Beware of listening to what happened between . .
    . Ahmad ibn Hanbal and al-Harith al-Muhasibi. If you
    become busy with this I fear death for you. These are
    notable leaders in religion and their utterances have
    various explanations which some, perhaps, have mis-
    understood. As for us, we have no other course but to
    approve of them and keep quiet concerning what took
    place between them, just as what is done concerning
    what took place between the Companions, may Allah
    be well pleased with them . . . O you who are seeking
    guidance! . . . leave aside what took place between
    them, and busy yourself with what concerns you, and
    leave what does not concern you![26]

Dhahabi directs an avalanche of insinuations against some
of the earlier and later Sufis in his *Mizan al-itidal*, where he
says, after quoting derogatory reports against al-Muhasibi:

    Where are the likes of al-Harith al-Muhasibi!
    How then if Abu Zura saw the books of the later
    [Sufis], such as the *Qut al-qulub* of Abu Talib [al-

25 Abd al-Fattah Abu Ghudda, notes to al-Lucknawi's *Raf wa al-takmil* p. 420-
421.
26 Subki, *Qaida* p. 53.

Makki], and where are the likes of the *Qut*? How then if he saw *Bahjat al-asrar* of Abu Jahdam, and *Haqaiq al-tafsir* of al-Sulami, then he would jump to the ceiling! How then if he saw the books of Abu Hamid al-Tusi [Imam Ghazali] . . .? the Ghunya of shaykh Abd al-Qadir [Jilani] . . . *Fusus al-hikam* and *al-Futuhat al-makiyya* [of Ibn Arabi]?[27]

Such assertions should be treated as instructed by Suyuti, who rejected them:

Don't let Dhahabi's mumbling deceive you, for he went so far as to mumble against Imam Fakhr al-Din ibn al-Khatib [al-Razi], and against one who is greater than the imam, namely: Abu Talib al-Makki the author of *Qut al-qulub*, and against one who is greater than Abu Talib, namely: Shaykh Abu al-Hasan al-Ashari, whose fame has filled the firmaments! And Dhahabi's books are filled with that: *al-Mizan*, *al-Tarikh*, and *Siyar al-nubala*. Are you going to accept his words against such as these? Never, by Allah! His word is not accepted concerning them; rather, we fulfill their right over us, and we render it to them in full.[28]

5.1. REFUTATION OF DUBIOUS OBJECTIONS TO *TASAWWUF*

QUESTIONS AND ANSWERS

Q. What about those who condemn al-Junayd's statement that the true *murid* stays away from the scholars of knowledge?

A. This is not what Imam al-Junayd said. Ibn al-Qayyim relates:[29]

Abu Abd al-Rahman al-Sulami said [in his *Tabaqat al-sufiyya*]: I heard Muhammad ibn Mukhlid say: I heard Jafar say: I heard al-Junayd say: The truthful seeker has no need for the scholars of knowledge (*al-murid al-sadiq ghaniyyun an al-ulama*).

---

27 Dhahabi, *Mizan al-itidal*, (1:430 #1606).

28 Suyuti, in his vindication entitled *Qam al-muarid bi nusrat Ibn al-Farid* (The taming of the naysayer with the vindication of Ibn al-Farid) as quoted by Imam al-Lucknawi in *al-Raf wa al-takmil fi al-jarh wa al-tadil* (p. 319-320).

29 Ibn al-Qayyim, *Madarij al-salikin* (2:366).

He also said: I heard al-Junayd say:

> When Allah desires goodness for the seeker, He
> makes him flock to the Sufis and prevents him from
> accompanying those who read books (*idha arada
> allahu bi al-muridi khayran awqaahu ila al-Sufiyya
> wa manaahu suhbat al-qurra*).

Allah said, "*Only he will prosper who comes to Allah with a
sound heart*" (26:89) and therefore ordered us to keep company
not merely with the scholars, but with the truthful ones; "*O
Believers! Be wary of Allah and keep company with the truthful
ones!*" (9:119). Al-Izz ibn Abd al-Salam mentions that the Sufis
are those meant by Allah's saying, "*Allah's party*" (5:56, 58:22),
precisely because, according to his definition, *tasawwuf* is "the
betterment of hearts, through whose health bodies are healthy,
and through whose disease bodies are diseased." He considers
the knowledge of external legal rulings an understanding of the
law in its generalities, while the knowledge of internal matters
is an understanding of the law in its subtle details.[30] In a celebrated *fatwa* he gives priority to the gnostics, or Knowers of
Allah (*arifin*), over the jurists and says:

> A sign of the superiority of the gnostics over the
> jurists is that Allah effects miracles at the hands of
> the former, but never at the hands of the latter, except
> when they enter the path of the gnostics and acquire
> their characteristics.[31]

This is the reality to which al-Junayd is referring. Those
who object to the above statements have forgotten or have
blinded themselves to the fact that the goal of creation is worship of Allah and knowing Him, not the accumulation of knowledge—even if it is knowledge of sharia! Therefore, al-Junayd's
words will not be understood by Westernized students of Islam
who have embraced the pursuit of knowledge and abandoned
the goal of knowledge. In fact, it is a form of polytheism (*shirk*)
that is characteristic of Iblis, whose superficial knowledge of

30 Al-Izz ibn Abd al-Salam, *Qawaid al-ahkam* (Dar al-sharq li al-tibaa,
1388/1968) 1:29, 2:212.
31 Al-Izz ibn Abd al-Salam, *Fatawa*, ed. Abd al-Rahman ibn Abd al-Fattah
(Beirut: Dar al-marifa, 1406/1986) p. 138-142.

Allah's revelations was so vast, yet did not give him an iota of wisdom.

There are abundant illustrations of al-Junayd's words as we have seen.[32] Another example of the superiority of a Sufi's company over that of the scholars is given by Bishr al-Hafi. Ibn Sad, in his *Tabaqat*, and others relate that Abu Nasr Bishr al-Hafi (d. 227) considered the study of hadith a conjectural science in comparison to the certitude of belief imparted by visiting Fudayl ibn Iyad (d. 187).[33]

Qasim al-Jui and Fudayl ibn Iyad are not only scholars of knowledge but they are the teachers of the greatest scholars of knowledge and the imams of righteousness and Godwariness among the Salaf. Ibn Taymiyya lists Fudayl ibn Iyad as one of the early Sufi shaykhs and mainstream Islamic authorities:

The great shaykhs mentioned by Abu Abd al-Rahman al-Sulami in *Tabaqat al-sufiyya* and Abu al-Qasim al-Qushayri in *al-Risala*, were adherents of the school of mainstream Islam and the school of *ahl al-hadith*, such as Fudayl ibn Iyad, al-Junayd ibn Muhammad, Sahl ibn Abd Allah al-Tustari, Amr ibn Uthman al-Makki, Abu Abd Allah Muhammad ibn Khafif al-Shirazi, and others. Their speech is found in the *sunna*, and they composed books about the *sunna*.[34] We have also seen Dhahabi's words in praise of al-Jui from his *Siyar alam al-nubala*.

Therefore, al-Junayd's statement does not recommend abandoning the scholars of knowledge. On the contrary, he advised the favor of such teachers over the book-scholars whose main concern is the transcription and the collection of books of hadith. Memorizers are many, but few are those who practice what they have memorized. This is even more true for the Quran than it is for hadith, as Imam Ibn Sallam (d. 224) related:

> The reciters of Quran are three types: the first type take the Quran as a merchandise by which to earn their bread; the second type uphold its letters and lose its laws, aggrandizing themselves over the

32 Ibn Abi Hatim, *Sifat al-safwa* (2/2:200 #763).

33 See Ibn Sad, *Tabaqat* (ed. Sachau) 7(2):83; al-Arusi, *Nataij al-afkar al-qudsiyya* (Bulaq, 1920/1873); and Abd al-Wahhab al-Sharawi, *al-Tabaqat al-kubra* 1:57.

34 Ibn Taymiyya, *al-Safadiyya* (Riyad: matabi hanifa, 1396/1976) 1:267.

people of their country, and seeking gain through it from the rulers. There are many memorizers of Quran that belong to that type. May Allah not increase them. Finally, the third type have sought the healing of the Quran and placed it on the sickness of their hearts, fleeing with it to their places of prayer, wrapping themselves in it. Those have felt fear and put on the garment of sadness. Those are the ones for whose sake Allah sends rain and victory over the enemies. By Allah! That kind of memorizer of Quran is more rare than the red sulphur. [35]

It is symptomatic of today's corruption when young men who could be acquiring knowledge from practicing scholars, instead waste their time speaking against the great shaykhs of old. The *hafiz* and historian of Damascus, Ibn Asakir, cautioned against letting our tongues loose against the scholars. He said:

Know, brother, that the flesh of scholars is poisonous (i.e. whoever backbites them is liable to poisoning, for the Quran likens backbiting to eating the flesh of one's dead brother), and the Way of Allah concerning those who insult them is well-known. So, whoever insults the scholars of this *umma* by his tongue, Allah will afflict him in this very world by death of the heart.

This is unfortunately the state of affairs with many nowadays, because today Islam is taught with words and books by people who do not practice purely or purify themselves in practice. Instead they are eager to censure and condemn others; and that is also the practice of those who are misguided by them. This was described in the many hadiths that state, "They will order people and not heed their own warning, and they are the worst of people."[36]

Such was not the way of the Companions, such as the *ahl al-suffa*, concerning whom the following verse was revealed." *And restrain thyself with those who call upon their Lord at morning and evening, desiring His countenance, and let not*

---

35 Al-Hasan al-Basri in *Fadail al-quran* (p. 60 #4).

36 Reported on the authority of Umar, Ali, Ibn Abbas, and others. These were collected by Abu Talib al-Makki in the chapter entitled "The Difference between the scholars of the world and those of the hereafter" in his *Qut al-qulub fi muamalat al-mahbub* (Cairo: Matbaat al-maymuniyya, 1310/1893) 1:140-141.

*thine eyes turn away from them, desiring the adornment of the
present life; and obey not him whose heart We have made neg-
lectful of Our remembrance so that he follows his own lust, and
his affair has become all excess"* (18:28).

Nor was this the way of Abu Bakr al-Siddiq, concerning
whom Bakr ibn Abd Allah said. "Abu Bakr does not precede you
for praying much or fasting much, but because of a secret that
has taken root in his heart."[37] Nor was this the way of the *tabiin* such as Hasan al-Basri, Sufyan al-Thawri, and the later
generations of Sufis who looked back to them. Al-Qushayri
relates that al-Junayd said, "*Tasawwuf* is not the profusion of
prayer and fasting, but wholeness of the breast and selflessness."[38] Nor was superficial knowledge the way of the recognized imams who emphasized doing-without (*zuhd*), and the
acquisition of true piety (*wara*) and truthfulness above the
mere fulfillment of obligations.

Imam Nawawi said:

> Al-Shafii said, may Allah have mercy on him,
> "Only the sincere one (*mukhlis*) knows hypocrisy
> (*riya*)." This means that it is impossible to know the
> reality of hypocrisy and see its hidden shades except
> for one who resolutely seeks (*arada*) sincerity. That
> one strives for a long time searching and meditating
> and examining at length within himself until he
> knows or knows something of what hypocrisy is. This
> does not happen for everyone. Indeed, this happens
> only with the special ones (*al-khawass*). But for a
> given individual to claim that he knows what
> hypocrisy is, this is real ignorance on his part.[39]

Imam Ahmad composed two books with *zuhd* and *wara* as
their respective titles. In the first he places the knowledge of
saints above the knowledge of scholars, as shown by the following report by his student Abu Bakr al-Marwazi:

---

37 Related by Ahmad with a sound chain in *Kitab fadail al-sahaba*, ed. Wasi Allah
ibn Muhammad Abbas (Makka: Muassasat al-risala, 1983) 1:141 (#118).

38 Al-Qushayri, *Risalat kitab al-sama* in *al-Rasail al-qushayriyya* (Sidon and
Beirut: al-maktaba al-asriyya, 1970) p. 60.

39 Nawawi, *Bustan al-arifin fi al-zuhd wa al-tasawwuf* (The garden of the gnostics in asceticism and self-purification p. 53).

I heard Fath ibn Abi al-Fath saying to Abu Abd
Allah (Imam Ahmad) during his last illness, "Invoke
Allah for us that he will give us a good *khalifa* (successor) to succeed you." He continued, "Who shall we
ask for knowledge after you?' Ahmad replied, 'Ask Abd
al-Wahhab." Someone who was present there related
to me that he said, "But he does not have much learning–" Abu Abd Allah replied, "He is a saintly man
(*innahu rajulun salih*), and such as he is granted success in speaking the truth."[40]

The same emphasis on inner perfection is placed by Imam
Malik in his saying, "Religion does not consist in the knowledge
of many narrations, but in a light which Allah places in the
breast." Ibn Ata Allah quoted Shaykh Muhyiddin ibn Arabi as
saying, "Certainty (*al-yaqin*) does not derive from the evidences
of the mind but pours out from the depths of the heart."

This is why many of the imams of religion cautioned against
thirst for knowledge at the expense of training the ego. Imam
Ghazali left the halls of learning in the midst of a prestigious
career to devote himself to self-purification out of concern for
his own soul. At the outset of his new life he wrote his magisterial *Ihya ulum al-din*, which begins with a warning to those
who consider religion to consist merely in jurisprudence.

The same warning was addressed to all those who take the
narration of hadith for the purpose of religion by the greatest
of the *huffaz*, or hadith masters, of his time and one of the early
Sufis, Sufyan al-Thawri (d. 161). He said, "If hadith was a good
it would have vanished just as goodness has vanished . . .
Pursuing the study of hadith is not part of the preparation for
death, but a disease that preoccupies people." Dhahabi comments:

By Allah he has spoken the truth . . . Today, in our
time, the quest for knowledge and hadith no longer
means for the hadith scholar the obligation of living
up to it, which is the goal of hadith. He is right in

40 Ahmad, *Kitab al-wara* (Beirut: Dar al-kitab al-arabi, 1409/ 1988) p. 10.

what he said because pursuing the study of hadith is
other than the hadith itself.[41]

It is for the purpose of "the hadith itself," for the purpose of
living up to the *sunna* of the Prophet (☙), and to the manners
of the Holy Quran,[42] that the great masters of self-purification
forsookthe pursuit of science as a worldly allurement, in favor
of the acquisition of *ihsan*, or excellence of character. That is
the meaning of the statements of Imam al-Junayd about the
sufficiency of the truthful seeker from the scholars of knowledge.

William Chittick quotes, in his compilation of Sufi teaching:

> The great scholars of the age split hairs in all the
> sciences. They have gained total knowledge and com-
> plete mastery of things that have nothing to do with
> them. But that which is important and closer to him
> than anything else, namely his own self, this your
> great scholar does not know.[43]

He also quotes:

> That iniquitous man knows hundreds of superflu-
> ous matters in the sciences, but he does not know his
> own spirit.

> He knows the properties of every substance, but
> in explaining his own substance he is like an ass.

> "I know everything permitted and not permitted
> by the Divine Law." How is it you do not know if you
> yourself are permitted or an old crone?

> You know that this is lawful and that is unlawful,
> but look carefully: Are you lawful or unlawful?

---

41 Dhahabi as cited in Sakhawi, *al-Jawahir wa al-durar fi tarjamat shaykh al-
islam Ibn Hajar* (al-Asqalani), ed. Hamid Abd al-Majid and Taha al-Zayni (Cairo: wizarat al-awqaf, al-majlis al-ala li al-shuun al-islamiyya, lajnah ihya al-turath al-islami,
1986) p. 21-22.

42 Living up to the *sunna* of the Prophet is the same as living up to the manners
of the Holy Quran according to the well-known hadith of Aisha concerning the disposition of the Prophet.

43 From the *Fihi ma fihi* of Jalaluddin Rumi, quoted from *The Sufi Path of Love:
the Spiritual Teachings of Rumi* by W. C. Chittick, p. 148.

You know the value of every merchandise, but you
do not know your own value–that is stupidity.

Yet you know every auspicious and inauspicious
star, but you do not look to see if you yourself are auspicious or dirty-faced.

The spirit of all the sciences is only this: to know
who you will be on the Day of Resurrection.[44]

Finally, he quotes Ibn al-Arabi as writing:

Two ways lead to knowledge of Allah. There is no
third way. The person who declares Allah's Unity in
some other way follows his own authority in his declaration.
The first way is the way of unveiling. It is an
incontrovertible knowledge which is actualized
through unveiling and which a person finds in himself. He receives no obfuscations along with it and is
not able to repel it. He knows no proof for it by which
it is supported except what he finds in himself . . .
This kind of knowledge may also be actualized
through a divine self-disclosure given to its posses-
sors, who are the messengers, the prophets, and some
of the saints.
The second way is the way of reflection and reasoning (*istidlal*) through rational demonstration
(*burhan aqli*). This way is lower than the first way,
since he who bases his consideration on it can be visited by obfuscations which detract from his proof, and
only with difficulty can he remove them.[45]

Q. What about the stories related by Abd al-Wahhab al-
Sharani and the books of Ibn Arabi that apparently contain
contradictions of the Sharia?
A. It is a wise phrasing of this question to use the modifier
"apparently." Appearances can be very misleading, and reality
can be vastly different from the illusion that motivates those
who object, through carelessness or unscrupulousness, to these

---

44 From the *Mathnawi* of Jalaluddin Rumi, Book 23, vv. 2648-54, quoted from *The Sufi Path of Love: the Spiritual Teachings of Rumi* by William C. Chittick, p. 128.
45 Adapted from William C. Chittick, *The Sufi Path of Knowledge*, p. 169, from Ibn al-Arabi's *al-Futuhat al-makkiyya* (I 319.27).

great scholars. Such persons were responsible for the recent anti-Sufi books that came forth from the inkwells of "Salafi" learning. Three of these books are:

• *al-Kashf an haqiqat al-sufiyya* (Unveiling the reality of Sufis),[46]
• *Ila al-tasawwuf ya ibad Allah* (Run to *tasawwuf*, O servants of Allah),[47] and
• *Hiwar ma al-Maliki fi radd munkaratihi wa dalalatihi* (Debate with al-Maliki for refuting his denounced and misguided stances),[48] a despicable attack on Shaykh Muhammad ibn Alawi.

Such books thrive on strange or distorted interpretations without any attention to context and verification. They are examples of how to write without intellectual honesty. The antidotes to such books are, respectively:

• Shaykh Abd al-Qadir Isa's 700-page book *Haqaiq an al-tasawwuf* (Realities from *tasawwuf*)[49]
• Shaykh Ahmad al-Qatani's 300-page refutation entitled al-*Hujja al-mtah fi al-radd ala sahib kitab ila al-tasawwuf ya ibad Allah* (The practical demonstration in refuting the author of the book "Run to *tasawwuf*")[50]
• The 160-page refutation of the attack on Shaykh al-Maliki, entitled *al-Tahdhir min al-ightirar bi ma jaa fi kitab al-hiwar* (Warning against the delusions fostered by the book "Debate with al-Maliki") by the two shaykhs of al-Qarawiyyin Abd al-Hayy al-Amruni and Abd al-Karim Murad.[51]

46 Mahmud Abd al-Rauf al-Qasim *al-Kashf an haqiqat al-sufiyya* (Amman: al-maktaba al-islamiyya, 2nd edition, 1413).

47 Abu Bakr ibn Jabir al-Jazairi, *Ila al-tasawwuf ya ibad Allah* (Cairo: Matbaat al-madani, 1408/1987).

48 By Abd Allah ibn Mani. Published in Riyadh by al-Riasa al-amma li idarat al-buhuth al-ilmiyya wa al-ifta wa al-dawa wa al-irshad!

49 Abd al-Qadir Isa, *Haqaiq an al-tasawwuf* (Dimashq: Warathat al-muallif, 1993).

50 Ahmad al-Qatani, *al-Hujja al-mutah fi al-radd ala sahib kitab ila al-tasawwuf ya ibad Allah* (Cairo: maktabat jumhuriyyat Misr, 1992).

51 Abd al-Hayy al-Amruni and Abd al-Karim Murad, *al-Tahdhir min al-ightirar bi ma jaa fi kitab al-hiwar* (Fes: s.n., 1404/1984).

The last book complements other authoritative refutations such as:

- Shaykh Yusuf al-Sayyid Hashim al-Rufai's excellent 150-page book *Adilla ahl al-sunna wa al-jamaa al-musamma al-radd al-muhkam al-mani ala shubuhat Ibn Mani* (The proofs of Sunnis entitled: The decisive and categorical refutation of the dubious issues raised by Ibn Mani)[52]
- The book of Shaykh Rashid ibn Ibrahim al-Marikhi of Bahrayn entitled *Raf al-astar an shubuhat wa dalalat sahib al-hiwar* (Exposing the dubious and misguided positions of the author of the "Debate with al-Maliki")
- The book of the savant, the Shaykh al-Sayyid Abd Allah ibn Mahfuz al-Haddad Alawi al-Husayni al-Hadrami entitled *al-Sunna wa al-bida*.

The fact is that Abd al-Wahhab al-Sharani (d. 973) is a major scholar of the tenth Islamic century who possessed unequalled knowledge of the recognized Schools in his time. His books on *tasawwuf* are in the tradition of the great classics of earlier times, such as those by al-Qushayri, al-Harawi al-Ansari, and al-Sulami. However, it is established that the original text of Sharani's books was mutilated and corrupted by his enemies even in his own time, in the same way that enemies of the *Shaykh al-akbar* corrupted his books after his time.

The great historian Abd al-Hayy ibn al-Imad al-Hanbali said:

> Certain groups bore envy towards al-Sharani, so they falsely attributed words to him that evidently contravened the Law, as well as certain deviant beliefs and questions that violated consensus. Because of this, Allah brought disgrace to those enviers and gave the shaykh victory over them. He was a strict adherent to the *sunna* and truly god-wary.[53]

---

52 Yusuf al-Sayyid Hashim al-Rifai, *Adilla ahl al-sunna wa al-jamaa al-musamma al-radd al-muhkam al-mani ala shubuhat Ibn Mani* 7th ed. (Kuwait: Matabi dar al-siyasa, 1410/1990).

53 Abd al-Hayy ibn al-Imad al-Hanbali, *Shadharat al-dhahab* (8:374).

Abd al-Wahhab al-Sharani, *Lataif al-minan wa al-akhlaq* (The kind gifts and refined manners 2:190).

Imam Abd al-Wahhab al-Sharani himself wrote:

Of the favors bestowed on me by Allah Almighty is fortitude in the face of the envious enemies who falsified my books with words that plainly contradict the sharia after the success of my book *al-Bahr al-mawrud fi al-mawathiq wa al-uhud.* When the latter came out, the scholars of the recognized schools in Egypt wrote approvingly of it and the people rushed to make copies of it until about forty copies were in circulation. Envious people tricked some of my unwitting associates by borrowing their copies and interpolating into them scores of leaves reflecting false beliefs, matters that contravene the consensus of Muslims, tales, and jokes from Juha [a folktale character] and [Ahmad ibn Yahya] Ibn al-Rawandi [a Shii author]. So they poured into this new mould the creases of my book in so many places that they became its new authors. Then they brought out these books for sale on the book market, on the day in which students come. They looked into those leaves and saw my name on them, and those who had no fear of Allah bought them and began to take them around to the scholars of al-Azhar, producing thereby a great *fitna.*[54]

The people continued on their round of the mosques, the markets, and the houses of princes for about a year, during which the Shaykh Nasr al-Din al-Luqani, with the Hanbali Shaykh al-Islam and Shaykh Shihab al-Din ibn al-Halabi, would always come to my defense. All this was happening without my knowledge. One of our beloved friends at al-Azhar finally sent word to me about it. I then sent my personal copy which contained the written appraisal of the scholars. They examined it and found nothing of what the enviers had interpolated.

Shaykh Abd al-Qadir Isa said:

Similarly they falsified what was in the books of Shaykh Muhyiddin ibn Arabi. Al-Sharani said in *al-Yawaqit wa al-jawahir* (1:9), "Ibn Arabi was a strict

54 Abd al-Qadir Isa, *Haqaiq an al-tasawwuf* (p. 508).

adherent of the Book and the *sunna* and he used to say, "Whoever lets fall the balance of the Law from his hand for one instant perishes . . ." All that contradicts the letter of the law and the doctrine of the assembly of the scholars in his books has been falsely interpolated in them." This was told to me verbatim by Sayyidi Abu Tahir al-Maghribi, who produced for me his copy of *al-Futuhat al-makkiyya* which he had compared to the Shaykh's hand-written copy in the city of Qunya. I saw in that copy none of the spurious passages which I had detected and suppressed before, at the time I prepared an abridgment of the *Futuhat!*[55]

The great scholar of the late Hanafi school Ibn Abidin said:

> What I have ascertained beyond doubt is that some of the Jews have attributed fabrications to the shaykh, may Allah sanctify his secret.[56]

A circumstantial proof of the above is that the copy of the *Futuhat* that was in Ibn Taymiyya's hands contained nothing that would raise any objection on his part, despite his excessive strictness. He said:

> I was one of those who, previously, used to hold the best opinion of Ibn Arabi and extol his praise, because of the benefits I saw in his books, such as what he said in many of his books, for example: *al-Futuhat, al-Kanh, al-Muhkam al-marbut, al-Durra al-fakhira, Matali al-nujum*, and other such works.[57]

Ibn Taymiyya goes on to say he changed his opinions, not because of anything in these books, but only after he read the tiny *Fusus al-hikam*, which the contemporary scholar Mahmud Mahmud Ghurab believes contained at least eighty-six spurious passages! Ghurab holds that they contradict the *Futuhat*, which must be given precedence since there is a manuscript copy of this massive work in the author's own handwriting, while there is no such copy of the *Fusus*.

---

55 Ibn Abidin, in his commentary on *al-Durr al-mukhtar* (3:303).

56 Ibn Taymiyya, *Tawhid al-rububiyya* in *Majmua al-fatawa al-kubra* (Riyad, 1381) 2:464-465.

57 Ibn Arabi, Sharh *Fusus al-hikam*, ed. M.M. Ghurab (Damascus: matbaat Zayd ibn Thabit, 1405/1985).

GLOSSARY

ahkam: legal rulings.

ahl al-bida wa al-ahwa: the People of Unwarranted Innovations and Idle Desires.

ahl al-sunna wa al-jamaa: the Sunnis; the People of the Way of the Prophet and the Congregation of Muslims.[1]

*aqid*a pl. *aqaid*: doctrine.

azaim: strict applications of the law. These are the modes of conduct signifying scrupulous determination to please one's Lord according to the model of the Prophet (ﷺ).

bida: blameworthy innovation.

faqih, pl. *fuqaha*: scholar of *fiqh* or jurisprudence; generally, "person of knowledge."

faqir, pl. *fuqara'*: Sufi, lit. "poor one."

fatwa, pl. *fatawa*: legal opinion.

fiqh: jurisprudence.

fitna: dissension, confusion.

hadith: saying(s) of the Prophet, and the sciences thereof.

hafiz: hadith master, the highest rank of scholarship in hadith.

haqiqi: literal.

hashwiyya: uneducated anthropomorphists.

hijri: adjective from *hijra* applying to dates in the Muslim calendar.

hukm, pl. *ahkam*: legal ruling.

ibadat: worship, acts of worship.

ihsan: perfection of belief and practice.

ijtihad: personal effort of qualified legal reasoning.

isnad: chain of transmission in a hadith or report.

istinbat: derivation (of legal rulings).

jahmi: a follower of Jahm ibn Safwan (d. 128), who said: "Allah is the wind and everything else."[2]

jihad: struggle against disbelief by hand, tongue, and heart.

kalam: theology.

khalaf: "Followers," general name for all Muslims who lived after the first three centuries.

khawarij: "Outsiders," a sect who considered all Muslims who did not follow them, disbelievers. The Prophet said about them as related by Bukhari: "They will transfer the Quranic verses meant to refer to disbelievers and make them refer to believers." Ibn Abidin applied the name of khawarij to the Wahhabi movement.[3]

madhhab, pl. *madhahib*: a legal method or school of law in Islam. The major schools of law include the Hanafi, Maliki, Shafii, and Hanbali and Jafari.

majazi: figurative.

manhaj, minhaj: Way, or doctrinal and juridical method.

muamalat (pl.): plural name embracing all affairs between human beings as opposed to acts of worship *(ibadat)*.

muattila: those who commit *tatil*, i.e. divesting Allah of His attributes.

muhaddith: hadith scholar.

muhkamat: texts conveying firm and unequivocal meaning.

mujahid, pl. *mujahidin*: one who wages *jihad*.

mujassima (pl.): those who commit

---

1 See the section entitled "Apostasies and Heresies" in our *Doctrine of Ahl al-Sunna Versus the "Salafi" Movement* p. 60-64.

2 See Bukhari, *Khalq afal al-ibad*, first chapter; Ibn Hajar, *Fath al-bari, Tawhid*, first chapter; and al-Baghdadi, *al-Farq bayn al-firaq*, chapter on the Jahmiyya.

3 al-Sayyid Muhammad Amin Ibn Abidin al-Hanafi, *Radd al-muhtar ala al-durr al-mukhtar, Kitab al-iman, Bab al-bughat* [Answer to the Perplexed: A Commentary on "The Chosen Pearl," Book of Belief, Chapter on Rebels] (Cairo: Dar al-Tibaa al-Misriyya, 1272/1856) 3:309.

tajsim, attributing a body to Allah.

mujtahid: one who practices *ijtihad* or personal effort of qualified legal reasoning.

munafiq: a dissimulator of his disbelief.

mushabbiha (pl.): those who commit *tashbih*, likening Allah to creation.

mushrik, pl. *mushrikun*: one who associate partners to Allah.

mutakallim, pl. *mutakallimun*: expert in *kalam*.

mutashabihat (pl.): texts which admit of some uncertainty with regard to their interpretation.

mutazila: rationalist heresy of the third century.

sahih: sound (applied to the chain of transmission of a hadith).

salaf: the Predecessors, i.e. Muslims of the first three centuries.

salafi: what pertains to the "Salafi" movement, a modern heresy that rejects the principles of mainstream Islam

shafaa: intercession.

sharia: name embracing the principles and application of Islamic law.

suluk: rule of conduct, personal ethics.

tawil: figurative interpretation.

tafwid: committing the meaning to Allah.

tajsim: attributing a body to Allah

tajwid: Quran reading.

takyif: attributing modality to Allah's attributes.

tamthil: giving an example for Allah.

taqlid: following qualified legal reasoning.

tariqa: path, specifically the Sufi path.

tasawwuf: collective name for the schools and sciences of purification of the self.

tashbih: likening Allah to His Creation.

tatil: divesting Allah from His attributes.

tawassul: seeking a means.

tawhid: Islamic doctrine of monotheism.

tazkiyat al-nafs: purification of the self.

usul: principles.

wasila: means.

BIBLIOGRAPHY

Abidin, *Hashiyat radd al-muhtar ala al-durr al-mukhtar.*

Abidin, *Shifa' al-alil wa ball al-ghalil fi hukm al-wasiyya bi al-khatamat wa al-tahalil.*

Adawi, Ali, *Hashiyat al-Adawi ala sharh Abi al-Hasan li-risalat Ibn Abi Zayd al-musammat kifayat al-talib al-rabbani li-risalat Ibn Abi Zayd al-Qayrawani fi madhhab Maalik* (Beirut?: Dar Ihya' al-Kutub al-Arabiyah, <n.d.>).

Ajiba, *Iqaz al-himam fi sharh al-hikam* (Cairo: Halabi, 1392/1972).

Ajluni, *Kashf al-khafa wa muzil al-albas.*

Alawi, Ahmad, *Knowledge of God.*

Alwani, Taha Jaber, *Usul al-fiqh al-islami: Source Methodology in Islamic Jurisprudence*, ed. Yusuf Talal DeLorenzo (Herndon, VA: IIIT, 1411/1990).

Amruni, Abd al-Hayy and Abd al-Karim Murad, *al-Tahdhir min al-ightirar bi ma ja'a fi kitab al-hiwar* (Fes: s.n., 1404/1984).

Arabi, *Sharh Fusus al-hikam*, ed. M.M. Ghurab (Damascus: matbaat Zayd ibn Thabit, 1405/1985).

Arusi, *Nata'ij al-afkar al-qudsiyya* (Bulaq, 1920/1873).

Imad, *Shadharat al-dhahab* (1350/1931).

Isa, Abd al-Qadir, *Haqa'iq an al-tasawwuf* (Dimashq : warathat al-mu'allif, 1993).

Ahmad, *al-Zuhd* (Beirut: dar al-kutub al-ilmiyya, 1414/ 1993).

Ahmad, *Kitab al-wara* (Beirut: Dar al-kitab al-arabi, 1409/ 1988).

Ahmad, *Kitab fada'il al-Sahaba*, ed. Wasi Allah ibn Muhammad Abbas (Mecca: Mu'assasat al-risala, 1983).

Ahmad, *Musnad.*

Allah, Ibn Ata', *Hikam.*

Allah, Ibn Ata, *Kitab al-hikam.*

Allah, Ibn Ata, *Lata'if al-minan fi manaqib Abi al-Abbas.*

Allah, Ibn Ata', *Sufi Aphorisms (Kitab al-hikam)*, trans. Victor Danner (Leiden: E.J. Brill, 1984).

Ansari, al-Harawi, *Tabaqat al-Sufiyya*, Mawlayi ed. (1983).

Ansari, Zakariyya, *Sharh al-risala al-qushayriyya* (Cairo: dar al-kutub al-arabiyya al-kubra, 1330/1912).

Arberry, A.J. Ed. "Jami's Biography of Ansari" in *The Islamic Quarterly* (July-December 1963).

Arberry, A.J., *Sakhawiana: A Study Based on the Chester Beatty Ms. Arab. 773* (London: Emery Walker Ltd., 1951).

Arna'ut, Shuayb, *Ibn Hibban Sahih.*

Ashari, Abu al-Maali Rukn al-Din Abd abd al-Malik ibn Abd Allah ibn Yusuf al-Juwayni al-Naysaburi al-Shafii, *Kitab al-irshad ila* qawati al-adilla fi usul al-itiqad.

Ashari, Abu al-Maali Rukn al-Din Abd abd al-Malik ibn Abd Allah ibn Yusuf al-Juwayni al-Naysaburi al-Shafii, *Nihayat al-matlab fi dirayat al-madhhab.*

Athir, *al-Nihaya.*

Baghawi, *Sharh al-Sunna.*

Baghdadi, Abd al-Qahir, *al-Farq bayn al-firaq* (Beirut: dar al-kutub al ilmiyya, n.d.).

Baghdadi, Abd al-Qahir, *Kitab Usul al-Din.*

Baghdadi, Abd al-Qahir, *Usul al-din.*

Baghdadi, al-Khatib, *Tarikh Baghdad.*

Barr, Ibn Abd, *Jami bayan al-ilm wa fadlih.*

Basri, Al-Hasan, *Fadail al-quran.*

Basri, Hasan, *Ihya.*

Bayhaqi *Dalail al-nubuwwa.*

Bayhaqi, *Shuab al-iman.*

Bayhaqi, *Sunan al-Bayhaqi.*

Biqai, *Masra al-tasawwuf aw tanbih al-ghabi ila takfir Ibn Arabi wa-tahdir al-ibad min ahl al-inad* (The destruction of *tasawwuf*, or: The warning of the ignoramus concerning the declaration of Ibn Arabis disbelief, and the cautioning of Allahs servants against the People of Stubbornness).

Bukhari, *Sahih Bukhari.*

Bukhari, *Tarikh.*

Chittick, W. C., *The Sufi Path of Knowledge.*

Chittick, W. C., *The Sufi Path of Love: the Spiritual Teachings of Rumi.*

Dawadari, *al-Durr al-fakhir fi sirat al-malik al-Nasir* (1960).

Dhahabi, *Mizan al-itidal.*

Dhahabi, *Mujam shuyukh al-Dhahabi, al-Mujam al-kabir,* ed. Muhammad Habib al-Hayla (Taif: Maktabat al-Siddiq, 1408/1988).

Dhahabi, *Siyar alam al-nubala,* ed. Muhammad ibn Hasan Musa (Jeddah: Dar al-andalus, 1995).

Dhahabi, *Tadhkirat al-huffaz* (Beirut: Dar al-Kutub al-Ilmiyah).

Ghazali, *al-Munqidh min al-dalal* (Damascus 1956).

Ghazali, *The remembrance of death.* Trans. T.J. Winter.

Gilani, Abd al-Qadir, *al-Ghunya li talibi tariq al-haqq* (p. 840).

Hadi, Ibn Abd, *Bad al-ilqa bi labs al-khirqa,* ms. al-Hadi, Princeton Library Arabic Collection.

Hajar, *al-Durar al-kamina* (1348/1929).

Hajar, *al-Isaba.*

Hajar, *Fath al-bari* (1989 ed.).

Hajar, *Hadi al-sari,* ed. Ibrahim Atwa Awad (Cairo, 1963).

Hakim, *al-Madkhal ila marifat al-iklil*, ed. & trans. James Robson, *An Introduction to the Science of Tradition* (London: Royal Asiatic Society of Great Britain and Ireland, 1953).

Hakim, *al-madkhal li ilm al-hadith*".

Hanbal, Ahmad ibn, *al-Zuhd*, 2nd. ed. (Beirut: dar al-kutub al-ilmiyya, 1414/1994).

Hanbali, Abd al-Hayy ibn al-Imad, *Shadharat al-dhahab*.

Hanbali, Ibn Rajab, *Istinshaq nasim al-uns min nafahat riyad al-quds* (Inhaling the breeze of intimacy from the whiffs of the gardens of sanctity).

Hanbali, Yusuf ibn Abd, *Bad al-ilqa bi labs al-khirqa* (The beginning of the shield in the wearing of the Sufi cloak).

Harawi, *Kitab sad maydan*.

Hatim, Ibn Abi, *Sifat al-safwa*.

Haytami, *Fatawa hadithiyya*.

Haytami, Ibn Hajar, *Fatawa hadithiyya* (Cairo: al-Halabi, 1970).

Haythami, *Majma al-zawaid*.

Huwjiri, *al-Risala*. B.R. Von Schlegell trans., *principles of Sufism* (Berkeley, Mizan Press, 1990).

Huwjiri, *Kashf al-mahjub*, trans. R.A. Nicholson (Karachi: dar al-ishaat, 1990).

Ibrahim, Muhammad Zaki, *Usul al-wusul* (Cairo: 1404/ 1984).

Isfahani, Abu Nuaym, *Hilyat al-awliya*.

Isnawi, Jamal al-Din, *Tabaqat al-Shafiiyya*.

Jami, Abd al-Rahman, *Nafahat al-uns*, ed. M. Tauhidipur, 1336/1957.

Jamra, Ibn Abu, *Bahjat al-nufus sharh mukhtasar sahih al-bukhari*.

Jawzi, *al-Muntazam*.

Jawzi, *Kitab al-qussas wa al-mudhakkirin*.

Jawzi, *Sifat al-safwa* (Beirut: dar al-kutub al-ilmiyya, 1403/1989).

Jawziyya, Ibn Qayyim, *al-Fawaid*, ed. Muhammad Ali Qutb (Alexandria: dar al-dawa, 1412/1992).

Jazairi, Abu Bakr ibn Jabir, *Ila al-tasawwuf ya ibad Allah* (Cairo: matbaat al-madani, 1408/1987).

Junayd, *Kitab dawa al-arwah*, ed. & trans. A.J. Arberry in *Journal of the Royal Asiatic Society* (1937).

Jurjani, Al-Sharif Ali ibn Muhammad. *Kitab al-tarifat* (Beirut: dar al-kutub al-ilmiyya, 1408/1988).

Kathir, *al-Bidaya wa al-nihaya* (1351/1932).

Kathir, *Tafsir*.

Keller, Nuh, *Reliance of the Traveller*.

Khaldun, *Shifa al-sail li tahdhib al-masail*.

Kutabi, Ibn Shakir, *Fawat al-wafayat*.

Lucknawi, *al-Raf wa al-takmil fi al-jarh wa al-tadil.*
Majah, *Sunan.*
Makdisi, George, "Ibn Akil."*Encyclopedia of Islam.*
Makdisi, George, "Lisnad initiatique soufi de Muwaffaq ad-Din ibn Qudama," in *Cahiers de lHerne: Louis Massignon* (Paris: Editions de lHerne, 1970).
Makki, Abu Talib, *Qut al-qulub fi muamalat al-mahbub* (Cairo: Matbaat al-maymuniyya, 1310/1893).
Maksidi, George, "Ibn Taimiya: A Sufi of the Qadiriya Order," in *American Journal of Arabic Studies I* (Leiden: E.J. Brill, 1974).
Maksidi, George, "The Hanbali School and Sufism," in *Boletin de la Asociacion Espanola de Orientalistas* 15 (Madrid, 1979).
Maliki, Ibn al-Arabi, *Aridat al-ahwadhi.*
Manzur, *Lisan al-arab.*
Maqrizi, *Kitab al-suluk* (1934-1958).
Mawdudi, Abu al-Ala, *Mabadi al-Islam.*
Muhasibi, *Kitab al-Wasaya,* ed. Abd al-Qadir Ahmad Ata (Cairo, 1384/1964).
Mundhiri, *al-Targhib.*
Muslim, *Sahih Muslim.*
Nabahani, *Jami karamat al-awliya* (1381/1962).
Nawawi, *al-Maqasid fi al-tawhid wa al-ibada wa usul al-tasawwuf* (The purposes in oneness, worship, and the foundations of self-purification). Cf. Nuh Keller, *Al-Maqasid: Imam Nawawis Manual of Islam* (Evanston: Sunna Books, 1994).
Nawawi, *al-Tibyan fi ulum al-quran.*
Nawawi, *Bustan al-arifin fi al-zuhd wa al-tasawwuf* (The garden of the gnostics in asceticism and self-purification). (Beirut: dar al-kitab al-arabi, 1405/1985).
Nuaym, *Hilyat al-awliya* (The adornment of the saints).
Qari, Ali, *al-Asrar al-marfua* (Beirut 1985 ed.).
Qari, Ali, *Mirqat al-mafatih sharh mishkat al-masabih.*
Qari, Ali, *Sharh ayn al-ilm wa-zayn al-hilm* (Cairo: Maktabat al-Thaqafa al-Diniyya, 1989).
Qasim, Mahmud Abd al-Rauf, *al-Kashf an haqiqat al-sufiyya* (Amman: al-maktaba al-islamiyya, 2nd edition, 1413).
Qatani, Ahmad, *al-Hujja al-mutah fi al-radd ala sahib kitab ila al-tasawwuf ya ibad Allah* (Cairo: maktabat jumhuriyyat Misr, 1992).
Qayyim, *Madarij al-salikin.*
Qayyim, *Rawdat al-muhibbin wa nuzhat al-mushtaqin* (The garden of the lovers and the excursion of the longing ones) (Beirut: Dar al-kutub al-ilmiyya, 1983).
Qudama, *Mukhtasar minhaj al-qasidin li Ibn al-Jawzi,* ed. M.

Ahmad Hamdan and Abd al-Qadir Arnaut, 2nd. ed. (Damascus: maktab al-shabab al-muslim wa al-maktab al-islami, 1380/1961).

Qushayri *Kashf al-mahjub*. (Nicholson trans. p.).

Qushayri, *al-Risala*, as translated by Rabia Harris, *Sufi Book of Spiritual Ascent* (Chicago: KAZI Publications, 1997).

Qushayri, *Risalat kitab al-sama* in *al-Rasail al-qushayriyya* (Sidon and Beirut: al-maktaba al-asriyya, 1970).

Qushayri, *Tartib al-suluk fi tariq Allah.*

Rajab, *Dhayl ala tabaqat al-hanabila* (Damascus, 1951).

Razi, Fakhr al-Din, *Itiqadat firaq al-muslimin.*

Rifai, Yusuf al-Sayyid Hashim, *Adilla ahl al-sunna wa al-jamaa al-musamma al-radd al-muhkam al-mani ala shubuhat Ibn Mani* 7th ed. (Kuwait: Matabi dar al-siyasa, 1410/1990).

Saadat, Abu, *Taj al-maarif.*

Sad, *Tabaqat* (ed. Sachau).

Safadi, Salah al-Din Khalil ibn Aybak, *al-Wafi bi al-wafayat* (Wiesbaden, 1962-1984) 1:274-277.

Saffarini, *Ghidha al-albab li-sharh manzumat al-adab* (Cairo: Matbaat al-Najah, 1324/1906).

Sakhawi, *al-Daw al-lami* (Beirut: dar maktabat al-hayat, 1966).

Sakhawi, *al-Jawahir wa al-durar fi tarjamat shaykh al-islam Ibn Hajar (al-Asqalani)*, ed. Hamid Abd al-Majid and Taha al-Zayni (Cairo: wizarat al-awqaf, al-majlis al-ala li al-shuun al-islamiyya, lajnah ihya al-turath al-islami, 1986).

Sakhawi, *al-Maqasid al-hasana.*

Sakhawi, *al-Qawl al-badi fi al-salat ala al-habib al-shafi* (The admirable doctrine concerning the invocation of blessings upon the beloved intercessor) (Beirut: dar al-kutub al-ilmiyya, 1407/ 1987).

Salam, Al-Izz ibn Abd [al-Maqdisi], *Hall al-rumuz wa mafatih al-kunuz* (Cairo: matbaat nur al-amal).

Salam, Al-Izz ibn Abd, *Bayn al-sharia wa al-haqiqa aw hall al-rumuz wa mafatih al-kunuz* (Cairo: matbaat nur al-amal, n.d.).

Salam, Al-Izz ibn Abd, *Fatawa*, ed. Abd al-Rahman ibn Abd al-Fattah (Beirut: dar al-marifa, 1406/1986).

Salam, Al-Izz ibn Abd, *Qawaid al-ahkam* (Dar al-sharq li al-tibaa, 1388/1968).

Sharani, *al-Tabaqat al-kubra* (1355/1936).

Sharani, *Lataif al-minan wa al-akhlaq* (Cairo, 1357).

Sharawi, Abd al-Wahhab, *al-Tabaqat al-kubra.*

Shafii, *Diwan*, (Beirut and Damascus: Dar al-fikr).

Sharani, Abd al-Wahhab, *Lataif al-minan wa al-akhlaq* (The kind gifts and refined manners).

Shatibi, *al-Itisam* (Beirut: dar al-kutub al-ilmiyya, 1415/1995).

Shatibi, *al-Itisam min al-kutub*, quoted in *al-Muslim: majallat al-ashira al-muhammadiyya* (Dhu al-qida 1373).

Shatibi, *al-Muwafaqa fi usul al-sharia* (Cairo:al-maktaba al-tijariyya al-kubra, 1975).

Shattanawfi, *Bahjat al-asrar.*

Subki, *Muid al-niam wa mubid al-niqam.*

Subki, *Qaida.*

Subki, *Tabaqat al-shafiiyya* (1324/1906).

Subki, *Tabaqat al-shafiiyya al-kubra.*

Subki, *Tabaqat al-shafiiyya.* Chester Beatty Library, ms. 3184 (2).

Subki, Taj al-Din. *Tabaqat al-shafiiyya.*

Suyuti, *al-Durr al-manthur.*

Suyuti, *al-Jami al-saghir.*

Suyuti, *al-Tibb al-nabawi.*

Suyuti, *Husn al-muhadara fi akhbar misr wa al-qahira* (1299/).

Suyuti, *Jami al-Kabir.*

Suyuti, *Qam al-muarid bi nusrat Ibn al-Farid* (The taming of the naysayer with the vindication of Ibn al-Farid).

Suyuti, *Tayid al-haqiqa al-aliyya wa-tashyid al-tariqa al-shad-hiliyya,* (The upholding of the lofty truth and the buttressing of the Shadhili path) ed. Abd Allah ibn Muhammad ibn al-Siddiq al-Ghumari al-Hasani (Cairo: al-matbaa al-islamiyya, 1934).

Tabarani, *al-Awsat.*

Tabarani, *al-Kabir.*

Tabarani, *Majma al-zawaid.*

Taymiyya, *al-Ihtijaj bi al-qadar* (Cairo: al-matbaa al-salafiyya, 1394/1974).

Taymiyya, *al-Risala al-Safadiyya* (Riyad: matabi hanifa, 1396/1976).

Taymiyya, *al-Safadiyya* (Riyad: matabi hanifa, 1396/1976).

Taymiyya, *al-Sufiyya wa al-fuqara.*

Taymiyya, *Majmu fatawa Ibn Taymiyya.*

Taymiyya, *Majmua al-fatawa al-kubra.*

Taymiyya, *Majmuat al-rasail wa al-masail* (Beirut: lajnat al-turath al-arabi).

Taymiyya, *Qaida fi al-tawassul wa al-wasila*, ed. Rabia ibn Hadi Umayr al-Mudkhali.

Taymiyya, *Qaida jalila.*

Taymiyya, *Risalat al-ibadat al-shariyya wal-farq baynaha wa bayn al-bidiyya.*

Taymiyya, *Tawhid al-rububiyya* in *Majmua al-Fatawa al-kubra* (Riyad, 1381).

Tirmidhi, Al-Hakim, *Adab al -muridin*, ed. Abd al-Fattah Abd Allah Baraka (Cairo: Matbaat as-saadat, 1976).

Wahhab, *Al-Tabaqat al-kubra al-musamma bi Lawaqih al-anwar fi tabaqat al-akhyar* (1374/1954) (Reprint, Beirut: dar al-fikr, n.d.).

Winter, T.J. Trans. *Ghazalis "Remembrance of Death"* (Cambridge: Islamic Texts Society, 1989).

Yafii, *Mirat al-janan* (1337/1918).

Zarruq, Ahmad, *Qawaid al-tasawwuf* (Cairo, 1310).

Zayd, Ibn Abi, *al-Jami fi al-sunan*.

Zirikly, *al-Alam* (1405/1984).

INDEX TO QURANIC VERSES

GENERAL INDEX

ENCYCLOPEDIA OF ISLAMIC DOCTRINE SERIES